Criminal Justice
Recent Scholarship

Edited by
Marilyn McShane and Frank P. Williams III

A Series from LFB Scholarly

The Punitive State
Crime, Punishment, and Imprisonment across the United States

Natasha A. Frost

LFB Scholarly Publishing LLC
New York 2006

Library of Congress Cataloging-in-Publication Data

Frost, Natasha.
The punitive state : crime, punishment, and imprisonment across the United States / Natasha A. Frost.
p. cm. -- (Criminal justice recent scholarship)
Includes bibliographical references and index.
ISBN 1-59332-176-7 (alk. paper)
1. Criminal justice, Administration of--United States. 2. Punishment--United States. 3. Imprisonment--United States. I. Title. II. Series: Criminal justice (LFB Scholarly Publishing LLC)
HV9950.F793 2006
364.973--dc22

2006014614

ISBN 1-59332-176-7

Printed on acid-free 250-year-life paper.

Manufactured in the United States of America.

CONTENTS

INTRODUCTION

Because of its comparatively high rates of imprisonment, the United States is frequently depicted as the most punitive country in the Western world, but is it fair to depict the United States as the most punitive place when punishment practices vary so dramatically across the states? In this book I ask, and try to answer, one central question. What do we mean by "punitive" and how do we measure it? Only after we have fully defined and operationalized the construct of punitiveness can we make any assertions as to how punitive a particular place is, whether that be any particular state or the United States more generally.

WHY IMPRISONMENT?

The focus of this study is on punitiveness through imprisonment as opposed to incarceration or social control more generally. Throughout this book, "imprisonment" refers to the incarceration of those serving sentences of more than one year in state prisons (because this is a study of state-level variation, those imprisoned in federal facilities are excluded from the analyses). Although studies of incarceration generally include those confined in jails and occasionally include juveniles detained in juvenile detention facilities, scholars occasionally use the word "incarceration" to refer to what I will call "imprisonment". For consistency, throughout this book, I substitute "imprisonment" for "incarceration" if these scholars were referring to imprisonment of more than one year in a state or federal prison. When used, the term "incarceration" refers more generally to confinement.

Clearly imprisonment, or for that matter even the more general incarceration, is not the only criminal justice response that could be included in a discussion of increasing punitiveness. As prison and jail populations have expanded, so have a whole host of alternative methods of coercive social control. Moreover, most of the alternatives to incarceration have become add-ons and, as Stanley Cohen (1985) has noted, the net of punitive social control has only widened. Gordon (1990) similarly argues that the growth in punitiveness manifests in both an overt "control through confinement" strategy and a more covert "control through surveillance" strategy, a combination she refers to as the "justice juggernaut." Gordon argues that growth in non-confinement alternatives has outpaced, and played a greater role in, increasing the punitive reach of the justice system than the more obviously punitive control through confinement strategies.

The focus on imprisonment can be justified because by most accounts imprisonment is qualititatively different from other forms of punishment. Stanley Cohen, for example, distinguishes between exclusionary punishments that cast out the offender and inclusionary punishments that integrate the offender (see Cohen, 1985, at p. 219 for a thorough discussion). Exclusionary punishments separate offenders from society, removing them either literally through banishment, death, or confinement or symbolically through branding or excommunication. Inclusionary punishments on the other hand keep the offender in the community, ostensibly allowing the retention of familial and societal ties while under some form of criminal justice supervision. Probation, community service, and electronic monitoring are all examples of more inclusive punishment. Under Cohen's classification, imprisonment is the only exclusionary punishment used with any regularity today. (Capital punishment is also an exclusionary penalty, but one that has not been used with any regularity over the past few decades. Moreover, not all states authorize capital punishment. Twelve states have no death penalty provision and the death penalty provisions in two states (New York and Kansas) were invalidated by courts in 2004 (Death Penalty Information Center, 2004)).

One might argue that all the various forms of confinement should be included in an analysis of punitiveness. In this study, however, jail and juvenile detention center confinement are excluded. Holleran and Spohn (2004) have recently argued that prison sentences are both quantitatively and qualitatively different from jail sentences, and that the two should, therefore, be distinguished in studies of sentencing outcomes. Prison sentences are quantitatively different from jail sentences because prison sentences typically entail a period of imprisonment of more than one year, while jail sentences entail incarceration of less than one year. Holleran and Spohn argue that prison and jail sentences are also qualitatively different in that the types of offenders housed in each type of institution are different (with jails typically housing misdemeanants and first time, low level felony offenders and prisons housing those convicted of serious felonies or repeat offenders) and that the post-incarceration consequences that follow are different. They argue that prison sentences are more stigmatizing and more destructive of family and employment relationships than are jail sentences, and that the collateral consequences, or as Jeremy Travis (2002) might call them "invisible punishments," (such as housing and welfare restrictions and, in most states, restrictions on the right to vote) typically follow only a prison sentence (though it should be noted that some of these collateral consequences typically follow a *felony conviction* not a prison sentence per se).

In addition to the insights offered by Holleran and Spohn on the qualitative differences between prison and jail, I would add that prisons are widely recognized as serving the function of post-conviction punishment. Jails, while used to punish misdemeanants and felony offenders sentenced to less than a year, also confine those detained while awaiting trial. According to the most recent Department of Justice figures more than sixty percent of those incarcerated in jails across the nation are pre-trial detainees (Harrison & Karberg, 2004). While time spent in jail under pre-trial detention no doubt feels like punishment, the government's stated purpose for detaining these inmates is not punishment per se. Moreover, most jails are administered by local or county governments and I employ a state-level analysis. Perhaps most importantly, jail data and prison data come from different sources that are not particularly comparable. Although comprehensive prison data are collected each year through the National Corrections Reporting Program (NCRP), comprehensive jail data are collected every five years through the Census of Jails (the most recently published census of jails was conducted in 1999 (Stephan, 2001)). The Annual Census of Jails providing intercensal estimates of the size of jail populations. Due in part to the high turn-over in jail populations, jail data lack the specificity and detail of prison data. The NCRP includes a file for each *inmate* admitted or released over the calendar year, while the Annual Census of Jails includes a summary file of total admissions and releases for each *facility*. Moreover, NCRP prison data from most states include data on time served in jails for those offenders admitted to or released from prisons. Juveniles are excluded because they are by and large processed through the juvenile justice system (Harrison and Karberg (2004:5) report that at mid-year 2003 only "0.2% of all state prisoners were under age 18") and again, for some of the same reasons, the data are not particularly comparable.

It seems important to note at the outset that the argument made in this book does not require a "punitive turn". The conceptual argument and the empirical analyses that follow would be relevant whether punitiveness had increased, decreased, or remained stable. The early chapters that focus on the punitive turn are included to set the conceptual and methodological arguments in a broader context. Although not essential to the argument made, the sheer scale of imprisonment indicative of the punitive turn underscores importance of more comprehensively understanding "punitiveness" in this historic moment.

ACKNOWLEDGMENTS

I once said that virtually everything that I know, I know because I have had the opportunity to work so closely with Todd Clear over the past seven years. That's an awkward way of saying that I cannot thank Todd enough for his belief in me and for his unwavering support of my work.

CHAPTER 1

THE PUNITIVE TURN

By most accounts, criminal justice policy in the United States has taken a decidedly 'punitive turn.' In the past two decades, we have seen the United States prison population increase by almost 350 percent from 319,598 prisoners in 1980 to 1,410,404 at mid-year 2004 and the jail population increase by 288 percent from 183,988 inmates in 1980 to 713,990 at mid-year 2004 (Harrison and Beck, 2005a). At mid-year 2004, more than two million inmates were housed in prisons or jails and the overall incarceration rate reached 726 inmates per 100,000 residents (Harrison and Beck, 2005a). Of course all of this incarceration comes with a price-tag. In 2001, state prison expenditures for adult correctional facilities reached 29.5 billion dollars (Stephan, 2004). Between 1982 and 2001, state governments increased their expenditures on corrections by over 500 percent, with the 9.9 percent average annual percent change in expenditures for corrections constituting the largest increase among justice expenditures overall (Bauer & Owens, 2004).[1] Put a different way, the per capita expenditures on corrections rose from $39 in 1982 to $200 in 2001 (an increase of over 400 percent). Moreover, in 2001, thirteen percent of all state and local public employees were employed by the justice system, and a third of all state criminal justice employees worked in corrections (Bauer & Owens, 2004).

During this period of increased incarceration, we have also seen the introduction of (1) sentencing guidelines that limit judicial discretion at sentencing, (2) mandatory sentences and mandatory minimums that stipulate statutorily required minimum terms of imprisonment for certain offenses, (3) truth-in-sentencing statutes that require that certain offenders serve fully 85 percent of their sentences, (4) more stringent habitual offender legislation, often in the form of a "three-strikes and you're out" initiative, that allows for a sentence of 25 years to life upon the third felony conviction, (5) expanded restrictions on the use (and in some states the complete elimination) of discretionary parole release, (6) post-imprisonment civil commitment for those who have completed their court-imposed sentences but are still deemed 'dangerous,' and (6) sex offender registration and notification statutes that require that sex offenders register and continually update their personal information with the state – in some cases for life, and that the community be notified when certain sex offenders are released into the community. The list of punitive measures introduced during this time period goes on and on (see Garland, 2001).

We have also seen the return of some of the more degrading forms of punishment previously associated with by-gone days. Chain-gangs have returned with a new fervor in recent years, as has the death penalty. There here have been calls from one well-known criminologist to reinstitute the use of corporal punishment (Newman, 1995), from others to more vigorously pursue shaming penalties of either the reintegrative or disintegrative type (Braithwaite, 1999; Kahan, 1996; see also Tonry, 1999b & Kahan, 1999), and most recently one scholar (Oleson, 2002) argued that we should subject convicted offenders to punitive comas rendering them unconscious for days, months, even years.

HAS THERE BEEN A PUNITIVE TURN?

Although there is a fairly substantial, and growing, body of literature documenting the increasingly punitive nature of American criminal justice policy, not everyone agrees that there has indeed been a punitive turn. While making an argument that increasing the use of imprisonment does in fact work as a strategy for reducing crime, Charles Murray (1997) implicitly argues that we have actually become less punitive over the past five decades, at least in terms of the use of imprisonment. To make this argument, Murray has to find a way to explain how a quadrupling of the prison population actually represents a reluctance to use imprisonment. Murray uses the 1950s as a reference period for a time when the risk of imprisonment, which he defines as the number of imprisonments per 1000 crimes committed, was relatively high and the crime rate relatively low. Allegedly in a rational cost-benefit calculus, aspiring criminals in the 1950s realized that because the risk of imprisonment was relatively high, crime 'did not pay.' Murray goes on to argue that beginning in the early 1960s the risk of imprisonment in the United States began to substantially and rapidly decrease falling "by 64 percent in just 10 years" (1997:16). Murray provides a figure documenting the crime rate (per 100,000 residents) and imprisonment risk (per 1,000 crimes) between 1950 and 1993. His figure is replicated here (Figure 1.1) using Bureau of Justice Statistics data covering the years 1960 to 2000.[2]

Figure 1.1: Crime Rate per 100,000 Residents and Prisoners per 1,000 Crimes, 1960-2000

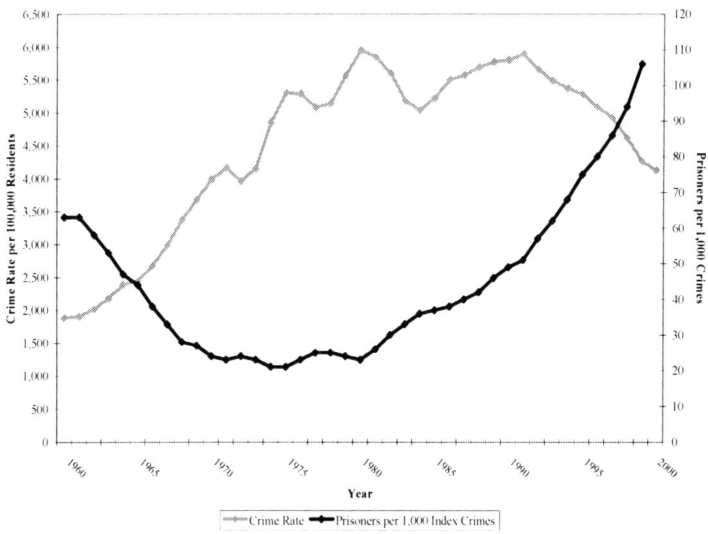

To bolster his argument that prison works – and implicitly, that we have become less punitive, Murray points out that the figure demonstrates that as the United States began decreasing the risk of imprisonment in the 1960s, the crime rate began to climb.[3] Moreover, according to Murray, it was only when the risk of imprisonment reached its pre-1960s level that we began to see the crime rate decline.

Charles Murray's proposition was rebutted in a pair of articles appearing in the same volume. Jock Young (1997) contends that the direction of the causal relationship between the crime rate and the risk of imprisonment is likely the reverse of what Murray proposes. According to Young, as the rate of crime began to escalate quite dramatically for a whole host of reasons in the early 1960s, there was no way for the risk of imprisonment to keep up. Crime did not increase because the risk of imprisonment decreased, but rather the risk of imprisonment decreased because crime increased. Andrew Rutherford (1997) argues that the issue is Murray's choice of denominator (imprisonments per 1000 crimes). While conceding that imprisonment risk, as measured by Murray, indeed did go down and has since gone back up, Rutherford suggests that using reported crime in the denominator allows Murray to completely ignore the overwhelming evidence that the risk of imprisonment for residents of the United States has continuously increased over the period.

In addition to the insightful critiques of Murray's position offered by Young and Rutherford, I would argue that the proposition that prison works is to a certain extent contradicted by the very evidence Murray presents to suggest that it does. A closer look at this figure reveals that although we now have the risk of imprisonment back up to its pre-1960s level, the number of crimes per 100,000 population have not dropped to anywhere near their 1950s levels. If the risk of imprisonment works in deterring crime, and Murray claims that it does, our crime rate should now be hovering closer to two thousand crimes per 100,000 population rather than five thousand. Murray's own figure demonstrates that either deterrence through imprisonment risk worked much more effectively in the 1950s, or that imprisonment risk seems to have little to do with the level of crime.

Moreover, I would argue that the measure of imprisonment risk is actually the wrong one. The measure of imprisonment risk employed by Murray (the number of imprisonments per 1000 reported crimes) might be the right one if calculating the *cost of crime* from the perspective of the offender (though even this is questionable), but in terms of whether or not we have become *more or less punitive*, the more appropriate measure of imprisonment risk is the risk of imprisonment following a felony arrest (this measure indicates how much more or less likely imprisonment has become for the apprehended offender). In determining whether or not crime pays, a prospective criminal offender (assuming he or she makes some calculus of the attendant risks of committing a crime) would no doubt first and foremost consider the risk of apprehension.[4] Some (Blumstein & Beck, 1999; Langan, 1991; Wilson, 1994) would argue that it is in fact at the point of arrest that we have become either no more effective or markedly less effective in keeping up with crime.[5]

The fact that the imprisonment risk *per crime reported* remains fairly low – or in fact has decreased – says little about how punitive we are, particularly if the risk of imprisonment *per arrest* has increased. Because Murray's risk measure fails to isolate the point at which we have become less effective, it is difficult to say whether we have become more or less punitive. A measure of imprisonment risk per arrest, removes the confounding problem of the effectiveness of law enforcement, and more clearly says something about how much more inclined we are to imprison given the existence of a punishment eligible offender. More importantly, as will be argued consistently in this book, increasing the risk of imprisonment is only one way to become more punitive and indeed perhaps not the only important way in which some of the states have actually become more punitive.

Murray, however, is not alone in contending that there has been no punitive turn. Others (DiIulio, 1994a, 1999a; Wilson, 1995) have also used this measure of imprisonments per crime and similarly argued that we have become less punitive.[6] John DiIulio has argued, for example, that rather than engaging in an 'imprisonment binge,' the United States has "been recovering from the starvation diet it went on in the late 1960s and stayed on throughout the 1970s" (1994:16).[7] More recently,

Roger Matthews in an article provocatively titled "The myth of punitiveness," (2005) reviewed the empirical evidence for increased punitiveness and argued that such evidence "does not provide a convincing case to support the claim that punitiveness has played a central role in recent developments" (2005:195). Although Matthews concedes that "the American evidence is stronger," he contends that even in the United States "punitiveness is much less pronounced than many criminologists suggest" (Matthews, 2005:195).

Curry (1998) directly confronts Charles Murray and several other influential conservative thinkers, including James Q. Wilson and John DiIulio, and implicates them as responsible for the many misconceptions about American punitiveness. Curry contends that these prominent policy buffs and others like them have done more than their fair share to contribute to the spread of three myths about imprisonment: (1) that the United States, rather than being too punitive, is in fact too lenient in both who it sends to prison and for how long, (2) that prison works in terms of meaningful reductions in crime, and (3) that whatever the cost of imprisonment, in terms of cost-benefit (where the cost is imprisonment and the benefit crime prevention), increasing levels of imprisonment is a bargain.

In a dissection of the numbers used to perpetuate these myths, Curry demonstrates that with regard to the first of these myths, the figures are constructed in a downright misleading way – calculating the chances of imprisonment and the length of imprisonment per crime, often whether reported or not. Curry contends that this method leads to a sizeable distortion of both the risk of imprisonment for, and of the harshness of the sentence imposed on, the actual punishment eligible offender. The second myth is perpetuated through both a failure to distinguish between violent crime and all other crime in claiming crime prevention benefits, and a failure to acknowledge that in the absence of the prison build-up there would have been other crime prevention alternatives in its place.[8] As Curry remarks: "Making the claim that crime would have been far worse without the prison boom, in short, tacitly assumes that the *alternative* was to do nothing. But doing nothing was never on anyone's crime control agenda" (1998:65, emphasis in original). These scholars perpetuate the third myth through at once underestimating the cost of imprisonment and overestimating the cost of crime.[9] They overestimate the cost of crime by including what Curry calls "intangibles," (the highly subjective 'costs' of pain and suffering) and underestimate the cost of imprisonment through ignoring the "hidden" costs of imprisonment (which might include, for example, the cost of public assistance, substitute care, and delinquency when a caretaker is imprisoned). A more even-handed analysis would either include or discount both the intangible and hidden costs of crime and imprisonment – rather than addressing one while discarding the other.

With a few exceptions, it seems most agree that there has been a punitive turn and that the reliance on imprisonment over the past few decades is unprecedented. As Cullen, Fisher and Applegate (2000:2) note "virtually all contemporary commentaries on correctional policy begin, almost ritualistically, by chronicling – and most often decrying – the seemingly endless roster of policies designed in recent years to inflict increasing amounts of pain on offenders". Cullen (1995:341) additionally argues that "only the culturally illiterate would be unaware that a movement has been afoot to expand the use of penal harm in the United States." Rates of imprisonment in the United States are now so high that even some of the more conservative commentators are no longer willing to say that what we need is more imprisonment. John DiIulio, for example, who once proclaimed we should "let 'em rot" (1994b) recently argued that "two million prisoners are enough" (1999b). Most also agree that, at least in terms of imprisonment, the United States began to engage in a full scale expansion of punitiveness in 1973, the first year in which the imprisonment rate began to increase following a period of decrease (Zimring, 2001). The punitive turn gained momentum in the early 1980s, with imprisonments growing at a previously inconceivable pace, and has resulted in a six-fold increase in imprisonment in the thirty years between 1973 and 2003.

THE NATIONAL PICTURE

The punitive turn in American criminal justice policy over the past few decades has had a significant impact on the size of the population under correctional supervision. According to the latest U.S. Department of Justice report (Harrison & Beck, 2005a), as of mid-year 2004, more than two million (2,131,180) people are in prison or jail in the United States. The mid-year 2004 figures represent an increase of 2.3 percent over mid-year 2003. Based on that figure, one in every 138 U.S. residents is currently incarcerated (Harrison and Beck, 2005a). Including the population under some form of correctional supervision (probation, parole, or jail/prison) the numbers are even more staggering: in 2004, more than 6.5 million Americans are living under some form of correctional supervision. By comparison, in 1980, our prisons and jails housed just over 500,000 people, and under 2 million (1,840,000) people were under correctional supervision. To put it another way, in 2004, we have more people in prison or jail than we had under any form of correctional supervision just twenty-five years ago.

In 1995, the United State's incarceration rate surpassed that of South Africa and since then, the U.S. has incarcerated more of its residents than any other nation in the world (Chambliss, 2001). The United States incarceration rate of 715 inmates per 100,000 residents far exceeds the incarceration rates of the Western European countries, all of which have rates of less than 200 inmates per 100,000 residents (Roberts, Stalans, Indermaur, & Hough, 2003). As depicted in Figure 1.2, the U.S. incarceration rate is more than five times that of several comparable European nations.

In terms of imprisonment, at yearend 2004, a total of 1,433,793 persons were currently serving sentences of more than one year, with 1,274,656 serving such sentences under state jurisdiction and 159,137 under federal jurisdiction (Harrison and Beck, 2005b). Although the imprisonment rate increased by only 1.8 percent between yearend 2003 and yearend 2004, the prison population saw its biggest increase in four years between midyear 2002 and midyear 2003, increasing by 40,983 inmates (or 2.9 percent) (Harrison and Karberg, 2004). As of yearend 2004, the average imprisonment rate in the United States stood at 486 prisoners per 100,000 population (Harrison and Beck, 2005b).

Figure 1.2: International Rates of Incarceration 2003

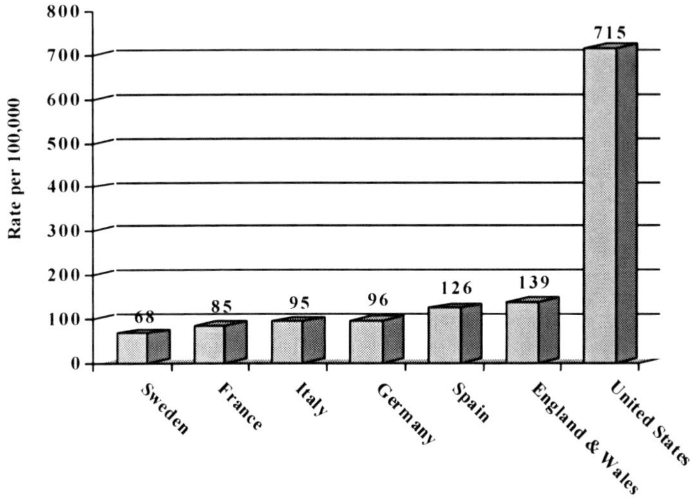

Source: U.S. Rate (Harrison & Karberg, Bureau of Justice Statistics, 2004), European Rates (Walmsley, Home Office, 2003)

INCREASING PREVALENCE

Perhaps even more disturbing than these raw figures are the prevalence statistics released in a recent Bureau of Justice Statistics Special Report, *Prevalence of Imprisonment in the U.S. Population, 1974-2001* (Bonczar, 2003).[10] According to this report, the increase in imprisonment over the past thirty years, has meant that far more people have experienced imprisonment than ever before (prevalence) and that if rates remain unchanged, we can anticipate that far more will experience imprisonment in their lifetime (lifetime likelihood).[11]

Bonczar reports that in 2001, approximately 1 in every 37 adults had served time in prison, and that if imprisonment rates remain unchanged, 6.6 percent of all U.S. citizens born in 2001 will serve time in a prison during their lifetime. Of course this 'experience of prison' is not evenly distributed across the population. Males and minorities are more likely to have experienced prison than females or whites. Although men born in 2001 are far more likely to experience prison than are females (11.3 percent versus 1.8 percent), the "imprisonment binge," as Austin and Irwin (2001) have called it, has certainly not left women behind. In fact, due to more rapidly growing imprisonment rates among women, the lifetime likelihood of imprisonment has increased more for women than it has for men. While men born in 2001, are just over three times more likely to serve time in prison than were those born in 1974, women similarly situated are six times more likely (Bonczar, 2003).

Some of the most disturbing figures in the 'prevalence report' concern the growing racial disparities in imprisonment and the likelihood that, without some substantial policy changes that will affect sentencing more generally, these disparities will likely not abate. Despite constituting only 13 percent of the United States population, Bonczar reports that "at year end 2001 nearly as many blacks (2,166,000) as whites (2,203,000) has ever served time in prison" (2003:5). Blacks and whites each constituted 39 percent of those who ever served time in a prison, while Hispanics accounted for the remaining 18 percent. Bonczar further reports that 16.6 percent of all black males have served time in prison, a number six times higher than the 2.6 percent of white men that have had such an experience. If Bonczar's lifetime likelihood predictions bear out, the future does not look any brighter. Again, given that the 2001 rates of imprisonment remain unchanged, one in three black males born in 2001 can expect to go to prison in their lifetime (contrasted with one in seventeen white males).

INCREASING SEVERITY

Not only are we punishing more and more people through imprisonment, we are apparently punishing them more harshly - imposing longer sentences on those who are sentenced to custody. Austin and Irwin (2001) argue the ever increasing imprisonment rate in the United States is largely a function of increasing sentence lengths, and not so much the result of increasing commitments. Others (Roberts, Stalans, Indermaur, & Hough, 2003, citing Brown & Langan, 1999), while acknowledging that the United States imposes lengthier sentences than other comparable nations, argue that both the average sentence length and the ratio of prison commitments to convictions in the U.S. have remained relatively stable (at least since 1990). Roberts et al. therefore suggest that the increasing imprisonment in the 1990s must be due to an increase in the number of convictions and cite evidence that in the six years between 1990 and 1996, the number of convictions increased by 20 percent (2003:17). This statistic, which covers only the period from 1990 to 1996, obscures changes in the average sentence length and conviction to imprisonment ratios both before and after the fairly limited period of study.

Time served, or length of stay (LOS), is an equally important determinant of severity. While sentences imposed say something about punitiveness, there have historically been a number of 'safety-valves' or 'back-end adjustments' that have allowed for post-sentencing downgrading of the severity of punishment. Largely because of these back-end adjustments, until recently it was highly unusual for a sentenced offender to serve even half of their court imposed sentence. Actual time served is therefore a purer measure of severity in punishment because while sentences imposed may be symbolically important, time served tells us how punitive we are in practice.

Michael Tonry, citing a report of a National Academy of Science Panel, points out that, in addition to a tripling of the prison/jail population, the "average time served per violent crime also *tripled* between 1975 and 1989" (1995:166, emphasis added). Truth-in-sentencing laws, which require that offenders' serve 85 percent of their sentence, will almost certainly further increase the length of stay for offenders sentenced under these statutes. Because LOS statistics are typically based on prison release cohorts, there is a lag between the time inmates begin serving longer sentences and the time that these lengthier stays show up in official release statistics. While the average LOS has only increased from about 24 to 25 months in recent release cohorts, as the population of inmates sentenced under truth-in-sentencing statutes approach release, LOS averages will further increase to as much as 28 months (Austin & Irwin, 2001). As Austin and Irwin point out these differences, while small in terms of time, have a surprisingly significant effect on the size of the prison population:

> Unless there is a drop in prison admissions, an increase of only three months in the average LOS from twenty-five to twenty-eight months will produce a 12 percent increase in the national prison population. Based on the current national prison population of approximately 1.3 million, the prison population would increase by about 155,000 inmates (2001:141).

THE PUNITIVE SENTENCING POLICIES

A number of policy initiatives, most of which directly impact criminal sentencing, have spread across the states over precisely the same period in which we have seen the size of the prison population quadruple. Marc Mauer (2001) has argued that changes in sentencing policy are the most significant factor in the growth of imprisonment over the past 30 years. The sentencing policies that are most frequently described as integral to the punitive turn, whether to drive or counteract that turn, include determinate sentencing, sentencing guidelines, mandatory sentencing, three-strikes type habitual offender sentencing, and truth-in-sentencing. In Chapter 5, a number of empirical studies measuring the effect of these policies on punishment outcomes are discussed in greater detail. For now, it seems sufficient to briefly describe these initiatives and their anticipated effects on prison populations.

Determinate Sentencing

The first dramatic change in sentencing policy came with the advent of the determinate sentence and the concomitant formal abolition of discretionary parole. Beginning in 1976, states began to switch from an indeterminate sentencing scheme – which stipulated a fairly broad range of sentence to allow for discretionary parole release upon evidence of rehabilitation – to one of determinacy - with more narrow sentence ranges and release determined by the sentence minus any good time. The advent of the determinate sentence came with the decline of faith in rehabilitation which coalesced around the publication of Robert Martinson's now infamous 1974 article, "What Works? – Questions and Answers about Prison Reform." In that article, Martinson asked what worked, reviewed an abundance of empirical work, and ultimately argued that with regard to rehabilitation, it seemed that nothing really worked.[12] Prior to the publication of this article, rehabilitation, and the indeterminate sentencing scheme that accompanies the goal of rehabilitation, had been attacked by those from the left and from the right. Those on the right, who had begun to depict criminal offenders as intractable, irredeemable, and undeserving of our sympathies, felt that indeterminate sentences often led to lenience in punishment and lobbied for the pursuit of more retributively oriented punishment. Those on the left, dismayed with the amount of discretion afforded to judges and correctional authorities, argued that when the sentence was indeterminate and release was dependent upon the whim of a parole board, potential abuses would likely follow.

Beginning with California and Maine in 1976, states began to abandon the indeterminate sentence and replace it with the determinate sentence (See Table 1.1). By 2002, seventeen states had adopted a determinate sentencing scheme (Stemen, Wilson, & Rengifo, 2003). Still, although most states have effectively abandoned 'rehabilitation' as their correctional goal, the majority of states retain the indeterminate sentencing scheme and continue to allow for discretionary parole release.

The effect of the switch from indeterminate to determinate sentencing in terms of punitiveness remains contested. Some (Zimring & Hawkins, 1991; Blumstein, 1988) argue that determinate sentencing leads to increases in prison populations because the abolition of discretionary parole release effectively disables a mechanism for back-end adjustments.

Table 1.1: Adoption of Determinate Sentencing by State, 1976-2002

State	Year
California	1976
Maine	1976
Indiana	1977
New Mexico	1977
Illinois	1978
Minnesota	1980
Florida	1983
Washington	1984
Oregon	1989
Delaware	1990
Kansas	1993
Arizona	1994
North Carolina	1995
Mississippi*	1995/2000
Virginia	1995

* Discretionary Parole Release Abolished 1995/Reinstated 1995/Abolished 2000
Source: Stemen, Wilson, and Rengifo (2003)

Stemen et al. (2003) point out that determinate sentencing could potentially increase prison populations in two ways, through increasing admissions and increasing length of stay. While judges had almost complete discretion under indeterminate sentencing schemes, determinate sentencing often reduces the ability of a judge to impose a non-incarceration sentence and prison admissions might therefore increase. Moreover, because determinate sentences specify either a specific term or a narrow range of term, these sentences might be harsher in the first instance and coupled with the absence of discretionary parole release, might lead to longer lengths of stay.

Marvell and Moody (1996), on the other hand, have argued that the anticipated effect of these laws depends to a large extent on the objectives or intentions of those passing the laws. If the objective in establishing determinate sentencing was to 'get-tough' on crime and increase the deterrent value of penalties through increasing prison terms for offenses, then clearly these laws would likely increase prison populations. Conversely, Marvell and Moody (1996) argue that if the intention was either to limit prison growth or to endorse a just-deserts oriented sentencing philosophy, then these laws might be expected to decrease overall punitiveness. Reitz (2001) too notes the importance of considering the underlying objectives of determinate sentencing in projecting its impact. Reitz describes some determinate sentencing structures as 'misconceived,' and sums up the mixed views regarding sentencing structure arguing that "there is, in short, no obvious correlation between the overarching structure that a jurisdiction chooses to erect for sentencing decisions and such things as the harshness, lenity, or distribution of punishments" (Reitz, 2001:231). In other words, in terms of whether the switch from indeterminate to determinate sentencing has increased or decreased punitiveness, the answer seems to be 'it depends' and it seems it depends, to a certain extent, on the establishment of sentencing guidelines.

Sentencing Guidelines

Shortly after the advent of the determinate sentence, states began to adopt sentencing guidelines. Sentencing guidelines, which specify a fairly narrow range of sentence for a convicted offender given his/her current offense and prior record, were heralded as an effective way to reduce disparity in sentencing and were adopted in states with both determinate and indeterminate sentencing structures (Bureau of Justice Statistics, 1998). Sentencing guidelines come in two forms, presumptive and voluntary, and in the majority of states the guidelines have been developed by an independent sentencing commission (Reitz, 2001). Presumptive sentencing guidelines specify the expected or 'presumed' range of punishment for a given offense/offender and require that the judge impose a sentence within that range or, if departing from that range, provide a written justification for doing so. Voluntary guidelines, which are not quite as rigorous, provide appropriate ranges of sentences that the judge may choose to consider.

In states with voluntary guidelines, judges can sentence outside of the suggested range at their own discretion.

Minnesota was the first state to adopt sentencing guidelines in 1980, and since that time a total of nineteen states have adopted either presumptive or voluntary sentencing guidelines. As depicted in Table 1.2, states tended to adopt presumptive guidelines in the initial period and voluntary guidelines as time passed.

Table 1.2: Sentencing Guideline Adoption by State, 1980-2002

State	Year	Type
Minnesota	1980	Presumptive
Alaska	1981	Presumptive
Pennsylvania	1982	Presumptive
Florida	1983	Presumptive
Maryland	1983	Voluntary
Washington	1984	Presumptive
Wisconsin*	1985/1999	Voluntary
Delaware	1987	Presumptive
Oregon	1989	Presumptive
Tennessee	1989	Presumptive
Kansas	1993	Presumptive
Arkansas	1994	Voluntary
North Carolina	1995	Presumptive
Virginia	1995	Voluntary
Ohio	1996	Voluntary
Missouri	1997	Voluntary
Oklahoma**	1997-R	Voluntary
Utah	1998	Voluntary
Michigan	1999	Voluntary

* Guidelines Adopted 1985/Repealed 1995/Reinstated 1999
** Guidelines Adopted 1997/Repealed 1999
Source: Stemen, Wilson, & Rengifo (2003)

Frase (1995) has argued that sentencing guidelines were initially envisioned as a way to provide a mechanism for greater control over the size of prison populations and would therefore likely slow growth. A handful of states explicitly require that the sentencing commission consider capacity in their formulation of guidelines, and have in some cases been quite successful in slowing the growth of their prison populations relative to other states (see Marvell, 1995; Nicholson-Crotty, 2004). Tonry (1993) has argued that conversely states wishing to expand their prison population can instruct their sentencing commission to develop pro-growth sentences and some have also done so quite successfully. Overall, Tonry notes that state sentencing commissions have "managed to make sentencing more accountable, more consistent, and less disparate in it impact on minority group members" (Tonry, 1996:64) and ultimately argues that:

> sentencing commissions and their guidelines have proven themselves as the most effective prescription thus far offered for the ills of lawlessness, arbitrariness, disparity, and discrimination that were widely believed to characterize indeterminate sentencing (1996:71).

It is important to note that although sentencing guidelines have received a more positive reception than any of the other sentencing policy changes, there has been a rather vocal critical response (see Altschuler, 1991; Savelsberg, 1992). Most of the criticism of sentencing guidelines targets the federal sentencing guidelines that took effect in 1987. The federal sentencing guidelines are routinely criticized for their rigidity and for virtually eliminating judicial discretion. The federal guidelines are also frequently described as too harsh, though Tonry (1996) notes that harshness was the objective, and so, on their own terms, they could be described as quite successful. Many have noted that the experience of the states that have adopted guidelines has been markedly different from the experience of the federal government. Minnesota, the first state to enact sentencing guidelines, has managed to keep its imprisonment rate far below the national average and its guidelines are often heralded for playing a central role in that control of the size of the prison population. Richard Frase (2000) notes that state guidelines differ in some key respects from the federal guidelines. Among the differences, Frase identifies both the greater flexibility and the comparative simplicity of state guidelines. He additionally notes that guidelines differ significantly across states arguing that some states guidelines "are so flexible that they are hardly 'guidelines' at all" (2000:426). Like Tonry (1996), Frase ultimately concludes that "state sentencing guidelines have proven to be much better than any other sentencing system which has been tried or proposed" (2000:426).

The impact of determinate sentencing and sentencing guidelines on punitiveness remains contested with some arguing that each might increase punitiveness, and others arguing that each more effectively controls punitiveness than the alternatives. The remaining three sentencing policy shifts, mandatory sentencing, three-strikes, and truth-in-sentencing are the most frequently cited punitive 'tough on crime' initiatives, and all three were expected to drastically increase punitiveness and result in significant prison population growth.

Mandatory Sentencing

Mandatory sentencing statutes stipulate that offenders sentenced for an offense for which there is a mandatory term be sentenced to that term without exception. According to Reitz (2001), the mandatory sentence approach can be understood as the adoption of determinate sentences offense by offense. Between the mid-1970s and mid-1980s, this offense by offense determinate approach has been pursued by all states for certain offenses regardless of whether the state formally switched to a determinate sentencing scheme (Tonry, 1996). A number of states, for example, have enacted mandatory terms of life in prison without the possibility of parole for aggravated murder. In contrast to mandatory sentencing, mandatory *minimum* sentencing provisions stipulate the minimum time to be served for the commission of a particular offense. Under mandatory minimum sentencing, a judge, while not required to impose the maximum sentence for a given offense, is not permitted to sentence to less than the required minimum. Additionally, some state provisions specifically restrict eligibility for parole to ensure that parole boards do not release the offender until the minimum term has been served (Reitz, 2001). Like determinate sentencing structures, mandatory penalties were enacted to reduce discretion and decrease disparity. According to Reitz:

> The motivating rationale [behind mandatory sentences] is that every scenario of that type should result in an identical sentence, with perfect uniformity across offenders and zero discretion exercised by government officials (such as judges and parole boards) at the case level (2001:229).

Since 1970, all fifty states, regardless of overall sentencing structure, have adopted one or more mandatory minimum sentencing provisions. According to the *1996 Survey of State Sentencing Structures* (Bureau of Justice Assistance, 1998), mandatory minimum provisions typically apply to five classes of offenders or offenses: (1) repeat or habitual offending, (2) drunk driving offenses, (3) drug offenses, (4) weapon offenses, (5) sex offenses. The BJA survey included a category for 'other offenses' to capture offenses with mandatory minimum penalties that are not of the primary five types.[13]

Mandatory minimum sentences, which were allegedly enacted to act as deterrents, produce equality in sentencing, circumvent discretion, and reduce disparity, have been attacked as failing on each of these grounds (see Merritt et al., 2006). Because they impose particularly harsh penalties for certain specified offenses, mandatory sentences were expected to deter commission of the offenses targeted. As noted by Tonry (1996), there is little evidence supporting deterrence generally. National advisory panels, including the National Academy of Science's Panels on Research on Deterrent and Incapacitative Effects (Blumstein, Cohen, and Nagin, 1978) and on Understanding and Control of Violent Behavior (Reiss and Roth, 1993), have concluded that the evidence for deterrence is marginal at best. With regard to the deterrent effect of mandatory penalties more specifically, Tonry (1996) identifies five major empirical works that have assessed mandatory sentences provisions in practice.[14] All five empirical studies suggest that, given deterrence does work, the deterrent effects of mandatory sentences are likely to be marginal primarily because the law itself tends to be seen as too harsh by many central actors in the criminal justice system, and these actors, from the police to the prosecutors and the judges, often go out of their way to circumvent the laws and avoid imposing the mandatory penalty (see also Merritt et al., 2006; Tonry, 2006).

With regard to equality, Tonry (2001a) points out that the equality principle requires not only that similar cases be treated similarly, but also that different cases be treated differently. He argues that mandatory sentences focus entirely on treating similar *crimes* similarly "but at the cost of ignoring differences in [offenders] lives and circumstances that many judges (and others) believe ethically relevant to thinking about just punishments" (Tonry, 2001a:6). The mandatory sentencing laws leave no room for either an assessment of individual culpability beyond prior offense history or for the tailoring of a sentence to fit that culpability. So, while these laws achieve equality in one sense (offense based), they violate the equality principle in another (offender based).

Nor have mandatory sentences necessarily reduced discretion. Many have argued that mandatory sentences have simply transferred discretion from judges who once determined appropriate punishment to the legislature that enacts these penalties (often in conflict with the recommendations of the states sentencing commission's guidelines) and most importantly to the prosecutors who have complete discretion in the charging of offenses and plea-bargaining of cases (Frost, 2006; Reitz, 2001; Tonry, 1996). According to some, prosecutors have liberally used their discretion in the charging of offenses when mandatory minimums apply – and have tended to use the threat of mandatory minimum terms as a useful card to play in their favor in the plea-bargaining process (see Merritt et al. 2006). With regard to federal mandatory minimums, the U.S. Sentencing Commission (1991) reported that prosecutors infrequently charged mandatory minimum offenses, in effect circumventing the laws before the case even got to court. Others have reported that prosecution, defense counsel and judges have at times conspired to alter the facts of the case to avoid the mandatory minimum or willfully disregard the stipulated sentence (see Tonry, 1996, 2001a, 2006).

It can also be argued that these laws have done more to create disparity than to eliminate it. Michael Tonry (1996) has documented situation after situation where mandatory sentences result in disparate punishment caused primarily by either the use of discretion by prosecutors in charging an offense or by judges and juries refusal to convict on the offense for which a mandatory penalty is stipulated and perceived as unjust. Tonry concludes that:

> patterns of circumvention are generally ad hoc and idiosyncratic with the result that sentencing disparities are often extreme: among like situated offenders, some will be sentenced to the ten- or twenty-year minimum sentence and others, benefiting from circumventions, will receive much less severe sentences (2001a:21).

While much of the disparity associated with mandatory minimums comes from circumvention of the laws (see Merritt, Fain, and Turner, 2006), in some cases disparities are written right into the law.[15]

Many, if not most, scholars consider mandatory minimum penalties unjust and unfair. John DiIulio recently decried mandatory minimum drug penalties arguing that "to continue to imprison drug-only offenders mandatorily is to hamstring further a justice system that controls crime in a daily war of inches, not miles" (DiIulio, 1999a:48). Franklin Zimring argues more generally that "the mandatory term is a huge expansion of punishment, rendering excessive outcomes in many cases to ensure sufficiency of punishment in a very few that might otherwise escape their just deserts" (Zinring, 2001:164). Members of the judiciary have come to agree. In an address to the American Bar Association, the moderately conservative Supreme Court Justice Anthony Kennedy recently spoke out against mandatory minimum penalties. During that address, Kennedy proclaimed that he "[accepts] neither the wisdom, the justice nor the necessity of mandatory minimums. In all too many cases they are unjust" and added that "our resources are misspent, our punishments too severe, our sentences too long." (Associated Press, 2003).

Mandatory sentences were expected to contribute to growing punitiveness through both increasing the number of offenders sentenced to terms of imprisonment (Langan, 1991) and increasing the average severity of sentences imposed on the classes of offenders or offenses sentenced under these provisions. That said, while clearly mandatory minimums have contributed to an increase in the severity of sentences for some of the targeted offenses, Tonry (1996) suggests that due largely to the ability of prosecutors to exert their discretion and to judges often successful attempts to circumvent the sentences, mandatory minimums have failed to drastically increase sentence severity overall.

Three-strikes

The three-strikes and you're out laws that were enacted in twenty-four states over a period of just three years (1993-1995) require lengthy sentences upon the third conviction for a serious, usually violent, felony.[16] The preceding characterization of three-strike laws requires numerous qualifications. State laws vary as to how many strikes are needed for an offender to be considered 'out,' what offenses count as strikes, and what it means to be 'out.' In a series of publications, James Austin and colleagues (Clark, Austin, and Henry, 1997; Austin, Clark, Hardyman, and Henry, 1999; 2000) provide a concise summary of the variation in three-strikes laws across states that I rely on here to note the following. First, not all states require three-strikes for the often dramatically enhanced penalties to ensue. While twenty states have a third strike provision, some states impose enhanced penalties on the second strike for certain serious or violent felonies and three states count someone 'out' upon commission of the fourth felony.[17] Definitions as to what constitutes a strike also vary across states with most states including an array of statutorily specified violent felonies. A few states however count non-violent offenses such as drug offenses as strikes or simply specify that penalties can be significantly enhanced following the commission of any three felonies.[18] Just as the number of strikes required and the strike offenses vary, so to does the meaning of 'you're out'. In some states, the court can double or triple the sentence specified by law for that offense. In other states, the sentences on the second, third, or fourth strike range from twenty-five years to life in prison with or without the possibility of parole. Some states mandate that the sentence be imposed, while others simply 'allow' for the enhancement. In sum, there is no such thing as "a" three-strikes and you're out law – there are twenty-four states that have enacted some sort of more stringent habitual offender sentencing borrowing the "so many strikes and you're out metaphor" from baseball.

These three-strike type sentencing enhancements are, at least in theory, particularly punitive sentencing enhancements for repeat offenders and were therefore expected to quite significantly increase prison populations through lengthening the average time served for certain offenders with certain offense histories. Many (Clark et al., 1997; Zimring, 2001; Zimring et al., 2001) contend, however, that for the most part these laws were written to "bark louder than they bite" thereby appeasing the public's thirst for retribution while having a negligible effect on the size of prison populations.[19]

With the exception of California's atypical three-strikes law, these laws were expected to have minimal impact on prison populations for several reasons. First and foremost, most states already permitted an enhancement of the sentence for repeat offenders. Clark et al. (1997) note that all but one of the states passing three-strikes type legislation in the mid-1990s already had significantly enhanced penalties for the commission of second, third, and fourth offenses – some even already had the mandatory life without parole requirement. In some of the states, the 'new' law expanded the types of offenses that 'counted' as strikes and in others it lengthened the sentence that was to be imposed, but in practice these changes have meant very little. Offenders sentenced under the provisions were already serving long sentences prior to the passage of the legislation. Moreover, in many states, the three-strikes laws are quite narrowly tailored, requiring that each strike be one of the statutorily prescribed felonies. In other words, an offender can commit any number of felonies, and while the sentence imposed will likely increase with each consecutive offense under pre-existing habitual offender laws, s/he will only be eligible for the lengthy three-strikes sentence after having committed the prescribed number of *strike eligible felonies.*

In sum, while three-strike laws indeed impose harsh sentences for repeat violent offenders, the new provisions are, according to many, not much harsher than the laws that already existed in almost every state. Additionally, as noted by Zimring and colleagues (Zimring, 2001; Zimring et al., 2001), the vast majority of offenders serving three-strike sentences are in California. Zimring (2001) notes that more offenders are serving strike sentences in California than in all other three-strikes states combined, and adds that most of three-strike inmates are serving second strike enhancements rather than the third strike 25 to life sentences.[20]

Truth-in-Sentencing

Of all the sentencing policy changes reviewed here, the advent of truth-in-sentencing legislation is likely to have the largest impact on prison populations into the future. Truth-in-sentencing (hereafter TIS) laws require that violent offenders serve a specified portion of their court imposed sentence (usually 85 percent) before becoming eligible for parole (Ditton & Wilson, 1999). Depending upon the source consulted, between five and nine states enacted 85 percent TIS laws before 1994, with Washington enacting thc first TIS law in 1984.[21] As part of the 1994 Crime Act, Congress authorized 'incentive grants,' referred to as VOI-TIS (Violent Offender Incarceration and Truth-in-Sentencing) grants, to encourage the adoption of stringent truth-in-sentencing legislation. To receive the grants, which provide financial assistance in the form of prison construction and expansion funds, the states must either already have in place (or enact) legislation that meets the federal standard that violent offenders serve a minimum of 85 percent of their sentence prior to release or demonstrate that they are increasing the sentences of those sentenced to prison for violent offenses. According to Sabol et al. (2002), under this standard all states received some VOI/TIS funding, though they note that in 1996, the law was amended to require the 85 percent standard be implemented within three years to qualify for the grants.[22] Twenty-nine states had (or have enacted) TIS laws meeting or exceeding the 85 percent requirement. Utah qualifies for the grant funding because although it has not adopted a TIS law, in practice its time served meets the federal standard (Sabol et al., 2002). Of the remaining twenty states, eleven have TIS laws that do not meet the 85 percent requirement and nine have not formally enacted TIS legislation at all (See Table 1.3).

TIS laws are expected to quite dramatically increase time-served for violent offenses, though there is debate over how much this increase in severity can be attributed *exclusively* to TIS laws. Having analyzed the effect of TIS laws in seven states, Sabol et al. argue that while "truth-in-sentencing reforms are associated with large changes in prison population outcomes... the changes are more appropriately associated with broader sentencing reforms than with truth-in-sentencing in particular" (2002:vii).

A Bureau of Justice Statistics analysis of time served by violent offenders released in 1993, 1995, and 1997 (Ditton & Wilson, 1999) reveals that while the percentage of the sentence served for these offenders has indeed been going up (from 47 percent in 1993, to 51 percent in 1995, to 54 percent in 1997), the average maximum sentence has been going down (from 98 months, to 95 months, to 93 months respectively) though not enough to counteract the more stringent percent of sentence requirements: the average time served has increased from 43 to 46 to 49 months over the period. These averages underestimate time served because they reflect time served of only those offenders that were released and underestimate the impact of TIS because most of those released in this period were not sentenced under TIS requirements. Ditton and Wilson additionally project that while violent offenders actually *released* in 1996 served an average of 45 months (or just over half of their average sentence), violent offenders *sentenced* in 1996 (and required to serve 85 percent) will likely serve an average of 88 months before release. Clearly, to the extent that they are consistently implemented, TIS laws will dramatically increase time-served for violent offenders, and contribute to continued growth in prison populations. As TIS laws are a relatively recent sentencing development and have not been fully implemented, the impact of these laws cannot yet be fully assessed.

Sentencing Policy Changes

To summarize, there have been fairly dramatic sentencing changes across the states over the past three decades. The switch in some states from indeterminate to determinate sentencing schemes has by some accounts decreased overall punitiveness and by others increased it (see Reitz, 2001 for a concise summary). The critical response to the development of sentencing guidelines has to a certain extent depended upon the nature of the guidelines adopted. The federal sentencing guidelines, considered unduly rigid and excessively harsh, have frequently been criticized not just by scholars but by members of the judiciary and other commentators. On the other hand, those guidelines that have been drafted by commissions that were explicitly instructed to consider capacity and prison population growth tend to be assessed in a much more positive light. Mandatory sentences have certainly resulted in harsher sentencing for some offenders but can be, and often are, circumvented. Three-strikes sentencing appears to be more symbolically punitive than it is actually punitive and has, for the most part, had little impact largely due to preexisting habitual offender laws. Truth-in-sentencing, however, by all accounts will likely have a significant impact on state prison populations – an impact that will not be fully realized for some time to come.

Although these sentencing changes tended to spread quite rapidly across the states, as noted in the previous sections, mandatory minimums aside, not all states have adopted all of these policies. Table 1.3 is a summary table depicting the adoption of these various policies by state. Within the table, the number in parentheses indicates either the year of adoption, or in the case of mandatory minimums, the number of mandatory minimum provisions a state had enacted by 1996.[23] Data for this table come primarily from Bureau of Justice Assistance's report *1996 Survey of State Sentencing Structures* (1998).[24] Empirical studies of the effects of these sentencing policy changes are discussed in Chapters 3 and 5.

Table 1.3: Sentencing Policies Adopted by State, 1976-2002

State	Determinate Sentencing	Sentencing Guidelines	Mandatory Minimums	Three-Strikes	Truth-in-Sentencing
AL			**X** (4)	**X** (1995)	
AK		P (1981)	**X** (3)		Other
AZ	**X** (1994)		**X** (5)		**85%+**
AR		V (1984)	**X** (5)		Other
CA	**X** (1976)		**X** (5)	**X** (1994)	**85%**
CO			**X** (6)	**X** (1994)	Other
CT			**X** (5)	**X** (1994)	**85%**
DE	**X** (1990)	P (1987)	**X** (6)		**85%**
FL	**X** (1983)	P (1983)	**X** (3)	**X** (1995)	**85%**
GA			**X** (6)	**X** (1995)	**85%**
HI			**X** (3)		
ID			**X** (3)		100% min
IL	**X** (1978)		**X** (6)		**85%**
IN	**X** (1977)		**X** (3)	**X** (1994)	50%
IA			**X** (4)		**85%**
KS	**X** (1993)	P (1993)	**X** (1)	**X** (1994)	**85%**
KY			**X** (5)		**85%**
LA			**X** (6)	**X** (1994)	**85%**
ME	**X** (1976)		**X** (2)		**85%**
MD		V (1983)	**X** (4)	**X** (1994)	50%
MA			**X** (3)		75% min
MI		V (1999)	**X** (5)		**85%**
MN	**X** (1976)	P (1980)	**X** (3)		**85%**
MS	**X** (1995)		**X** (6)		**85%**
MO		V (1997)	**X** (6)		**85%**
MT			**X** (6)	**X** (1995)	
NE			**X** (3)		50%
NV			**X** (2)	**X** (1995)	100% min
NH			**X** (5)		100% min
NJ			**X** (5)	**X** (1995)	**85%**
NM	**X** (1977)		**X** (3)	**X** (1994)	

State	Determinate Sentencing	Sentencing Guidelines	Mandatory Minimums	Three-Strikes	Truth-in-Sentencing
NY			**X** (4)		**85%**
NC	**X** (1995)	P (1995)	**X** (3)	**X** (1994)	**85%**
ND			**X** (4)	**X** (1995)	**85%**
OH	**X** (1996)	V (1996)	**X** (6)		**85%**
OK		V (1997)	**X** (2)		**85%**
OR	**X** (1989)	P (1989)	**X** (4)		**85%**
PA		P (1982)	**X** (6)	**X** (1995)	**85%**
RI			**X** (6)		
SC			**X** (4)	**X** (1995)	**85%**
SD			**X** (4)		
TN		P (1989)	**X** (4)	**X** (1995)	**85%**
TX			**X** (4)		50%
UT		V (1998)	**X** (4)	**X** (1995)	**85%**
VT			**X** (2)	**X** (1995)	
VA	**X** (1995)	V (1995)	**X** (2)	**X** (1994)	**85%**
WA	**X** (1984)	P (1984)	**X** (3)	**X** (1993)	**85%**
WV			**X** (6)		
WI	**X** (1997)	V (1985/99)	**X** (6)	**X** (1994)	**100%** +
WY			**X** (1)		

VARIATIONS IN IMPRISONMENT

There has been a lot of interest in the aforementioned fluctuations in the imprisonment rate in the United States over the past three decades. In 1973, Blumstein and Cohen, noting that punishment rates had remained remarkably consistent over time (from the 1920's to the 1970's), offered empirical support for a Durkheim inspired "stability of punishment" thesis. Finding that the incarceration rate remained remarkably stable for the fifty years between 1920 and 1970, Blumstein and colleagues (Blumstein & Cohen, 1973; Blumstein, Cohen & Nagin, 1978) argued that self-regulating forces work to constrict the growth of incarceration. In a later study, Blumstein and Moira (1979), then applied the stability of punishment thesis to 47 of the fifty states, and reported further empirical support for the notion that punishment self-regulates. Since that time, as depicted in Figure 1.3, we have seen the incarceration rate grow in a way which makes it difficult to support Blumstein and colleague's stability thesis.

Figure 1.3: Growth in U.S. Imprisonment Rate, 1925 – 2000

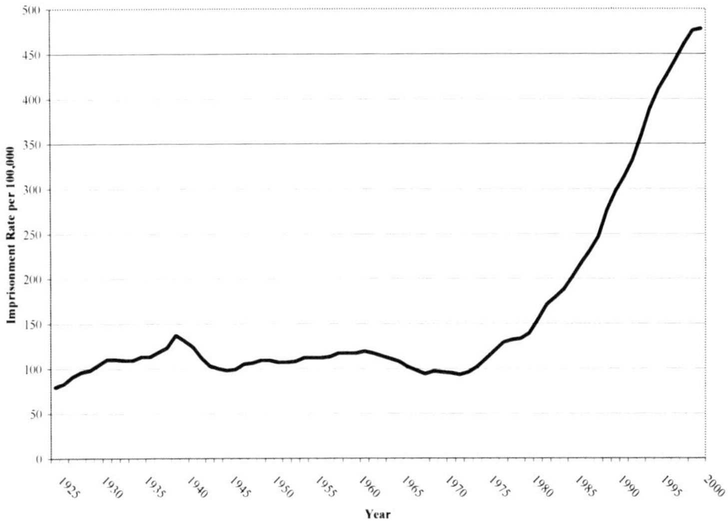

Data source: Maguire & Pastore (2003)

Somewhat unfortunately for Blumstein et al., the punitive turn began at almost exactly the point at which their examination of the alleged homeostatic nature of punishment ended. In sum, all evidence suggests that the practice of imprisonment is not quite as "homeostatic" as Blumstein and colleagues once asserted.[25] In defense of the "empirical feasibility" (to borrow a phrase from Chiricos and Delone, 1993) of his thesis at the time it was written, Blumstein himself notes that "clearly, some fundamental societal and political changes" contributed to the end of an era where "incarceration policy was largely within the control of functionaries within the criminal justice system" (Blumstein, 2002:451-452). In recent years there have been a number of attempts to explain the "fundamental societal and political changes" that contributed to the sudden and dramatic shift in the scale of imprisonment. The literature in this area is so vast that only some of the more influential theories are examined in any detail.

NOTES

[1] The average annual percent change in expenditures for police was 6.9 percent, and for the judiciary 8.8 percent. The expenditure and employment data reported here all come from the Bureau of Justice Statistics Bulletin, *Justice Expenditure and Employment in the United States, 2001*, authored by Bauer and Owens (2004). While none of the expenditure data are adjusted for inflation, according to Bauer and Owens, "expenditure on all justice functions... increased at a rate greater than inflation" (2004:3).

[2] The data that used to construct this figure come from Maguire and Pastore (2003).

[3] Murray might be advised to read Useem, Liedka, and Piehl's (2003) cautionary note about comparing UCR crime rates prior to the 1960s to those post-1960. As they note, the UCR's reporting methods underwent a substantial change in 1960, and as a result "The FBI recommends against using its crime data prior to 1960 in time-series comparisons" (Useem et al., 2003:29, n.4). Nils Christie's most recent work (2004) questions the utility of whole process of examining changes in crime when crime itself is such a fluid concept.

[4] Deterrence theorists frequently argue that it is some combination of both and involves a calculus of the probability of arrest times the expected punishment given an arrest. See the discussion in Chapter 11.

[5] Saunders and Billante (2002-03) expand Murray's thesis in an analysis of crime and imprisonment risk per crime in Australia, New Zealand, England and the United States. Saunders and Billante find a similar pattern to Murray and also see evidence of "a weakening in the willingness to use prison as punishment" (2002-03:8). They are, however, more cautious than Murray,

noting that as crime rates increased, the clearance rates over the same period decreased quite rapidly. Saunders and Billante ultimately assert that the "increasing the probability of getting caught appears no less important than increasing the severity of punishment that follows" (2002-03:8). Langan (1991) found that between 1974 and 1986 the arrest rate for each of six index crimes declined.

[6] Cullen (1995) points out that conservative criminologists frequently use imprisonments per crime as the measure of punitiveness and tend to go back to at least the 1960s to argue that we have ultimately become less punitive. Liberal criminologists, on the other hand, typically use either total prisoners or imprisonment rates as the measure of punitiveness, and begin their analysis of punitiveness in the 1970s (see also, Clear, 1994).

[7] DiIulio more recently recognized the imprisonment binge – at least in regard to drug offenders – arguing that "where drug-only offenders are concerned, in the late 1990s we have gone from prison bulimia to a prison binge" (DiIulio, 1999a:49).

[8] Curry points out that even the authors of those studies relied upon to buttress this claim (most notably, Marvell & Moody (1994) and Levitt (1996)) concede that the reduction in violent crime is likely to be minimal with more imprisonment. See also Spelman (2000a, 2000b) for a discussion of "diminishing returns" associated with increased imprisonment.

[9] Here Curry is particularly critical of John DiIulio. Curry argues that DiIulio's "work bears a curiously schizophrenic quality" (1998:76), in that DiIulio's rhetoric, particularly in the popular press (see DiIulio, 1994b, 1996, 2000), is quite forceful and equivocal, while his own research is considerably more guarded and tentative (see DiIulio & Piehl, 1991 &1995). Austin and Irwin (2001) are even more critical of the work of John DiIulio, they argue that:

> In making his statements on crime and the criminal justice system, DiIlulio [sic] has made use of the entire range of tactics employed by the academic apologists. He has uncritically accepted unverified, frequently outlandish statements of facts and built his own arguments on them. He has drawn conclusions from a single case – an anecdote. He has selected facts or relationships, plucked them from their full context, and then twisted them to suit his conservative agenda. Sometimes it appears he has just made things up (2001:238).

[10] All of the prevalence and lifetime likelihood estimates in the paragraphs that follow come from the Bonczar (2003) report.

[11] It is important to note that these prevalence and lifetime likelihood statistics only estimate the number that have experienced *prison* and the chances of future generations experiencing *prison*. Bonczar reports that this is because the data are not available for jail experiences. It is also important to note that these figures are based on first time imprisonment

[12] The strength with which Martinson made this declaration is contested with some suggesting that he declared nothing worked and then back-tracked (Feeley, 2003), and others noting that he never equivocally argued that *nothing* worked (See Cullen, 1995).

[13] The Bureau of Justice Assistance (1998) reports that the number of states reporting a mandatory minimum for an offense other than the primary five offenses targeted by this type of legislation tripled between 1994 and 1996. In 1994, only 11 states reported a mandatory minimum for some 'other' offense, by 1996 32 states reported these additional mandatory minimums.

[14] These include the U.S. Sentencing Commission Report, *Mandatory Penalties in the Federal Criminal Justice System* (1991), a study of New York's Rockefeller Drug laws (Joint Committee on New York Drug Law Evaluation, 1978), two studies of Massachusetts' mandatory one year prison term for the possession of an unlicensed firearm (Beha, 1977; Rossman, Froyd, Pierce, McDevitt, & Bowers, 1979), and one study of Michigan's mandatory two year prison term for the use of a firearm during the commission of a felony (Bynum, 1982).

[15] The distinction in mandatory minimum punishment for the possession of crack-cocaine versus powder cocaine is possibly the most widely criticized individual sentencing policy to have come to pass over the past few decades (see Donziger, 1996).

[16] Three strikes laws are a type of mandatory sentence.

[17] States with two strike provisions include: Arkansas, California, Connecticut, Georgia, Kansas, Montana, North Dakota, Pennsylvania, South Carolina, and Tennessee (Clark, Austin & Henry, 1997). Georgia has two and four strike provision and Louisiana three- and four-strike provision, (both stipulate that upon the fourth felony conviction of any type, the offender is sentenced to the maximum term for the fourth offense in Georgia and life without parole in Louisiana – Louisiana requires that one of the four felonies be one of the three-

strike offenses). Maryland has only a four-strike provision requiring that the offender serve life in prison without parole upon the fourth conviction for one of the statutorily listed offenses provided that the offender served prison terms for the first three offenses separately.

[18] Indiana, Louisiana and California include various drug offenses while North Dakota and Utah allow the enhanced penalties for the commission of a broad range of felonies (see Clark et al., 1997 for a concise description of variations in state laws).

[19] This phrase is borrowed from Zimring et al. (2001) who document the history of, and critique, the adoption of California's exceptional three-strike law in the book *Punishment and Democracy*.

[20] It is also worth noting that three strikes type legislation was not the only punitive legislation passed in the 1990s to bear a catchy soundbite name. Other legislation, such as Florida's "10-20-Life", legislation imposes increasingly harsh sentences for the use of a weapon during the commission of a crime (Zimring et al., 2001).

[21] There is some discrepancy between sources. According to Ditton and Wilson (1999), the five states with 85% TIS laws before 1993 are Delaware, Minnesota, Tennessee, Utah, and Washington. According to Sabol, Rosich, Kane, Kirk, and Dubin, (2002), there were nine states with 85% requirements prior to 1994 including Arizona, California. Georgia, Minnesota, Missouri, North Carolina, Oregon, Virginia, and Washington. There is also discrepancy between sources as to whether Delaware, Pennsylvania, and Michigan actually meet the requirement with Ditton and Wilson (1999) reporting that they do, and Sabol et al. (2002) reporting that they do not.

[22] The effect of the VOI/TIS grant program on the adoption of TIS laws is debated. Sabol et al. (2002:v), for example, report that thirty states left existing standards intact and only twenty adopted or altered their TIS laws in response to the grant program with twelve states "[increasing] the severity of their existing truth-in-sentencing laws" and eight states drafting new TIS laws.

[23] As noted above, the six mandatory minimum offense types identified in the survey are: repeat/habitual, drunk driving, drug offenses, weapon offenses, sex offenses and other offenses.

[24] The data were updated using the following sources: for determinate sentencing and sentencing guidelines: Stemen, et al. (2003); for three strikes:

Clark, et al.(1997); and for truth-in-sentencing: Ditton and Wilson (1999) & Sabol et al. (2002).

[25] Interestingly, Blumstein has not yet completely thrown in the towel with regard to his belief in the 'stability of punishment.' In his most recent work, Blumstein argues that "it is entirely possible that prison populations may have reached a new homeostatic level, but at a rate four times that which prevailed for 50 years" (2004:77).

CHAPTER 2

UNDERSTANDING THE PUNITIVE TURN

The increasingly punitive nature of American criminal justice policy since 1970 is only occasionally disputed: most agree that we have 'gotten tough' on crime with astounding results (at least in terms of the sheer volume of people imprisoned – though not necessarily in terms of returns, such as crime reduction, which continues to be hotly debated). Most also agree that the impetus for the punitive turn began in the late 1960s and early 1970s. Less agreed upon are the genesis of, and the forces driving, this punitive approach.

As to the genesis of the punitive turn, some (Garland, 2001; Young 1999) argue that fundamental cultural and labor-market changes that occurred as we transitioned from modernity (the post-war period) to late modernity (the late 1960s onward) have changed the way we experience the world around us, and consequently, changed our approach to social problems. Some (Parenti, 1999) argue that economic crises, and the need to control surplus populations in the wake of those crises, created and sustains the punitive turn. Others (Beckett, 1997; Bennett 1980; Feeley, 2003) emphasize political determinants arguing that, at least in the United States, a change in our approach to crime control can be almost wholly attributed to a conservatively oriented attack on the welfarist approach of the earlier period. Still more (Wilson, 1975) ignore massive structural, cultural, and political changes and argue that the punitive turn is simply a by-product of the public's demand that the government do something about increasing crime (in some cases without feeling the need to explain either the increase in crime or the changing public sentiment).

As to what might be driving punitiveness, the list of alternative explanations continues to grow. Increasing crime (Wilson, 1975), increasing fear of crime (Chambliss, 2001), increasing insecurity (Garland, 2001), increasing economic precariousness (Young, 1999), an increasing emphasis on individual responsibility (Garland, 2001; Young 1999; Beckett, 1997), and racism (both overt and covert) (Beckett, 1997; Parenti, 1999) are just a few of the constructs frequently implicated as driving forces behind continually increasing punitiveness. Though crime is clearly in some way related to imprisonment, at least in terms of creating the supply for punishment, due to the ambiguity in the evidence, few argue that changes in the level of crime alone can adequately explain variations in punitiveness. Because it seems that no one construct is capable of fully explaining the punitive turn, most theorists have tried to develop theories that incorporate a combination of structural, political, cultural and social determinants.

Confronted with the realities that increasing punitiveness was not simply a short-lived trend and that imprisonment has continued to increase even though crime rates have been declining substantially over the past decade, scholars have been all the more eager to explain the punitive turn.[1] Caplow and Simon note that "as much as possible, an interpretation of the incarceration rise should explain its rapidity, extent, and endurance" (1999:69). Some of the more influential recent theories of the punitive turn that have tried to do just that are presented in more detail in the pages that follow. These theories are described more fully because many of those doing empirical work to explain variations in punitiveness over time (or across places) turn to constructs identified in these theories to understand the punitive turn. Before turning to these theories a brief discussion of the issues of crime and race merit some attention.

CRIME

The most obvious predictor of variation in punishment is variation in crime. Even the most critical criminologists admit that imprisonment rates depend to a certain extent on crime rates. While punishment clearly depends upon the existence of crime, if punishment were strictly a function of the size of the crime problem in any given state, we could construct a crime rate ranking and infer the state's imprisonment rate ranking from it. Yet, as has been demonstrated time and again, crime and imprisonment do not track each other in any consistent fashion. As Jock Young argued, "[the idea] that there is a direct and obvious relationship between high risk of imprisonment and the level of crime... is a classic of common sense, yet it is as incorrect as its opposite, the rather irritating liberal assumption that the crime rate has nothing whatsoever to do with the imprisonment rate" (Young 1999a: 143). While it seems imperative to address the problem of crime in any discussion of the expansion of punishment, few who theorize the punitive turn argue that changes in crime rates can adequately explain changes in rates of imprisonment. Most of those who theorize the punitive turn simply include some discussion of the expected effects of changes in crime on changes in imprisonment.[2]

ENDURING RACISM

If there is one brute fact that should not be (yet often is) ignored in theorizing the punitive turn, it is the vast over-representation of minorities, particularly young black males and increasingly young Hispanic males as well, among the imprisoned population. Many (c.f. Tonry, 1995; Donziger, 1996; Mauer, 1999) have noted the racial undertones of some of the particularly punitive legislation (most notably the crack/cocaine distinction that imposes penalties 100 times greater in magnitude for the possession of crack than for the possession of cocaine). Many also suggest that the crime wars, and the war on drugs in particular, have been fought in a very specific locale – the largely minority neighborhoods of the inner city. Few, however, have offered a comprehensive framework for understanding the complete reversal of the ethnic composition of our prisons over the exact same period that is most frequently circumscribed as representing the punitive turn. To the extent that we have increasingly filled our prisons over the past few decades, we have increasingly filled them with young, inner city, minority, male drug offenders (Baadsager, Sims, Baer, and Chambliss, 2000).

Alex Lichenstein has argued that there have been two surges in the use of imprisonment, and that both disproportionately affected black Americans: the first followed the emancipation of African Americans in the 1860s, the second followed the civil rights movement of the 1960s. As Lichenstein (2001) points out, while the scale of imprisonment might have reached unprecedented levels in the more recent period, high imprisonment rates, particularly high Southern imprisonment rates, also proliferated following the Civil War and Reconstruction. The massive build up of imprisonment in this earlier period was also felt unevenly, with African American rates of imprisonment dramatically outpacing white imprisonment rates. Lichenstein uses Georgia as an example demonstrating that between 1871 and 1896, Georgia's imprisonment rate per 100,000 soared from 38 to 100. Following the surge, the imprisonment rate for blacks in Georgia was ten times that of the imprisonment rate for whites (150 and 15 respectively). Lichenstein argues that this increase suggests: "either a massive racial bias in the pattern of imprisonment or else the unlikely prospect that the state's white population was the most law-abiding citizenry in human history" (2001:192). Lichenstein goes on to argue that if the effect of imprisonment on whites was anything like its effect on blacks, there would be a national outcry against the punitive turn.

As will be discussed in the chapters that follow, most empirical work finds a significant positive relationship between race (usually measured as the percent of the population that is black) and imprisonment. The evidence for discrimination as a causal determinant of the relationship between race and imprisonment is at best mixed (see for example, Blumstein, 1982, 1993b; Langan, 1985). Intentional discrimination or not, Michael Tonry points out that "the rising levels of Black incarceration did not just happen" and argues that "they were the foreseeable effects of deliberate policies" (Tonry, 1995:4). Any theory that purports to explain the punitive turn is incomplete without a consideration of the disproportionate effects of that punitiveness on racial and ethnic minorities.

PUNITIVE PUBLIC SENTIMENT

There are several competing theories of the relationship between popular punitiveness and jurisdictional level punitiveness. While few argue that there is no relationship, there is disagreement as to the strength and direction of the relationship. Some argue that public opinion drives public policy, some that public policy shapes and directs public opinion, and others that the relationship is more complex and almost certainly reciprocal (with public opinion playing an important role in the development of public policy and political posturing affecting public opinion).

The 'democracy-at-work' thesis suggests that there is a direct link between popular punitiveness and the enactment of punitive policies (Beckett, 1997; Cullen, Fisher, and Applegate, 2001; Roberts et al., 2003). According to proponents of this model, increasing levels of crime in the late 1960s and early 1970s served as the genesis for increasing punitiveness. Put simply, we needed to get 'tough on crime' because crime was spiraling out of control. Moreover, according to this model, there is a direct unidirectional relationship between public opinion and public policy. As the public becomes increasingly fearful, it becomes increasingly punitive. Public punitiveness is depicted as a response to either rising crime itself, or to the feeling that crime is rising, and punitive crime policies are depicted as a legislative response to the fearful public's desire to see criminal offenders punished more harshly.[3] Under this conception, the public demands harsher punishment and the legislature delivers. Politicians, both Republican and Democrat, who press for harsh law and order policies often wholeheartedly adopt this thesis suggesting that they are enacting punitive legislation as a result of popular demand, and are therefore simply being responsive to their constituents.

While the democracy-at-work thesis is usually espoused by politicians and conservatively oriented policy types, Zimring, Hawkins, and Kamin (2001) present a seemingly pure case of democracy-at-work in their recent book *Punishment and Democracy*. In this work, they explore and attempt to explain the evolution of California's three-strike law that was ratified with overwhelming support by the people in a ballot initiative. While the enactment of California's three-strikes legislation is particularly interesting for its populist flair, it must also be stressed that it is unusual: very little criminal justice policy is ratified through voter referenda as California's three-strikes initiative was.[4] Perhaps because it is so straightforward, the democracy-at-work thesis is often criticized for being too simplistic. The thesis takes into account neither the complexity of the political process nor the complexity of public sentiment. A variation of the democracy-at-work thesis, variously referred to as populist punishment or penal populism, has been gaining popularity.

PENAL POPULISM

A number of scholars attribute the driving force behind some of the most punitive responses (imprisonment generally and particularly punitive legislation in particular) to a rise in what has alternately been called either "penal populism" (Roberts et al., 2003) or "populist punitiveness" (Bottoms, 1995). These scholars argue that pandering to an overly punitive public, politicians use the crime issue to their advantage advancing policies that are popular with the public with little or no regard for their outcomes in terms of fairness or effectiveness. Roberts et al. (2003:65) argue that "the difference between the Democracy at Work thesis and penal populism is a subtle one, to do with the intentions underlying political initiatives" and distinguish policies that are *responsive* to the public and policies that are *populist*. Populist policies are those which exploit punitive public sentiment and are pursued simply for political gain. Roberts et al. (2003) argue that while it is important to be responsive, "penal populists allow the electoral advantage of a policy to take precedence over its penal effectiveness" (2003:5), and warn that "sentencing reform guided by politics and provoked by public pressure proceeds down a one-way street of punitiveness" (2003:viii).[5]

Crucial to the penal populism perspective is the notion that these policies are not only ineffective and unwise, but also based on an uninformed understanding of public opinion. Public opinion regarding crime and punishment is complex and often contradictory. An abundance of previous research (see Roberts, 1992; Roberts and Stalans, 1997 and Cullen et al., 2000 for concise summaries) has demonstrated that the American public knows very little about the actual extent of crime or the nature of sentencing and punishment. Cullen et al. (2000:4) note this "lack of knowledge about crime is not an isolated domain of ignorance" and cite Kinder (1998) in arguing that the public is "awash in ignorance" about most policy issues. The public usually thinks policies are not punitive enough but also frequently lacks knowledge with regard to how punitive criminal justice policies actually are. When asked to sentence hypothetical offenders, subjects often come up with hypothetical sentences that are less, not more, severe than those actually imposed for similar offenses by the criminal justice system (Roberts and Stalans, 1997). Even where there is some knowledge, Roberts (1992) points out that very few people have had direct experience with the criminal justice system, and so most of the knowledge that the public does have is secondhand.

Cullen et al. (2000) provide an impressive review of research on public punitiveness that underscores the importance of considering the complex nature of public opinion. Although Cullen et al. find that across most of the studies the public is appropriately characterized as quite punitive, this punitiveness is, in their words, quite "mushy" (Cullen et al., 2000:58). The harshness expressed by the public in opinion polls and surveys, can be moderated quite significantly when one moves from probing 'global' attitudes about punishment generally to probing 'specific'attitudes about the suitability of particular punishments for individual offenders. Moreover, even though the public is quite punitive, Cullen et al. note that "policy makers invariably overestimate rather than underestimate the punitiveness of the public" (2000:66).

In both the democracy at work and penal populism perspectives, the development of punitive policies is seen as a bottom-up process with punitive public opinion driving public policy. The political elites are depicted as either being responsive to the public's demands (democracy-at-work) or exploiting the public's sentiment (penal populism). According to both perspectives, the public is punitive of its own accord. Others (Beckett, 1997) have characterized the relationship between punitive public opinion and punitive policy as a more insidious top-down process where political ideology initially shapes and then exploits public opinion for political gain.

POLITICAL EXPEDIENCY

In her book, Making Crime Pay (1997), Katherine Beckett most fully develops the argument that increasing punitiveness is a function of political expediency. According to Beckett, representations of crime and punishment are not influenced by criminological knowledge, but rather are constructed for political gain, usually to support a wider political ideology. Beckett traces the beginning of the punitive turn to the late 1960s when conservative political elites trying to win electoral support began to frame the problem of crime as one related to increased lawlessness associated with the excessive permissiveness of the welfarist approach to social problems. With clever use of imagery and rhetoric, criminal offenders, civil rights demonstrators, and welfare recipients were all implicated. Having framed the social problems of the time in terms of increased lawlessness, conservative politicians rallied for a 'get tough' law and order response. The call to law and order resonated with the public because it tapped into their own larger concerns (fear of crime, the sense that informal social control was breaking down, etc.).

According to Beckett and others (Chambliss, 2001; Austin and Irwin, 2001), the conservative crime control ideology was born out of a "southern strategy" initially meant to capture the southern white vote, but later deemed useful for securing the vote of white suburbanites. Conservatives, realizing that the black vote was out of their reach, adopted a strategy that would appeal to anxious whites. Beckett argues that the conservative strategy was first and foremost an attempt to redeem political standing among constituents after having suffered a great defeat with the success of the civil rights movement. As such, the conservative rhetoric of the time was patently racist. To appeal to southern whites, conservative politicians presented a picture of lawlessness that clearly implied that particular groups were responsible for the increasing lawlessness. Part of the conservative claims-making agenda included pairing the image of the welfare recipient and the criminal offender and depicting both as undeserving and coddled by the welfarist approach. Criminals were capitalizing on the leniency of the criminal justice system, and the poor on a welfare system that allowed people to get something for nothing. Both the recalcitrant criminal and the opportunistic welfare recipient were apparently allowed to flourish under excessive permissiveness of the Great Society programs. Both were also depicted as responsible for their own condition, a notion that appealed to the growing emphasis on individual responsibility in American culture. Beckett argues that the images of the criminal offender and the welfare recipient have so frequently been paired in the conservative political rhetoric that they have essentially become one.

The conservative strategy, which proved quite successful in securing the white vote, gained momentum as the years proceeded. As crime rates reached all time highs in the early 1970s, the call to law and order, initially touted as a response to the increased lawlessness of the civil rights era, turned into an all out 'war on crime.' The war on crime in turn spurned a "war on drugs." The war on drugs is particularly interesting because, by most accounts, the war on drugs has been fought in a very specific locale; the poor, urban, largely minority community.[6] Beckett argues that both of these wars, and more importantly the problems they profess to be attacking, have been largely constructed for political gain.

Beckett's theory, which builds upon the work of W. Lance Bennett (1980), is ultimately a theory of 'elite manipulation:' the public is manipulated by political elites into believing that crime is a social problem of utmost concern, and that increasingly punitive criminal justice intervention is the most viable, and perhaps only, appropriate response.[7] In defending her thesis emphasizing elite manipulation of public opinion, Beckett embarks upon a discussion of the difference between *public initiative* and *public receptivity*. She does so in the context of rebutting the claims of those who would argue that public punitiveness precedes punitive public policy. As the terms suggest, public initiative involves the public actively bringing crime to the agenda, while public receptivity requires only that the public be responsive to the call to law and order. The conservative ideology resonates with central values in American culture, particularly the cluster of values and beliefs around individualism, and the public responds to rhetoric that emphasizes these values.

In Beckett's theory, the media are the crucial middleman in the development of public punitiveness. The media plays a crucial role because the average citizen gets most of his or her information about crime and punishment from the media. In reporting on crime and punishment, the media rely heavily on government sources because they make good 'official' sources and tend to package information in ways that are useful (Bennett, 1980). Through this reliance, the media allows government sources, or claims-makers as Beckett refers to them, to shape the extent and nature of the conversation about crime, criminals, and appropriate punishments. In an indirect critique of Beckett's thesis, David Garland forcefully argues that the media's role, while important, should not be overemphasized:

> It is sometimes claimed that public support for punitive measures is a shallow media-generated phenomenon. The claim tends to be that tough-on-crime policies do not originate in any groundswell of public demand; that the public are not truly committed to these policies; and that such commitment that does exist has been artificially aroused and excited by media images and campaigns that misrepresent both crime and public sentiment. Public support for enhanced 'law and order' is, on this account, the fabricated result of manipulative political rhetoric and a rabble-rousing popular press… but it is a mistake to infer… that the voting public is easily and infinitely malleable, that mass support for law and order policies can be conjured up from nothing, or that newspapers and television can create and sustain a mass audience for crime stories without certain social and psychological conditions being already in place (Garland, 2001:146).

In developing his own theory of the punitive turn, Garland (2001) tries isolate those conditions that have served to transform American and British cultures from cultures of welfarism to cultures of control.

FROM PENAL WELFARISM TO A CULTURE OF CONTROL

In what Malcolm Feeley has called "the best and boldest analysis of the dramatic developments in the criminal process in England and the United States during the past quarter-century" (Feeley, 2003:127), David Garland (2001) traces the roots of the punitive turn to structural, political, and cultural changes that began to take shape in the 1960s and into the early 1970s. Garland emphasizes what he sees as "the most basic transformative forces of modern times: the economic force of capitalist competition and the political struggle for social and political equality" (2001:78), and then somewhat briefly describes marked changes in the capitalist market economy, family structure, demographics, social ecology, social life, culture, and the mass media (see Garland, 2001:77-89) arguing that these transformations "[have] ushered in profound changes in the way that life is lived – changes that have had important implications for issues of crime and its control" (Garland, 2001:78).

According to Garland then, it was also during this transition from modernity to late modernity that both our understanding of crime (its causes and remedies) and our experience of crime began to undergo significant transformations. When high rates of crime became a "normal social fact" and crime became much more salient as an issue, both the authorities and the populous slowly adapted. Garland argues that the initial government response was one of adaptation and denial. According to Garland, in the late 1960s and early 1970s the state adapted to this new reality by (1) professionalizing, rationalizing, and commercializing the business of justice thereby diffusing responsibility, (2) defining deviance down and lowering expectations,[8] (3) redefining the criteria by which success was to be measured, and (4) changing the focus from the causes of crime to the consequences of crime. In making these adaptations, the state effectively denied both responsibility for rising crime and its own power to do anything in the face of rising crime.

As for the rest of us, Garland builds a late-modern conception where crime is experienced (by just about everyone) not as an aberration but as an everyday inescapable reality. While Garland recognizes that "the collective experience of crime… is highly differentiated and stratified," (2001:148) he goes about describing this collective experience from the perspective of the professional middle classes (the professional practictioners, the liberal elites, and the educated middle classes). Garland contends it has been this group, who provided so much of the support for the penal welfarist approach, that has undergone the most significant transformation and whose adaptations to this new experience of crime have likely most strongly influenced the punitive turn. Garland argues that prior to the emergence of high crime rates as a social fact, the professional middle classes enjoyed the most social distance from the problem of crime, yet as we entered late-modernity several social changes worked together to increase the salience of crime particularly for this group. The changing ecology of life and structure of the household made this once relatively sheltered group quite suddenly more vulnerable to crime. The emergence of the automobile, white flight to the suburbs, the commute to work, two career families, high rates of divorce, and the like have fundamentally altered the lives of these middle class professionals, reducing the social distance between this section of the populous and everyday crime. According to Garland, in their highly routinized and scheduled lives, risk of criminal victimization has become just one more thing that these once comfortable liberal elites must now manage. They manage these risks with a fair share of resentment for the "new element of precariousness and insecurity [that] is built into the fabric of everyday life" (Garland, 2001:155).

Garland reserves a role for the media in the transformation of both culture and of the experience of crime. Just as structural and ecological changes made crime all the more salient, the advent of the television served to further reduce the social distance between the middle class professionals and the experience of crime. Additionally, the anxieties and resentments that have built up as a result of this new experience are played out again and again on television screens in programs that almost inevitably portray the victim as sympathetic, the system as failing, and criminals as "more numerous, more threatening, and more dangerous than they typically are" (Garland, 2001:158). Though he describes the media as an important ingredient in the creation of a crime complex, Garland is careful not to overemphasize their role in the creation of these sentiments:

> This is not to say that the media has *produced* our interest in crime, or that it has *produced* the popular punitiveness that appears as such a strong political current today... My point is rather that the mass media has tapped into, then dramatized and reinforced, a new public experience – an experience with profound psychological resonance – and in doing so it has *institutionalized* that experience (Garland, 2001:158, emphasis in original).

The adaptive approach initially taken by the state did little to calm the increasing anxieties and insecurities of the liberal elites that emerged in the wake of this new experience of crime. The government's defining down of deviance and retreat from the welfarist approach meant that middle class professionals were more frequently confronted with minor crime and disorder as they went about their daily lives. The state therefore launched a second, contradictory, and more overtly political crime control policy that sought to assuage public fears, and ultimately pandered to an overly punitive public driven more by anger and resentment about their increasing need to fear crime than by crime itself. For all of these reasons and more, through the 1980s and 1990s, the state embraced a more politically expedient expressive punitive approach to the control of crime.

Garland ultimately traces the transition from the old criminology with its emphasis on penal welfarism, to the new co-existing, and quite contradictory, criminologies of the self and other. The criminologies of the self and of the other stand as polar opposites, offer quite starkly different depictions of the problem of crime, and suggest quite drastically different solutions. In Garland's words:

> There is a *criminology of the self*, that characterizes offenders as normal, rational consumers, just like us: and there is a *criminology of the other*, of the threatening outcast, the fearsome stranger, the excluded and the embittered. One is

> invoked to routinize crime, to allay disproportionate fears and to promote preventative action. The other functions to demonize the criminal, to act out popular fears and resentments, and to promote support for state punishment (2001:137, emphasis in original).

Garland argues that it is the simultaneous existence of these two very different criminologies that has led to development of the seemingly schizophrenic approaches to crime control, with the criminology of the self, and its emphasis on rationality and the everyday experience of crime, increasing the popularity and prominence of control oriented theories and risk-reduction strategies, and the criminology of the other, with its us and them approach and focus on the evil of those who commit crime, leading to an increasing reliance on strategies of "punitive segregation".[9]

Garland's 'almost theory,' as Malcolm Feeley (2003) might describe it, is not without its critics including Jock Young and Feeley himself.[10] While recognizing the ambitiousness of Garland's project and commending him for reuniting the fields of criminology (with its emphasis on the causes of crime) and penology (with its emphasis on punishment), Young (2002) offers a strong critique, initially taking issue with the comparative strategy Garland employs. Most comparative research carefully addresses both similarities and differences. Young contends that Garland, through solely exploring similarities, completely loses sight of, indeed glosses over, some of the important differences between the United States and England. The similarities, of which Garland identifies many, are to Young nowhere near as important as the prominent differences including not only differences in levels of inequality, hand-gun ownership, racial animus, and the like, but perhaps more importantly in the profound differences in the level of crime (particularly lethal violence) and the scale of punishment (the very content of which Garland seeks to explain).

Young (2002) also regrets Garland's tendency to turn to the mundane, arguing that Garland, in formulating a "criminology of everyday life" essentially relegates the contributions of feminist, critical, and deprivation oriented criminologies to the proverbial dustbin while raising to a position of near exclusive prominence the more rationally-oriented (and mundane) criminologies of the routine activities, situational, opportunity, and control theorists. Young also contends that in his embrace of the criminology of the self, and the situational crime prevention type theories that go hand in hand with that particular strain of criminology, Garland loses touch with the essential character of both crime and punishment describing only one monolithic conception of crime and punishment in late modernity, where both are characterized as largely rational and mundane responses to an increasingly insecure everyday lived experience. Young does not deny that a whole amalgam of risk reduction/crime prevention strategies have emerged during his period as a result of a new experience of crime, he argues, however, that the experience described by Garland quashes perhaps more compelling accounts of the experience of crime:

> …the nature of crime and the response to it – is far from mundane… the actors are far from pallid creatures calculating the best manoeuvres through the social world in order to minimize risk and maximize contentment and that much of the dynamic behind crime is resentment and much of the response to it vituperative. Crime has its excitement, its drama, its seductions and punishment, like it, its vindictiveness, its hostility, its thinly concealed satisfactions" (Young, 2002:235-236).

Moreover, though Garland implicates a long list of factors as crucial to understanding the rise in crime, Young argues that one of the most prominent factors that might be isolated is conspicuously left off the list: "what, of course, is striking by its absence is the notion of the frustrations and drives which are engendered by societies which preach equality but are starkly unequal" (2002:233). Through their absence, it seems Garland is suggesting that the criminologies that have traditionally emphasized social exclusion and deprivation are no longer relevant or at least no longer capture the interest of researchers and criminologists. Young advises that the reader only need turn to some of the better ethnographies, among which he cites those of Elijah

Anderson (1999), Phillipe Bourgois (1995) and Jay Macleod (1995), to find research still oriented in the tradition of deprivation, though now relative rather than absolute.

Although he offers an overwhelmingly supportive critique, Feeley first notes that Garland has chosen to analyze changes that have taken shape in England and the United States, which he maintains are "deviant cases"or "outliers" in their recent over-reliance on increasingly repressive crime control measures.[11] Feeley then argues that Garland could have, and perhaps should have, taken on the political determinants of the punitive turn more explicitly suggesting that "the decline in penal welfarism and the embrace of a harsh culture of control can be accounted for in large part by the new political consensus that emerged in the 1970s and 1980s that rejects the welfare state and seeks to roll it back" (Feeley, 2003:122). He focuses his own discussion on describing those political transformations and explaining how the new ways of thinking about crime that emerged in the mid-1970s influenced the development of an overtly punitive crime control orientation. Feeley argues that a relatively small number of very influential intellectuals played a key role in this transformation. Feeley credits Martinson's (1974) proclamation that 'nothing works' in the realm of rehabilitation with dealing the final blow to the penal welfarist approach to crime, and James Q. Wilson's (1975) *Thinking About Crime*, with its admonition to stop worrying about root causes and start fighting crime by managing the risks, for providing a new direction once that final blow had been dealt. According to Feeley:

> Martinson's and Wilson's pieces had enormous influence in shaping subsequent crime policy. Martinson's article crystallized opposition not only to rehabilitation programs but to social programs designed to prevent crime more generally. Wilson's writings set forth an alternative set of concerns. Rather suddenly, social workers and traditional (i.e. structural) criminologists were out of fashion and out of favor (Feeley, 2004:120-121).

Feeley contends that a new breed of criminologists riding the wave of this neo-conservative tide scurried around performing cost-benefit analyses of various crime prevention strategies, designing the country out of its crime problem, and stipulating the conditions under which, through enhancing punishment, potential criminals (given they are rational calculators) would be deterred from committing crime. One need only turn to the vast literature on how many crimes might be prevented, or how much money might be saved (Zedlewski, 1987; see also Zimring and Hawkins, 1988), by imprisoning one chronic or serious offender (Greenwood & Abrahamse, 1982) to see evidence of some of these new criminologies hard at work.

Both Garland (2001), and more recently Christie (2004), implicate criminologists for providing the intellectual (and sometimes empirical) support for the dramatic expansion in crime control measures (though, somewhat ironically, Garland seems to find value in the work of the very intellectuals that led the charge against the penal-welfarist approach). Feeley critiques this perspective arguing that "criminologists did not change their stripes... they were swept aside. Invaders from other disciplines entered the field and took responsibility for providing the intellectual framework for the new criminology that fostered the harsh new culture of control" (2003:118). With no doubt some measure of satisfaction, Feeley notes that despite their influence on the politics of punishment and the development of this new criminology of everyday life, "to this day, many of the original insurgents and their protégés remain somewhat on the fringes of the field of criminology" (2003:121). I end the discussion of Garland on this point because indeed Young argues that, in *The Culture of Control,* Garland himself is guilty of 'sweeping aside' and rendering all but irrelevant the still influential, and perhaps ever more important, structural theories of social exclusion and deprivation.

FROM INCLUSION TO EXCLUSION

In an earlier discussion of exclusionary and inclusionary punishment, it was argued that as an integral part of the punitive turn, we have come to depend more and more on increasingly exclusionary punishments such as imprisonment. Young (1999a), Beckett and Western (2001), and perhaps even Garland (2001) would no doubt all argue that we have come to rely on such high levels of imprisonment because we have, as a society, become more exclusionary. In a series of works, Jock Young (1999a; 1999b) most fully describes the transition from an inclusive to an exclusive society.

Young (1999b) argues that societies are to a greater or lesser extent exclusionary or inclusionary in nature and that the nature of the society will to a large extent dictate their punishment strategy.[12] While inclusionary societies 'absorb' and incorporate their deviants, exclusionary societies 'spit them out' and segregate them. Young locates the transition from inclusion to exclusion in the late-1960s to early-1970s, describing the transition as one from modernity to late-modernity. Modernity, the post-war period, was characterized by a society bent on inclusion and assimilation. To paraphrase Young (1999b), in the modern period, we sought to assimilate our deviants, rehabilitate them, reform them, and mold them in the image of ourselves. Late-modernity, on the other hand (roughly 1970 to the present) is characterized by a culture that places an extreme emphasis on individualism, a labor market which selectively allows participation and arbitrarily doles out rewards, and a society in which a sizeable proportion of the population are experiencing economic and ontological insecurity.

Young argues that his theory of the ever more exclusive society explains increasing crime and increasing punitiveness equally well. We find the majority of crime at the lower end of the economic continuum because those occupying that space suffer from 'tantalizing exclusion'. The lower classes see the material rewards of gainful employment, are encouraged to become 'voracious' as consumers, but are given no meaningful opportunities to participate in the labor force through which they might attain the material goods. We should probably not then be surprised that those suffering from "tantalizing exclusion" turn to crime to either satisfy the consumerism our culture encourages or vent frustration at being a spectator in the great race for accumulation. Young can account for American exceptionalism in this regard because, in this framework, the United States can be characterized as a *uniquely* exclusionary society: one that to an extent unlike any other "holds firm to the values of meritocracy yet denies so many participation in the race" (1999a:21).

The middle classes, on the other hand, have become increasingly punitive as we moved from modernity to late modernity. According to Young, the middle classes previously enjoyed positions of relative stability, but in the transition to late modernity, that relative stability was replaced by a sense of overwhelming insecurity. Young characterizes the middle class position in late modern society as one of 'precarious inclusion.' While they are included in the labor market economy, their jobs, and therefore their lifestyles, are by no means secure. Not only are they fully aware that their position is precarious, they are keenly aware of the randomness with which rewards are distributed in late-modern capitalist society. According to Young, they perceive corruption at the upper end and unfairness at the lower end of the economic strata. From their perspective, those above them have secured rewards which they have by no means earned and those below seem to be trying to get something for nothing.

THE CONTROL OF MARGINAL POPULATIONS

Beckett and Western (2001) also develop an exclusion/inclusion theory that owes much to David Garland's influential book, *Punishment and Welfare* (1985) and Young's depiction of inclusive and exclusive societies, to explain recent trends in penal policy. They argue that penal policy and social policy are intimately related and that together they constitute a relatively coherent 'policy regime'. Both penal policy and social policy target the same group: those who are socially marginal.[13] Inclusive regimes, which tend to emphasize to social causes of marginality, make more concerted efforts to integrate those in society who are deemed socially marginal. In contrast, exclusive regimes tend to emphasize individual responsibility, depict the socially marginal as undeserving of our sympathy or our aid, and develop exclusionary policies for the control of these populations. Under this conception, imprisonment, an exclusionary penal policy for dealing with those who are socially marginal, can be contrasted with welfare, an inclusionary social policy for dealing with that same population. To the extent that we have become a more punitive society, we have done so to the detriment of social welfare of large, yet specific, sectors of the population.

THE CONTROL OF SURPLUS POPULATIONS, RACISM, AND POLITICAL EXPEDIENCY

Christian Parenti (1999) develops an argument that more explicitly and quite seamlessly merges the decline of penal welfarism, overt racism, political expediency and the control of surplus population theses in explaining the punitive turn. It is in the first section of his book, *Lockdown America: Police and Prisons in the Age of Crisis,* that Parenti provides a fascinating description of the emergence of the new law-and-order paradigm. He does so to develop a thesis that, while it was certainly politically expedient to ratchet up both the crime rhetoric and the punitive criminal justice policy (particularly in the mid-1960s and in all Presidential election years that followed), it was ultimately economic crises and the need to control a newly created surplus labor population that led to the punitive turn of the 1980s and 1990s. In the remaining two sections, Parenti provides a linear history of the developments in criminal justice policy as they relate to policing and punishment. In the pages that follow, I summarize the first section of the book which constitutes Parenti's theoretical contribution.

In *Lockdown America*, Parenti (1999) contends that it was Lyndon Johnson who, looking to divert attention from the failure of the war in Vietnam, began to envision a new war on the domestic front. Through consolidating and creating new federal drug enforcement agencies and encouraging Congress to establish the Law Enforcement Assistance Administration that would become so central to the emerging "war on crime", Parenti argues it was actually Johnson who "laid the initial groundwork for the tremendous combination of police power, surveillance, and incarceration that today so dominates domestic politics" (1999:6). Despite his acknowledgment of Johnson's role in creating the platform from which the war on crime would be launched, Parenti, like others (Beckett, 1997; Chambliss, 2001; Austin and Irwin,

2001) attributes the politicization of the crime issue to the "sunbelt Republicans," who amplified the rhetoric bringing crime to the forefront of their political agenda.

Parenti, through including a few telling quotes, demonstrates the tendency of these sunbelt Republicans to overtly link crime to the overly permissive penal welfarist approach to social problems more generally. Parenti cites the following passage from Goldwater in his failed 1964 Presidential bid:

> If it is entirely proper for the government to take away from some to give to others, then won't some be led to believe that they can rightfully take from anyone who has more than they? No wonder law and order has broken down, mob violence has engulfed great American cities, and our wives feel unsafe in the streets (Parenti, 1999:7).

Here the war on poverty is linked to increasing lawlessness, and not lawlessness in general, but rather the lawlessness of a very specific problem sector of society - the poor who had benefited from the welfarist approach for far too long.

Four years later, as Nixon made a presidential bid of his own, he too recognized the power of the law-and-order rhetoric and as demonstrated in the following private correspondence quite clearly weds race and crime: "I have found great audience response to this [law-and-order] theme in all parts of the country, including areas like New Hampshire where there is virtually no race problem and very little crime" (Parenti, 1999:7, citing correspondence between Richard Nixon and Dwight Eisenhower). Upon winning his Presidential bid in 1968, Nixon was faced with the reality that law enforcement was largely a local issue, and so, through a series of initiatives, set about a full-scale federalization of the enforcement of drug and organized crime activity, thereby launching the war on drugs that would become such an integral part of the punitive turn in the decades that followed. The blatant racism implicit in the new war on crime and drugs is perhaps made no more clear than in a diary entry of H.R. Haldeman, Chief of Staff to Richard Nixon, also cited by Parenti: "[President Nixon] emphasized that you have to face the fact that the whole problem is really the blacks. The key is to devise a system that recognizes this while not appearing to" (1999:12).

According to Parenti, the dual wars on crime and drugs that were launched with fervor during Nixon's administration, all but ground to a halt during the Ford and Carter administrations only to reemerge with a new voracity during the eight year tenure of Ronald Reagan. Integral to the decline in popularity of the law-and-order approach was the Nixon administration's own involvement in the Watergate scandal. At this point, Parenti (1999) departs from Beckett (1997), noting that the new approach to the 'law-and-order' problem that would emerge in the 1980s was not simply tied to the political expediency of uniting issues of poverty, race, drugs, and crime, but was also inextricably tied to the emergence during the late 1960s of troubling economic conditions.

Throughout the mid to late 1960s, unemployment was down and, as a result, the power of the working classes had increased substantially. Parenti argues that by the end of the 1960s, the working class began to leverage its newly acquired power through demanding higher wages, decreasing productivity through work slowdowns, and orchestrating strikes in virtually every sector. At the same time, industrial success and post-war profitability, which had reached unprecedented levels, began to show signs of cracking under the pressure. According to Parenti, by 1970, the market became saturated and consumer demand slowed dramatically in what he calls a classic "crisis of over-accumulation."(1999:32). In Parenti's words:

> At one level the crisis involved a simple contest between the classes. The share of output that went to profits *declined* while the share going to everything else, including the social wage, *increased.* The working class was too powerful, and from the management point of view, needed disciplining. (Parenti, 1999:37, emphasis in original).

As a result of the crisis, profits fell sharply, real wages remained high, and unemployment and inflation began to spiral upward. The economy became stagnant, and would remain so throughout the 1970s. Parenti argues that it was Carter's 1979 appointment of a new Federal Reserve Chairman that would lead to the proverbial tightening of the economic purse straps.

Enter Ronald Reagan. Parenti argues that the real disciplining of the working classes began when Federal Reserve Chairman Paul Volcker realized that "for the economic stagnation and low profits of the seventies to be vanquished the American people would have to learn how to work harder for less" (1999:38). Through successive increases in interest rates during the early years of Reagan's presidency, Federal Reserve Chairman Volcker intentionally sent the United States economy into a devastating yet "artificial" recession. For his part, Reagan, while cutting taxes for the wealthy, initiated his own attack against both organized labor and social programs that served to benefit the poor and working families. According to Parenti, "the Reagan administration's assaults on social spending were really about lowering the cost of doing business" (1999:41). Parenti goes on to explain how the economic restructuring of the early 1980s, while somewhat successful in turning the economy around, "created whole new classes of poor and desperate people. It was in response to this social crisis, created by the elite response to the profit crisis, that a new wave of criminal justice crackdown began" (1999:44).

By recognizing the integral role of the 1960s economic "crisis of over-accumulation" in the 1980s build up of repressive criminal justice mechanisms, Parenti manages to merge political and economic theories in describing the ascendancy of the rising tide of punitiveness – with the former taking precedence in the initial build-up under Nixon to effectively reinforce racial divisions and the latter in the launching of full-scale wars on crime and drugs initiated during eight years of "Reaganomics" to control surplus populations. The politicization of crime and punishment certainly did not decline during this new era, indeed Parenti carefully documents the ascendancy of the many politically expedient crime bills that were passed throughout Reagan's two terms and the terms of Bush and Clinton. Nor does Parenti lose sight of the centrality of race to the success of that politicization. Parenti argues, however, that the political interests took a backseat to the economic interest in "managing and containing the new surplus populations created by neoliberal economic policies, even when those populations [were] not in rebellion" (1999:45).

SUMMARY

The theories discussed in this chapter are important in that they identify constructs that are potentially integral to explaining the punitive turn.[14] Although the theories differ in their orientations, some common themes emerge. Crime, and perhaps more importantly the experience of crime, seems to be crucial to understanding the punitive turn. Related to the experience of crime is the increasingly punitive orientation of the public. Although the nature of the relationship between punitive public sentiment and punitive criminal justice policy continues to be debated, most reserve some role for increased public punitiveness in explaining our increasing tendency to impose greater harm on criminal offenders. Structural changes, economic fluctuations, and political divisions are also frequently identified as important factors in increasing punitiveness. Finally, race and class divisions and the problem of marginal or surplus populations often emerge as potential explanatory constructs. To the extent that one or more of these theories can explain the punitive turn, they should also be capable of explaining variations in punitiveness across places and of explaining changes across different types of punitiveness.

NOTES

[1] As evidence of that growth, in 1999, Michael Tonry (1999a) identified five dominant explanations for the punitive turn; by 2004, Tonry had expanded this list to eight, incorporating three additional explanations that had emerged in just five years (see Tonry, 2004).

[2] As discussed in Chapter 1, Charles Murray (1997) is a notable exception.

[3] See Tyler and Boeckmann (1997) for a study of the psychology of punitiveness at the individual level.

[4] As an interesting aside, California's three-strike provision is also uniquely punitive when compared to similar legislation in other states. No doubt some would argue that alone might be evidence that the people are actually more punitive and that the politicians are simply proposing punitive legislation to address growing public unrest. Others, including Zimring, Hawkins and Kamin themselves, would suggest that when Californians voted for Proposition 184, they understood neither the expansive breadth of the law they were endorsing nor the implications.

[5] Not all are quite so critical of penal populism (see Johnstone (2000) who argues for a participatory model of penal policy making).

[6] Though this focus is particularly pronounced in the War on Drugs, it is also true of the War on Crime.

[7] While Beckett's analysis only goes as far as 1991, it seems reasonable to assume that, if her theory is correct, the drive toward greater public punitiveness would have increased as Democrats began to jump on the get-tough bandwagon in greater numbers during the early 1990's. Crime, which dominated network news coverage from the late 80's through early 90's, has in recent years begun to slip at least in terms of its percentage share of network news coverage (Center for Media and Public Affairs). What is not clear is the effect, if any, that this waning popularity of crime stories has had on public punitiveness in the past few years.

[8] Defining deviance down means raising the threshold at which deviant behavior is targeted by the official criminal justice system response (in other words, criminalizing conduct less).

[9] Though Garland does not explicitly point this out, it is also likely the professional middle classes to whom the street criminal and the welfare recipient is 'the other.' To the lower and working classes, the criminal and the welfare recipient is not only unlikely to be 'the other,' but probably quite likely to be the brother, father, mother, sister, friend or neighbor. His 'criminology of the other', therefore, cannot explain the punitiveness of these classes as well as it does that of the professional middle classes. (For more on the criminology of the other, see Garland (2000) and Hallsworth (2000)).

[10] Feeley (2003) points out that Garland's book is as much a history of the present as it is a theory.

[11] Feeley (2003) later suggests that perhaps it is the United States that is the lone outlier and that England, while showing tendencies to head in the direction

of the United States, is actually still more like its Western European neighbors. Christie (2004), also noting the tendency of England (and Wales) to pursue American style policies in recent years, situates England as somewhere in between the United States and Western Europe. Not quite as punitive in its orientation as the United States, but simultaneously becoming significantly more punitive than its Western European counterparts. Christie suggests England is beginning to look more like Eastern Europe, a region that while notable for its punitiveness, is, with a few exceptions (Russia and the former Soviet republics among them), significantly less punitive than the United States. (see Christie, 2004: 63-65).

[12] It is by no means settled that an inclusive society is less punitive than an exclusive one. Nor is it self-evident that an inclusive society is in any way superior to an exclusive one. Moreover, as Young notes, exclusivity and inclusivity exist on a continuum, and societies are to a greater or lesser extent inclusive of exclusive (rather than one or the other).

[13] Though Beckett and Western never explicitly identify the members of the population that can be characterized as 'socially marginal,' by inference, the poor and the unemployed are socially marginal.

[14] In the recent book, *Thinking About Crime*, Michael Tonry (2004) argues that each of the theories of the punitive turn is inadequate and, perhaps not surprisingly, suggests that the only theory capable of explaining punitiveness across time and place is his own theory of cycles of sensibilities and moral panics.

CHAPTER 3

TRENDS IN IMPRISONMENT

Some social scientists have set out to empirically examine the relative contribution of political and societal changes to changes in imprisonment rates over time (here I present only studies that test explanations for changes in national trends in imprisonment – those that refine the analysis to test state-level variations are more directly relevant and are therefore covered in greater depth in the chapters that follow). Because empirical researchers only rarely set out to explicitly test a particular theory with all its nuances, it is virtually impossible to sort these studies into the categories presented in the previous chapter. That said, broadly speaking, most researchers doing empirical work test the ability of either economic, political, social or demographic variables to explain variations in punitiveness over time and when testing the explanatory power of one variable, tend to include one or more of the other variables as controls. Here the studies are sorted by reference to the variable the researcher hypothesizes is most related to increasing imprisonment. Moreover, because empirical work examining national imprisonment rate trends is voluminous and only indirectly relevant, only a few of the more representative studies are discussed at any length here. I describe the empirical work of this nature that has been most influential, and have therefore turned to the studies that are most frequently cited.[1]

CRIME

As noted in Chapters 1 and 2, few scholars argue that changes in crime rates, or trends in crime over time, can adequately explain changes in the level of imprisonment. There is also little evidence that imprisonment can effectively and consistently curtail crime. It seems crucial to note that in a study of the relationship between crime and imprisonment, crime can be conceived of as both an input and an output of imprisonment and might be specified as either an independent or dependent variable. Most obviously, as an independent variable, crime clearly might explain some of the variation in imprisonment rates over time. In times of increasing crime, one might expect increasing imprisonment and vice-versa. Much research has demonstrated that the relationship between crime and imprisonment is non-linear at best (Selke and Andersson, 2003). Some, such as Millie, Jacobson, and Hough are more equivocal arguing "it can be said with certainty that the increase [in the adult prison population] is not a product of increasing crime" (2003:382).

When specified as a dependent variable one might predict that imprisonment would reduce crime or increase crime. To the extent that imprisonment deters, rehabilitates, or effectively incapacitates criminal offenders, imprisonment might be expected to reduce crime. To the extent that imprisonment weakens informal social control, disrupts important networks, and is "destructive of life chances" (Simon, 2001) imprisonment might be expected to increase crime (see Clear, 1996, 2002; Clear, Rose, Waring and Scully, 2003; Fagan, 2004; Lynch and Sabol, 2004; Rose and Clear, 1998). Empirical work assessing the effect of either crime on imprisonment or imprisonment on crime has produced often conflicting results. When crime has been specified as an independent variable, some find that crime – particularly violent crime – predicts imprisonment (Taggart and Winn, 1993) and others find no significant relationship (Bowker, 1981). Similarly, when crime is specified as a dependent variable, some find that imprisonment reduces crime (Marvell and Moody, 1994; Levitt, 1996; Spelman, 2000a), some find it increases crime (Bowker, 1981), and others find no significant relationship between imprisonment and crime (Irwin and Austin, 2001; DeFina and Arvanites, 2002).[2] Ultimately, it is crime as an independent variable that counts more in a study of punitiveness. While crime as an independent variable tells us (to a certain extent) whether a punitive strategy is reasonable given the crime problem, crime as a dependent variable tells us to what extent that punitive strategy works.

Although few studies examine the relationship between crime and imprisonment singularly, most empirical work specifies crime as one among many independent variables potentially explaining variation in imprisonment rates. The findings with regard to the relationship between crime and imprisonment are therefore discussed within sections that discuss empirical work seeking to explain variations in imprisonment using a variety of potential explanatory variables. Suffice to say for now, broadly speaking, crime rates – particularly violent crime rates – tend to explain some of the variation in imprisonment rates across states and over time.

ECONOMIC DETERMINANTS

Many of the economically driven theories of imprisonment arise from the Marxist tradition and build on the early twentieth century work of Rusche and Kirchheimer (1939) who argued that punishment policy has historically been contingent upon labor market demands. In modern capitalist society, Rusche and Kircheimer's theory suggests most directly that when there is a large surplus of labor, we can expect to see large portions of the economically marginal population relegated to prisons. When labor is scarce, those same marginal populations are far more valuable to the economy, and prison populations are likely to decline.

Chiricos and Delone (1992) provide an impressive review of the body of empirical work that has amassed on the relationship between labor surplus (unemployment) and imprisonment. In their examination of 44 empirical studies, Chiricos and Delone find support for the "empirical plausibility" of a labor surplus explanation for levels of punishment (and imprisonment in particular). The empirical studies assessed by Chiricos and Delone, which varied in scope and methodology, measured the effect of unemployment on three types of punishment outcomes: overall prison populations, prison admissions, and sentence severity. Chiricos and Delone report that researchers using the overall prison population as the dependent variable were more likely to find a significant positive relationship between unemployment and crime (64 percent) than were those that focused on either prison admissions (60 percent) or sentence severity (25 percent). Of additional interest, researchers who employed the state as the level of measurement were among the least likely to find a positive relationship between unemployment and imprisonment (finding a positive relationship 85 percent of the time and a significant positive relationship only 34 percent of the time). While recognizing that support for the theory depends to a large extent on the choice of dependent variable, the level of measurement, and the control of potentially confounding variables, Chiricos and Delone (1992) argue that the accumulated body of empirical work provides "empirical plausibility" for the labor surplus perspective initially developed by Rusche and Kirchheimer (1939).

Although those who look to economic determinants to explain fluctuations in imprisonment have most frequently turned to unemployment levels as the explanatory variable, more recently scholars have taken an interest in economic inequality (see Christie, 2000; Melossi, 1993; Young, 1999b). Put simply, economic inequality measures gauge the distance between the 'haves' and the 'have nots'. As with the studies of unemployment and imprisonment, studies assessing the effect of economic inequality on levels of imprisonment have produced often contradictory findings. The economic inequality studies typically explore the relationship between inequality and imprisonment across states and are primarily discussed in Chapter 5 (though see also the discussion of Jacobs and Helm's (1996) below).

POLITICAL DETERMINANTS

In a series of works, Katherine Beckett (1994; 1996; 1997; see also Beckett and Sasson, 2000) has examined the relationship between political claims-making, media attention, and punitive public opinion. In *Making Crime Pay* (1997), Beckett tested her own theory and empirically demonstrated that on a national level punitiveness is linked to a broader agenda, closely aligned with the conservative political position, which paints certain segments of society as unredeemable. To reach that conclusion, Beckett examined national trends in political initiative around crime and drugs, media reporting of crime/drug issues, and public opinion/concern about crime and drugs as social problems. In her 1997 analysis, Beckett measured political initiative by reference to "the number of speeches, statements, policy initiatives, or summaries pertaining to crime or drugs made by federal officials and reported in the mass media" (1997:116, n.12), media coverage by counting the number of stories indexed under various crime and drug headings in print and television media indexes, and public opinion by the number of people identifying crime or drug issues as the "most important problem facing the nation" in Gallup and New York Times opinion polls.[3] In an analysis of political initiative, media coverage and public opinion during the "war on crime" from 1964 to 1974 and the "war on drugs" from 1985 to 1992, Beckett demonstrated that on a national level fluctuations in public opinion follow (rather than precede) political initiative around crime and drug issues, which in turn precedes media coverage.

Beckett is not the only researcher to empirically test the role of political determinants in increasing punitiveness. In a series of studies, David Jacobs and colleagues (Jacobs and Carmichael, 2001; Jacobs and Helms, 1996, 1997, 2001) employ time-series analyses of data on a variety of political and economic determinants and test their effects on levels of imprisonment. One of these studies explored state-level variation (Jacobs and Carmichael, 2001) and is therefore discussed in Chapter 6. The most recent study (Jacobs and Kleban, 2003) explores political determinants of imprisonment rates cross-nationally. The remaining two (Jacobs and Helms, 1996; Jacobs and Helms, 2001) attempted to explain the political determinants of imprisonment at the national level, the former using annual prison admission rates per capita and the latter using annual imprisonment rates per capita and are therefore discussed here.

In Jacobs and Helms (1996) first study of determinants of variation in imprisonment at the national level, the researchers, covering the period from 1950 to 1990, employed prison admission rates per capita as their dependent variable. Their independent variables included crime (measured by the crime rate and the crime rate squared to account for what they called a threshold hypothesis – a hypothesis that crime results in more vocal calls for punitive responses after it eclipses a certain threshold[4]), income inequality (measured in the first instance by the gap between the wealthy and all others, and in the second by the GINI index – a measure of the gap between the poor and all others), political conservatism (measured by the political affiliation of elected officials – the President, the percentage of Republican Governors, U.S. Senators and U.S. Representatives – and the percentage of citizens that identify themselves as Republican in Gallup polls), unemployment and economic growth (rate and per capita Gross Domestic Product respectively), a demographic variable (percent of young males between the ages of 14 and 25 years of age), and family breakdown (out of wedlock births measured as a five year moving average lagged by 19 years).

In the final analysis, Jacobs and Helms found that crime rates squared (but not traditional unadjusted crime rates), family breakdown, income inequality (but only inequality between the wealthy and all others) and political conservatism predict fluctuations in imprisonment rates; unemployment, economic growth, and the percentage of young males in the population did not. Jacobs and Helms (1996) argue that their findings suggest that economic determinants, the most frequently posited of the 'causes' of fluctuations in imprisonment, have been overemphasized, and that family breakdown (and the attendant breakdown in informal social control), political conservatism, and "the political potency of the affluent" (1996:349) are the strongest predictors of changes in imprisonment practices over time.

In a second and similar analysis of the determinants of changes in imprisonment over time, Jacobs and Helms again test the theory that "punishment is an inherently political process" (2001:191). In this work, they change the dependent variable from annual prison admissions to annual imprisonment rates, slightly modify their measurement of the political determinants of imprisonment, add a measure of race (the percent of the population that is non-white), and employ a time-series design covering the years from 1953 to 1998. Here the politically-oriented independent variables include whether a Republican President held office, whether it was a presidential election year, the percentage of Republicans holding govenorships or positions in the state legislatures, and a count of the consecutive years a Republican was president. Additionally, they include a dummy variable for the Clinton years because they contend that Clinton's unorthodox crime control agenda, which led to continual increases in imprisonment during the years of his administration, may constitute a "potentially idiosyncratic Democratic administration" (Jacobs and Helms, 2001:178). They include all of the remaining independent variables with the exception their former measure of income inequality between the wealthy and all others.

Once again, Jacobs and Helms (2001) find that political explanations, both manifest and latent, best explain variation in imprisonment policy. Unemployment was once again a non-significant contributor to changes in imprisonment, and they found no support for the notion that racial threat plays a significant role in increasing calls for more punitive responses to crime (although racial threat was measured simply by the percentage of the population that was non-white). Here crime and income inequality (as measured by the Gini index), while not significant in their earlier study, were significantly related to changes in imprisonment rates but the income inequality effect was delayed – with income inequality taking about two years to impact imprisonment rates. Interestingly, they find support for their hypothesis "that reactions to crime in the Clinton years were exceptional" (Jacobs and Helms, 2001:182), and find that holding the years of the Clinton administration constant "sharpens the distinction between Republican and Democratic administrations before the Clinton presidency on law-and-order issues" (2001:182).

PARTITIONING GROWTH IN PUNITIVENESS OVER CRIMINAL JUSTICE STAGES

All of the previously discussed empirical work has tested the effects of various variables on imprisonment rates which might be referred to as the end result of growing punitiveness. Others have tried to partition the growth in punitiveness to isolate the stage of the process at which we have actually become more punitive. Bureau of Justice Statistic's statistician Patrick Langan (1991) undertook such an analysis. Langan first notes that the size of prison populations depends on the flow in to prison and the flow out of prison. Langan reports that in most of the years between 1926 (the first year in which national prison data were collected) and 1990, prison admissions have outpaced releases.[5] The flow in to prison can grow with changes in demographics or with changes at any one of three criminal justice stages: reporting of crime, arrests, and convictions resulting in a sentence of imprisonment. The flow out can slow when sentences to prison grow in length, when release mechanisms are effectively disabled, and when actual time served increases as a result. Examining national data from 1940 to 1988, Langan finds that after 1973 (the year most often isolated as the beginning of the punitive turn), the median time served in prison was actually lower than it was in the pre-1973 period, and therefore proceeds to analyze only changes in the stages at which the flow in to prison might be expected to increase prison populations through increasing admissions.

Having discounted the importance of the flow out of prison, Langan analyzes the effect of changing demographics, reported crime and arrest rates, and imprisonment risk across six index offenses on prison population growth from 1974 to 1986.[6] Langan finds that there has been some growth at each of the stages, but that the vast majority of growth in prison populations (51 percent) is attributable to the increasing risk of imprisonment following a felony arrest. Demographic changes, particularly the 40 percent growth in the number of blacks in their twenties between 1974 and 1986, explained 20 percent of the growth in admissions. While reported crime rates increased, Langan reports that this growth was to a large extent offset by declining arrest rates for each of the index offenses. Although not directly tested in his analysis, Langan asserts that increasing imprisonment risk is a function of both increasing convictions and increasing sentences to prison following a conviction. He feels confident in this assertion because sentences to jail and probation, which have also grown rapidly over this period, "together with prison sanctions constitute virtually 100% of the sentences felons receive" (Langan, 1991:1572), and therefore, there must have been increases in convictions.

Undoubtedly the empirical work of most interest here is Blumstein and Beck's (1999) analysis of variations in imprisonment over time partitioning the contribution of increasing punitiveness at each of the various stages along the crime-punishment continuum. Like Langan (1991), Blumstein and Beck are interested primarily in identifying the stages at which we have become more punitive, and assessing the relative contribution of each stage to the resulting escalation in the size of the prison population overall. This study is of particular interest because the analyses performed in the latter part of this dissertation extend their analysis of two of these stages to the state-level assessment of variations in punitiveness.

Blumstein and Beck (1999) identify four processing stages along the crime-punishment continuum that might have contributed to the increasing size of the United States prison population: the amount of crime, the number of arrests per crime, the number of commitments per arrest, and the average time-served per offense. The first two stages might be referred to as offense and apprehension phases respectively, while the latter two represent distinct components of the sanctioning phase. Blumstein and Beck measure the offense and apprehension phases by examining UCR reported adult offense and clearance rates, and find that over time (1980-1996), only 12 percent of the increase in imprisonment can be attributed to changes in these early stage phases of the process (notably the vast majority of the 12 percent can be attributed to changes at the offending stage (11.5 percent) and only a negligible amount (one half of one percent) to increasing police effectiveness at effecting arrests). Ultimately Blumstein and Beck find that "the remaining 88% [of the growth in imprisonment] is attributable to increases in the imposition of sanctions, primarily in the decision to incarcerate (51%) and secondarily in the time served by those incarcerated (37%)" (1999:43).

Blumstein and Beck's analysis involves a sub-analysis of these four stages based on six offense types (murder, sexual assault, aggravated assault, robbery, burglary, and drug offenses) "that account for three-quarters of state prison populations" (1999:20). Blumstein and Beck point out that the 12 percent contribution that offense rates make to the increase imprisonment can be predominantly attributed to changes in the level of drug offending (measured by drug arrests due to the lack of data on drug offending), and find that when drug offenses are removed from the analysis, the sanctioning phases account for over 99 percent of the increase in the size of the incarcerated population. Moreover "the relative contribution of increasing rates of commitments and time served is reversed" (Blumstein and Beck, 1999:43) with commitments per arrest accounting for 41.5 percent of the increase and time served accounting for 57.7 percent. They explain the reversal of the relative contribution as a function of an escalating degree of imprisonment risk for drug offending with a much less notable trend in time served for those offenses.

Perhaps of greatest interest is a finding Blumstein and Beck report at the end of their study:

> For the state offenses, by 1996 the rates of crime for each of the offenses considered were on the decline, new commitments to prison had been flat since 1990, new admissions of parole violators had been flat since 1994, and yet prison populations continued to increase. *In recent years, only growth in time served is contributing to the growth in incarceration... time served is the single factor influencing prison population that has been increasing steadily during the 1990s.* (1999:55, emphasis added)

In a more recent analysis, Blumstein and Beck (2005) extend their analysis to 2001 and partition the period into two separate periods. Using 1992 as a break point between 1980 and 2001, Blumstein and Beck again find that growth in crime and arrests per crime explain almost none of the growth in imprisonment (though crime did explain some of the growth in the earlier period), and find that increases in the propensity to imprison contributed more to growth in the early period (1980-1992), and increases in the duration of imprisonment contributed more to growth in the later period (1992-2001).

PARTITIONING GROWTH IN PUNITIVENESS OVER TIME

Perhaps having read Blumstein and Beck's 1999 article, Franklin Zimring (2001), one of the most active scholars in the area of imprisonment policy research, suggests, somewhat tentatively, that the recent growth in imprisonment might be parsed into three eras of expansion. The first, which Zimring suggests began in the mid-1970s and continued through about 1985, was an expansion in the risk of imprisonment, particularly for lower-level offenders who previously would likely not have received a term of imprisonment.[7] The second era, which began around 1985 and continued through the early 1990s, represented a shift in emphasis from low-level felons to drug offenders, and a concomitant and more pronounced increase in the risk and duration of imprisonment for this particular class of offenders. The third and final era, which we are apparently still experiencing currently, is one not of increasing risk of imprisonment for either low-level felons or drug offenders, but one of increasing harshness in the length of time offenders serve for their transgressions, presumably regardless of offense (though Zimring is less specific about for whom this harshness is applicable). Zimring characterizes the transition from the second to the third era as follows:

> Here the shift in emphasis from 'lock 'em up' to 'throw away the key,' and I believe (without currently sufficient evidence) that the lengthening of sentences has begun during this period to play a much larger role in sustaining the growth of prison population (Zimring, 2001:162).

In an interesting critique of Zimring's periodization, James Jacob's (2001) points out that the middle era (1985-1992) essentially collapses into either the first or third era because, as postulated by Zimring, in the first era there was an increase in the *propensity to imprison* low-level offenders, in the second an increase in both the *propensity to imprison* and the *duration of imprisonment* for a certain group of low-level offenders (specifically drug offenders), and in the third an increase in the *duration of imprisonment*. The problem for Zimring is that he does not empirically back up his periodization with data.[8]

Without offering much by way of empirical support for his periodization of the imprisonment expansion, Zimring uses it as a point of departure for explaining the reasons for the shift into the third "throw away the key" era. Here he relies on "the new politics of punishment" (Zimring, 2001:162) implicating three quite specific changes in the way we have approached punishment policy through the 1990s up to the present. The first that criminal laws that were typically written to "bark much louder than they bite," with quite a distance between their "symbolic and operational content", in this new era have reversed course and bitten at least as hard, if not harder, than their bark is loud (Zimring, 2001:163). The second that criminal justice policy generally, and punishment policy more specifically, has become a "zero sum game" where imposing harm on those that we punish automatically benefits those that fall victim to them. When criminal justice policy is envisioned as a zero sum game, doing more harm to offenders is depicted as promoting greater good for the victim.[9] And the third that an increasing distrust of most of the central actors in the criminal justice process (police, judges, and parole authorities in particular) has led to legislation that reduces their discretion, which in turn has thwarted their ability to make downward or back-end adjustments to the severity of punishment.[10]

STATE-LEVEL VARIATION

Studies of imprisonment in the United States as a nation, while demonstrating overarching trends, fail to capture the uniqueness of experiences at the state level. Although as a nation the United States has become more punitive, there is notable variation across the fifty states. In the age of 'get-tough' legislation, states have adopted a punitive strategy to varying extents (as documented in Chapter 1, Table 1.3). While some states wholeheartedly embrace every in vogue punitive measure, others adopt very few.

Moreover, states at the high end of the imprisonment rate continuum have imprisoned at rates as much as ten times higher than those at the low end (Zimring and Hawkins, 1991:148). While most states have experienced increases in imprisonment levels in keeping with the national trend, the extent to which they have increased correctional control through imprisonment has varied greatly. Some states imprisonment rates are far lower than the national average and others greatly exceed it. Maine, for example, imprisoned 148 inmates per 100,000 residents in 2003, well below the national average of 480 inmates per 100,000 residents, while Oklahoma's imprisonment rate of 803 per 100,000, far exceeded the national average (Harrison & Karberg, 2004). To speak of the fifty states as a unified whole masks over significant variation in state imprisonment practices. As depicted in Figure 3.1, in terms of imprisonment, Maine, Minnesota, and North Dakota, for example, actually look more like Europe than they do their American counterparts.[11]

Figure 3.1: Incarceration Rates: Europe, United States, and Select U.S. States[12]

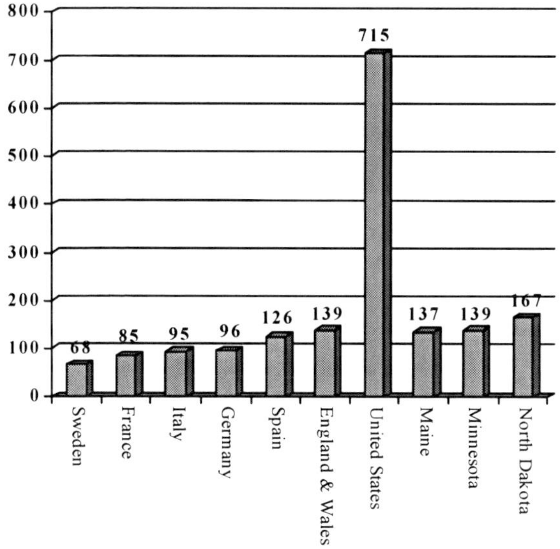

What makes one state more punitive than another? What best explains this state-level variation in punitiveness? Almost all studies of state-level variations in *punitiveness* are studies of state-level variations in *imprisonment*. Studies of state-level variations in punitiveness (i.e. imprisonment) can be classified into two broad areas – those that seek to *explore* the variation, and those that seek to *explain* it. Studies of each type will be reviewed in Chapters 4 and 5 respectively.

NOTES

[1] It is important to note however that research is often as frequently cited for its flaws as it is for its merits.

[2] It should be noted that each of these findings need qualifying as research rarely demonstrates that imprisonment reduces all types of crime. Levitt (1996), for example, found that imprisonment overall reduced both violent and property crimes, but that in an analysis of individual crime types only robbery and burglary were significantly reduced.

[3] While Beckett's theory was fairly well received when published (see Lyons, 2000; Simon, 2000; Sparks, 2000), Useem, et al. (2003) have criticized her measure of public opinion. Beckett's analysis relied upon the 'most important problem' (MIP) question that has been posed to the American public in Gallup opinion polls for most of the twentieth century. Useem et al. argue that because the question asked is: "What is the most important problem facing the country today?" (2003:15) responses might be particularly susceptible to salient events and sudden crises.

[4] By squaring the crime rate, Jacobs and Helms's analysis gives greater weight to higher crime rates.

[5] Admissions outpaced releases in 48 (or three quarters) of the 64 years between 1926 and 1990.

[6] Langan uses the term 'imprisonment rate' to refer to the number of imprisonments per 100 arrests – later in this study, this measure is referred to as 'imprisonment risk' – to avoid confusion, I will use the latter term here as the term "imprisonment rate" is usually used to describe prison populations per

100,000 population). The six offenses included the usual index offenses (murder, rape, robbery, aggravated assault, burglary, and larceny).

[7] Here imprisonment risk is used more appropriately than it was in Murray's (1997) analysis and refers to the risk of imprisonment following a felony arrest.

[8] Because measures of imprisonment risk and time-served by offense are attainable (and are likely fairly reliable for low-level and drug offenses), the feasibility of Zimring's parsing of the expansion into three eras could be empirically either demonstrated or refuted. This type of analysis is exactly that which is undertaken in the analysis section of this book.

[9] See also Zimring & Hawkins (2004).

[10] In an essay in the same volume, Jacobs (2001) ably critiques Zimring's characterization of the changes in the politics of punishment in the 1990's. Most notably he questions Zimring's use of California's three-strikes experience as an example of the first change when Zimring himself points out the uniqueness of California's experience in this regard. Zimring notes that the "The California version of Three Strikes has resulted in nine time as many prison terms as all of the 26 other three strikes laws in the United States combined" (2001:163).

[11] The rates for European countries and the United States are incarceration rates including those incarcerated in jails. The rates for the select states are imprisonment rates.

[12] Data Sources: International Rates (Walmsley, 2003); United States rates (Harrison & Karberg, 2004)

CHAPTER 4

EXPLORING VARIATIONS IN IMPRISONMENT

Although countless scholars have noted the substantial variation in the use of imprisonment across states (see for example Reitz, 2001; Christie, 2000; Currie, 1998; Cullen, VanVoorhis, and Sundt, 1996 to list but a few), most address national trends in imprisonment and simply note the state-level variation as a caveat. The comments of Cullen, et al. (1996) and Reitz (2001) are typical:

> The limits of our contribution, however, should be immediately confessed. It takes a good measure of hubris to suggest that that the 'American experience' with imprisonment can be boiled down to a discussion of two forms of crises [crowding crisis and crisis in conscience]. Prisons in the United States are part of an unwieldy, decentralized system that has an enormous amount of 'within group' variation. Accordingly, the reader should be aware that in our attempt to convey essential features of the current state of United States imprisonment, our analysis cannot escape the limits of reductionism. (Cullen et al., 1996:21, citation omitted).
>
> One preliminary caveat is needed. It is hard enough to compact three decades of complex national experience into a single book or chapter. The project is made more difficult, perhaps impossible, given that fact that there really is no such thing as "U.S. sentencing practice"... the states have varied

> greatly in their individual experiences of crime and their governmental responses to it. Much of the gross national data presented here, and the many sweeping authorial statements about U.S. attitudes and policy outlooks, merit a constant refrain of qualification and disclaimer (Reitz, 2001:223).

Despite the (sometimes reluctant) tendency to address the punitiveness of the United States generally, there have been many studies that document and a number of studies that more comprehensively explore state-level variation in imprisonment (usually controlling for levels of crime). Virtually all of these studies explore state-level variation in terms of variation in imprisonment rates rather than admission rates, imprisonment risk, or time-served. Some explore the variation cross-sectionally, while others do so longitudinally. Each of these studies attempts to document the wide variation in punishment practices across states. Studies that examine relative punitiveness of the states while in one way or another controlling for crime are included here rather than in the chapter that follows on explaining variations in punitiveness because none of the authors of these studies suggest that crime can wholly explain the variations in punitiveness.

VARIATIONS IN THE "SCALE OF IMPRISONMENT"

In their frequently cited book, *The Scale of Imprisonment*, Zimring and Hawkins (1991) explored state-level variations in imprisonment in a chapter suitably titled "Fifty-One Different Countries." Exploring the vast differences in rates of imprisonment across the states, Zimring and Hawkins note that there is more variation across the fifty states than there is across the countries in Western Europe. They report that in 1980 the imprisonment rate of the state at the upper end of the imprisonment spectrum (North Carolina) was ten times the rate of the state at the lower end (New Hampshire). In comparison, across Western Europe in 1977, the country at the upper end of the imprisonment rate spectrum (Finland) imprisoned at a rate just over four times that of the country at the lower end (Netherlands). When the variation in imprisonment across states is greater than the variation across countries, that variation is worth not only exploring but explaining.

Zimring and Hawkins also explored variation across time, finding that while all states had become more punitive, in terms of increasing imprisonment rates, over their periods of study (1950-1980 and 1980-1986), most had retained their punitiveness ranking relative to other states. In other words, states that were less punitive in the earlier period tended to remain less punitive in the later period (even though all states had moved in the direction of greater punitiveness through higher rates of imprisonment).

IMPRISONMENT, INCARCERATION, & TOTAL CONTROL RATES

In 1988 and 1989, James Austin and colleagues (Austin and Tillman, 1988; Austin and Brown, 1989), on behalf of the National Council on Crime and Delinquency, explored several methods of ranking states in terms of punitiveness. They ranked the fifty states and Washington D.C. according to imprisonment rate (the traditional measure of the size of the prison population per 100,000 residents), the total incarceration rate (a measure which included those serving custodial sentences in either prisons, jails, or juvenile detention centers), and the total control rate (a measure which added those on probation or parole to the total incarceration rate).

In the 1989 analysis of 1987 data (Austin and Brown, 1989), across all of the measures – the imprisonment, incarceration, and total control rates – Washington D.C. ranked as the single most punitive jurisdiction – its imprisonment and incarceration rates were more than double that of the next closest state. If you exclude Washington D.C., six states (Alabama, Arizona, Georgia, Louisiana, Nevada, and South Carolina) were among the top ten most punitive states in terms of both imprisonment and total incarceration rates, and only one state, Georgia, was among the top ten most punitive states across all three measures.[1] There was more consistency across the measures when examining states at the lower end of the punitiveness continuum: eight states (Iowa, Maine, Massachusetts, Minnesota, New Hampshire, North

Dakota, Utah, and West Virginia) were all among the ten least punitive states whether measured by imprisonment or total incarceration rate, while five states (Maine, New Hampshire, North Dakota, Utah, and West Virginia) were among the ten least punitive across all measures. Interestingly, Massachusetts, which is one of the *least punitive states* when measured by the imprisonment or incarceration rate, is among the top ten *most punitive states* when punitiveness is measured by the total control rate. In Austin and Brown's study (1989), California, a state often singled out for the sheer scale of its imprisonment system, is among the top ten most punitive states when measured by total incarceration or total control rates, but fails to make the top ten in terms of imprisonment rate (ranked 15th).[2] Although the imprisonment, total incarceration, and total control rates, are interesting in that they provide an overall picture of variations in the scale of various types of punishment across jurisdictions, they do not control for the levels of crime in each state.

To provide some measure of control for crime, Austin and Brown also calculate total control/crime ratios and rank the states accordingly. As explained by Austin and Brown:

> If the level of crime explains why states vary in their use of incarceration, probation and parole, one would expect to see little variation across the states in total control/crime ratios. States with relatively high rates of crime should have correspondingly high total control rates; states with low rates of control [sic] should have correspondingly low total control rates. But, in both cases, the total control/crime ratios would be similar. (Austin and Brown, 1989:4).

After calculating the ratios and ranking the states, Austin and Brown find, however, that there is great variation in these ratios – with states at the top of the ranking having as many as five times as many people under correctional control per crime as those at the bottom of the ranking. Georgia, a state that was among the most punitive across all measures of the scale of punishment, continues to be over-punitive relative to other states when crime is considered. Georgia has approximately 42 persons under some form of correctional control for every 100 reported crimes. By way of comparison, New Mexico has only 9 persons under correctional control per 100 crimes reported. Massachusetts, a state that ranks as one of the ten least punitive states using the traditional imprisonment rate measure (and is therefore likely considered a 'non-punitive' state in most studies that try to explain variations in punitiveness), has approximately 41 people under correctional control per 100 crimes, and again appears to be among the top ten over-punitive states when this control for crime is incorporated.

Finally, Austin and Brown calculate imprisonment and total control per arrest ratios, which represent the number of persons in prison or under correctional control per arrest, and rank the states according to these ratios.[3] In these analyses, Georgia continues to be the only state to make the 'top ten most punitive' list across all measures.

As noted by the researchers, "in some ways, the imprisonment to arrest ratio is a superior measure of punitiveness in that it reflects the use of the most punitive sanction, given the number of arrests made in that state for serious crimes" (Austin and Brown, 1989:5). By this measure, likely the most pure measure of punitiveness (though only in terms of imprisonment propensity), the wide variation across states persists. The most punitive states (Mississipi, Indiana, and South Dakota) imprisoned upwards of 70 people per 100 index crime arrests and the least punitive states (Minnesota, Montana, Colorado) imprisoned less than 20 people per 100 index crime arrests. The interesting cases in Austin and Brown's punitiveness rankings are those that seem particularly punitive using one measure and notably non-punitive using another. Here Massachusetts stands out as a prime example of a state that seems all over the place on the various punitiveness scales (ranking 45th in imprisonment rate, 42nd in total incarceration rate, but 5th in terms of total control rate, and 1st in terms of control/arrest ratio – with lower rankings indicating greater punitiveness). By way of explanation, it might be fair to characterize Massachusetts as a state that is somewhat reluctant to use imprisonment (hence its low imprisonment rate – 107 per 100,000 in 1987 - and average imprisonment to arrest ratio – 34 prisoners per 100 index crimes), but not so reluctant to impose some form of punishment (hence its high total control rate – 1,935 people under correctional control per 100,000 residents – and high total control/arrest ratio – 6 people under correctional control for each index crime arrest).

CRIME, ARREST, AND IMPRISONMENT

Like Austin and colleagues (1988; 1989), Selke and Andersson (1992) developed a model for assessing the relative punitiveness of the fifty states and Washington D.C.. Their somewhat more complex quantitative model, incorporating logged transformations of crime, arrest and imprisonment rates, allowed them to ultimately "create a qualitative ordering of the states in terms of their deviation… from the line denoting the average behavior of states in imprisoning criminal offenders while controlling for reported crime rates" (Selke and Andersson, 1992:225-226). Selke and Andersson then compared their ranking of the states to that of Austin and Tillman (1998) and found that, while their ranking of imprisonment rates controlling for crime rates produced a similar ranking to Austin and Tillman, there were some notable variations between them. At both the upper and lower ends of the 'punitiveness' spectrum, several of the ten states that Austin and Tillman (1988) identified as most and least punitive respectively (either by simple reference to their imprisonment rates or to their imprisonment rates controlling for arrests) were also identified as among the ten most and least punitive states using Selke and Andersson's more sophisticated model of imprisonment controlling for crime (including Minnesota, Rhode Island, Utah, North Dakota, and Massachusetts at the lower end of the punitiveness continuum, and Alabama, Nevada, South Carolina, Delaware and Louisiana at the upper end). At both ends of the continuum, however, there were a handful of states that moved quite significantly (Mississippi, for example was the most punitive using Selke and Andersson's model, while it was not even in the top ten using either of Austin and Tillman's models).

Because of the fairly high degree of consistency across punitiveness rankings between their own model and that of Austin and

Tillman, Selke and Andersson conclude that the state-level rankings that result from the various models do not differ substantially enough to suggest that the choice of model makes that much of a difference. They note, however, that because there are a few instances in which a state moved quite substantially up or down in its ranking, the more quantitatively sophisticated model of ranking punitiveness that they developed might be preferable.

PRESSURE TO CONFORM

Like Selke and Andersson (1992), others have also explored state-level variation in imprisonment to more explicitly explore the effect average punitiveness across states has on variations in punitiveness rankings among states. Testing a hypothesis that states might gravitate toward the national trend by adjusting their punitiveness due to 'pressure to conformity,' Ouimet and Tremblay (1996) classified states according to their punitiveness using a measure that accounted for levels of crime. They defined punitiveness by reference to imprisonment rates noting that in their study "a state is defined as more or less punitive if its imprisonment rate is higher or lower than expected given its crime rates" (Ouimet & Tremblay, 1996:111), and calculated a measure of punitiveness that took into account the difference between a state's actual imprisonment rate and its expected imprisonment rate given its crime rates. The resulting measure, which Ouimet and Tremblay called a "percentage deviation from the predicted value (PDPV)" measure, allowed them to classify some states as either under-punitive or over-punitive based on their crime rates (1996:112).

Ouimet and Tremblay hypothesized that 'pressure to conformity' would push the over-punitive states to lower their imprisonment rates and regress toward the mean in later periods to avoid being labeled as an outlier in terms of punitiveness. Analyzing changes in PDPV across three time periods (1972, 1982, and 1992), the researchers found that there was indeed high turnover in states that were identified as under or over punitive. Ouimet and Tremblay report that "only 3 states – Minnesota, New Mexico, and Massachusetts- managed to stay in the under-punitive list three times, whereas 1 state – South Dakota –

remained in the list of the 10 most overpunitive states" (1996:116). Ouimet and Tremblay's analysis is particularly interesting in the theory it advances – that those who administer the state's punitive apparatus might pay attention to the punishment levels of other states and adjust accordingly.

Although only a sampling of the studies that explore variations in punitiveness across states have been presented in any great detail, and keeping in mind that the authors of these studies use different methods for ranking the states and different time periods in constructing the rankings, it might prove useful to examine the variation in rankings across studies. Table 4.1 identifies those states that consistently rank among the most or least punitive across studies.

Table 4.1 demonstrates that state-level rankings are not particularly consistent across the studies. Granted each of these studies employs a somewhat different methodology but in all instances, the researchers are attempting to rank states according to their relative punitiveness controlling for crime. Only three states appear in the top and bottom ten across all three studies. An additional five states are among the most punitive and an additional four are among the least punitive in at least two of the studies. There are also some interesting anomalies across studies. Vermont, for example, ranks among the ten least punitive in Selke and Andersson's measure of imprisonment controlling for crime but is far more average across the other studies (ranking between 20th and 30th).

The articles discussed in this chapter suggest several things: 1) that there is indeed a large amount of variation in imprisonment across states, 2) that the state-level ranking depends to a certain extent on the methodology employed, and 3) that we do not yet fully understand the nature of the variations in punitiveness across states.

Table 4.1: Variations in Punitiveness Across States, Across Studies

Study	Austin and Brown (1989)	Selke and Andersson (1992)	Ouimet and Tremblay (1996)
Measure	Imprisonment /arrest ratio	Imprisonment controlling for crime	PPDV
Year	1987	1987	1992
Most Punitive			
	Mississippi	**Mississippi**	***South Dakota***
	Indiana	**Alabama**	**Oklahoma**
	South Dakota	***Nevada***	***South Carolina***
	South Carolina	***South Carolina***	**Ohio**
	Ohio	***South Dakota***	Michigan
	Alabama	**Louisiana**	Arizona
	Georgia	Virginia	***Nevada***
	Louisiana	North Carolina	New Jersey
	Oklahoma	Arkansas	Kentucky
	Nevada	Maryland	Wyoming
Least Punitive			
	Minnesota	***Minnesota***	**West Virginia**
	Montana	Rhode Island	***Minnesota***
	Colorado	**Washington**	***North Dakota***
	Utah	***Utah***	Tennessee
	North Dakota	***North Dakota***	Oregon
	West Virginia	Vermont	Maine
	Wisconsin	**Massachusetts**	**Massachusetts**
	Iowa	**Colorado**	Nebraska
	Washington	New Hampshire	***Utah***
	California	Hawaii	Illinois

Note: States in bold appear in the top or bottom ten in two of the three studies. States in bold italics appear in the top or bottom ten across all three studies.

NOTES

[1] In Austin and Brown's (1989) rankings, Alaska and Delaware were also among the top ten most punitive states in terms of imprisonment and total incarceration rates, and Delaware among the top ten most punitive across all three measures; however, because both of these states have combined prison and jail populations, their imprisonment rates are inflated and are substantially the same as their total incarceration rates. This is also the case for Connecticut, Hawaii, Rhode Island, and Vermont. I, therefore, leave these states out of the discussion when they appear among the top ten states by one or more of the various measures of punitiveness. When these states appear among the bottom ten this distinction matters less because these states are actually less punitive than they rank.

[2] According to Clear and Cole (2003), one in nine U.S. prisoners is imprisoned in California.

[3] Austin and Brown's (1989) prison/arrest ratio is the type of measure used later in this analysis to capture imprisonment risk.

CHAPTER 5

EXPLAINING VARIATIONS IN IMPRISONMENT

In addition to the studies that *explore* state-level variation in imprisonment, there are a number of studies, of varying degrees of sophistication, that attempt to *explain* state-level variations in imprisonment using one or more of the potential explanatory variables discussed in Chapter 2. Although the approaches vary in their orientation, scope, and method, they almost invariably use imprisonment rates as the dependent variable.[1] In this chapter, I review a few of the more recent attempts to empirically explain state-level variation in imprisonment. The first section of the review covers some of the more recent sentencing policy studies, and the second section three of the more methodologically sophisticated attempts to explain variation using a variety of social, structural, political, ideological, and demographic indicators.[2]

SENTENCING POLICY STUDIES

A number of recent studies (Marvell, 1995; Sorenson and Stemen, 2002; Nicholson-Crotty, 2004) explore the impact of sentencing guidelines on punitiveness across the states. As described in Chapter 2, sentencing guidelines were, by most accounts, expected to curb or at least stabilize the expansion of prison populations (Nicholson-Crotty, 2004).

Marvell's (1995) analysis included the nine states that had established presumptive sentencing guidelines by 1990.[3] According to Marvell, in six of the nine states, the sentencing commissions were instructed to consider capacity, while in the remaining three capacity was not a consideration. Marvell's analysis tested the effect of sentencing guidelines on two punishment outcomes, prison population and new court commitments to prison, and included five control variables (state and year dummies, a crime prone age control, serious crime rates, income, and employment). Marvell found that the states that specifically mandated the consideration of capacity in the development of sentencing guidelines experienced a slowing in the growth of the prison population in the years following the effective date of the guidelines, while those without the mandate did not. Interestingly, Marvell finds that even in those states with mandates to consider capacity, the sentencing guidelines did not slow pace of new court commitments to prison and, though sentence length is not a dependent variable in his analysis, argues that "the implication is that changes in prison population growth are due mainly to changes in prison term length" (1995:704).

Sorenson and Stemen (2002) make a significant contribution because theirs is the only analysis to assess the impact of a large number of policy variables on punishment and to include the full array of punishment outcomes that might be indicative of greater punitiveness. Their dependent variables include imprisonment rates, prison admission rates, average sentence length, and average time served. Sorenson and Stemen include sentencing guidelines, determinate sentencing, mandatory sentencing, truth-in-sentencing and three-strikes provisions (considered separately though they are a form of mandatory sentencing) as independent variables in their analysis of punishment outcomes. They additionally included a number of demographic, economic, ideological, crime, and systemic variables as controls. The limitation of their study was its cross-sectional design with the independent variables measured in 1996 predicting the dependent variables, lagged by one year, and measured in 1997.

While recognizing that the evidence for an effect of sentencing policy on prison population outcomes is ambiguous at best, Sorenson and Stemen suggest (though never explicitly hypothesize) that determinate, mandatory, three-strikes, and truth-in-sentencing policies would increase both the size of prison populations and rate of admissions to prison, and in the case of mandatory, three-strike, and truth-in-sentencing policies also increase sentence length and time-served. They suggested that sentencing guidelines, on the other hand, would reduce or at least slow the expansion of prison populations.

Somewhat surprisingly each of their sentencing policy variables were only weakly related to imprisonment and prison admission rates (and none of the zero-order correlations were significant). As reported by Sorenson and Stemen (2002) sentencing guidelines were slightly negatively correlated with both imprisonment rates and prison admission rates (-.12 and -.19 respectively), determinate sentencing and three-strikes policies were essentially unrelated to either imprisonment rates (-.02/.03) or prison admission rates (.01/.07), and truth-in-sentencing and mandatory sentencing policies were each more strongly related to imprisonment rates (.16/.22) than they were to prison admissions (-.02/.04) (See Table 1 in Sorenson & Stemen, 2001:464). The only correlations to approach significance were those between mandatory sentencing policies and imprisonment rates (p=.06) and between sentencing guidelines and admission rates (p=.09).

Sorenson and Stemen's cross-sectional design, large number of independent variables, and small sample size, precluded a comprehensive regression analysis. To conduct the regression, they had to eliminate many of their independent variables with only sentencing guidelines surviving. The regression indicated that although sentencing guidelines reduced both overall imprisonment rate and prison admission rate (by 72 and 55 per 100,000 respectively), they were not the strongest predictor of either (with percent black being the best predictor of imprisonment rates and index crime rate being the best predictor of prison admissions).

Additional analyses performed by Sorenson and Stemen compared sentence lengths and average time served of inmates in states with and without each of the sentencing policies. The sentencing policy variables were coded dichotomously allowing for a comparison of means between states with and without the various policies.[4] In this portion of the analysis they found that although determinate sentencing, presumptive sentencing guidelines, and mandatory sentencing provisions each had a significant effect on the average sentence length (with determinate and presumptive sentencing decreasing and mandatory sentencing increasing the average sentence length), none of the policy variables had a significant effect on the average amount of actual time served. Sorenson and Stemen recognize, as have others, that both truth-in-sentencing and three-strikes laws, predominately passed between 1994 and 1996 might not have had time to exert influence on average time served as most of those inmates sentenced under these policies had not yet been released by 1997 (the year in which their dependent variables were measured). Additionally, although Sorenson and Stemen do not make this inference, it might be argued that all of these sentencing policies, which ultimately appear to produce substantially the same outcomes in terms of time served, actually "bark louder than they bite."[5]

In the most recently published sentencing policy study, Sean Nicholson-Crotty (2004) also examines the effect of mandatory sentencing guidelines on imprisonment rates and prison admission rates. Building on the work of both Marvell (1995), Marvell and Moody (1996) and Sorenson and Stemen (2002), Nicholson-Crotty hypothesizes that mandatory sentencing guidelines explicitly linked to resources (e.g. those in effect in states that mandate a consideration of capacity) will either prevent or reduce growth in imprisonment rates and prison admissions, while those not linked to resources will increase growth. Nicholson-Crotty employs a pooled time-series design including all 50 states to examine the effect of mandatory sentencing guidelines on prison population fluctuations between 1975 and 1998.[6] In addition to his primary independent and dependent variables, Nicholson-Crotty included a host of control variables including demographic indicators (size of the crime and imprisonment prone population, percent black, population density, and total population), economic indicators (per capita income and unemployment rates), an ideological indicator, and crime rates.[7]

Nicholson-Crotty (2004) finds that indeed the linking of sentencing guidelines to correctional resources crucially affects imprisonment outcomes, particularly in regard to prison admission rates. In states where the guidelines were explicitly linked to resources, the introduction of guidelines "decreased the rate of admission to state prisons by an average of 29.8 inmates per 100,000 population each year" (2004:406). Conversely, in states where there was no linkage between the guidelines and correctional resources, average annual admissions increased by an average 13.9 inmates. While resource-linked guidelines had "no appreciable impact" on imprisonment rates, in states with no linkage, the guidelines increased the imprisonment rate by an average 34 inmates per 100,000 (Nicholson-Crotty, 2004:407). Three of Nicholson-Crotty's control variables also significantly predicted imprisonment rates (percent black, total population, and imprisonment prone population) and crime rates approached significance.[8] Nicholson-Crotty concludes that his findings "suggest a clear policy recommendation," and argues that "to ensure that mandatory guidelines do not increase commitment and incarceration rates, lawmakers must explicitly link sentencing recommendations to available correctional resources" (Nicholson-Crotty, 2004:408).

DEMOGRAPHIC, SOCIAL, STRUCTURAL, AND POLITICAL INDICATORS

Two empirical studies, those by Katherine Beckett and Bruce Western (2001) and David Greenberg and Valerie West (2001), measure the impact of a variety of potential explanatory variables on state-level imprisonment rate fluctuations over time. These empirical studies deserve particular attention because these two studies most fully test the explanatory power of variables identified as important to explaining the punitive turn in the theories discussed in Chapter 2. Moreover, it will be argued in the next chapter that these types of studies serve as the best examples of where a more refined dependent variable might provide a more nuanced understanding of variations in punitiveness across the states.

Control of Marginal Populations

Beckett and Western (2001) test their theory that social and penal policy represent a single 'policy regime' (discussed in Chapter 3), with a state-level analysis of imprisonment rates and welfare spending. If penal and welfare policies are in fact component parts of one social policy regime, it stands to reason that they will vary together and that they will be negatively related. Greater penal severity (in terms of increasing imprisonment) will be coupled with decreasing welfare expenditures. Conversely, states with more generous welfare policies will rely less on imprisonment because they have adopted a more inclusionary approach to dealing with the socially marginal. They hypothesize that states that have adopted an increasingly exclusionary penal policy will likely have supplemented this increasing punitiveness in the punishment realm with an increasingly exclusionary welfare stance in the social policy realm.

Beckett and Western examine the relationship between imprisonment and welfare across the states between 1975 and 1995. They measure imprisonment by reference to the imprisonment rate and welfare in terms of total spending on the promotion of welfare which included "measures states spending on Aid to Families with Dependent Children (AFDC), Supplemental Security Income (SSI), unemployment insurance, all non-tertiary education spending, food stamps, and Medicaid" (2001:49). They standardized and then summed the welfare measures to produce a composite "welfare generosity score". In addition to the primary independent variable (welfare generosity), Beckett and Western incorporate a number of additional independent variables including two measures of racial heterogeneity - the percent of the population that is black in the first model and the percent minority in the second, UCR measures of violent and property crime (measured separately), and measures of unemployment, poverty, urbanization, and republican political strength.

Beckett and Western ultimately find that the percent black and welfare generosity are the most important predictors of variations in imprisonment rates across the states. They find that both percent black and welfare generosity were strongly and significantly related to imprisonment rates by 1995 (percent black positively and welfare generosity negatively) and argue that "beginning in the 1980s, states with larger black populations are states that spent less on social welfare and also incarcerated at higher levels" (2001:54). The effect of both of these variables starts off fairly small in 1975 and grows as time passes so that, by 1995, the percent black and welfare generosity variables are more tightly coupled with imprisonment. The results for the model measuring racial heterogeneity by reference to the percent minority, rather than percent black, were notably weaker with percent minority in the earlier periods negatively related or unrelated to imprisonment and by the 1990s significantly positively related. With regard to their control variables, violent crime rates, poverty, and republican strength each positively impacted imprisonment rates, while property crime rates were negatively related. Beckett and Western conclude that indeed it seems that punishment and welfare "have come to form a single policy regime aimed at the governance of social marginality" and add that "states with larger poor and African-American populations and more Republican dominated legislatures have been more inclined to adopt this approach to social marginality" (2001:55).

Beckett and Western's analysis is not without its critics. In a response appearing in the same volume, David Greenberg, while conceding that "locking people up or giving them money might be considered alternative ways of handling marginal, poor populations – repressive in one case, generous in the other" (2001:81), argues that the analytical strategy employed to assess the coupling of these approaches that allegedly constitute a policy regime is problematic. Greenberg argues that:

> To the extent that these changes reflect a change in the thinking that lies behind both policies, using one variable to predict the other may be a little misleading. It is a little like using the length of people's left leg to predict the length of their right leg. Both are indicators of someone's height. If imprisonment and welfare are both products of the same mind-set, the critical issue is to understand the source of this mind-set and why it changed between the 1960s and subsequent decades, with consequences for both imprisonment and welfare (2001:84).

Crime, Race, Conservatism, Unemployment, Inequality, and Welfare

In 2001, David Greenberg and Valerie West published one of the most sophisticated attempts to explain state level variations in imprisonment. An empirical study conducted by Jacobs and Carmichael and published in the same year (2001) is very similar to that of Greenberg and West and therefore, is only discussed for the points at which it diverges from Greenberg and West in either its methods or its findings.[9] In a study of state-level variations in imprisonment, Greenberg and West (2001) use the imprisonment rate as the dependent measure and a nearly exhaustive list of independent variables including crime indicators (violent, property, and narcotics crime rates), demographic indicators (percent black, latino), fiscal indicators (state revenues, unemployment rate), and political indicators (political affiliation of the governor, percent of the population that is conservative). In their study, Greenberg and West include both cross-sectional and longitudinal analyses to examine variations in state punitiveness between 1971 and 1991.[10] The variables in their analysis accounted for between to 87 and 91 percent of the variation in state imprisonment rates.[11] Some of Greenberg and West's more interesting findings include those related to crime, political conservatism, race, unemployment, and welfare spending.

Punitiveness and Crime

Greenberg and West broke the crime rate down into its two component parts (violent and property crime) and additionally included a measure of drug arrests. They found that violent crime and drug arrest rates each significantly predicted imprisonment rates, but property crime rates did not, and note that "although growth in crime was not a major cause of higher prison populations, imprisonment rates have been higher, and have grown faster, in states with higher levels of victimizing crime, especially violent crime" (2001:638).[12] They conclude that their findings support the conclusion that imprisonment rates are neither "entirely determined" nor "entirely unrelated" to crime rates

(2001:638). In other words, crime rates – particularly violent crime rates – explain some, but not enough of the variation in state imprisonment rates between 1971 and 1991.

Punitiveness and Race

Greenberg and West also found that race, in terms of the percentage of the population that is black, is a significant predictor of state-level variations in punitiveness. Specifically they found that states with larger black populations were more punitive than states with smaller black populations and that these states became even more punitive as the size of the black population increased. They are quick to point out that these findings survive the usual claim that race is only significant because blacks live in high crime, high unemployment neighborhoods:

> It cannot be stressed too strongly that the coefficients for employment and race are direct effects, with crime rates controlled, and so they cannot be explained away by claims that crime rates are higher where there is more unemployment or where more blacks live (Greenberg & West, 2001:638).

Interestingly, the size of the latino population was not related to the size of the imprisoned population, nor was its growth related to imprisonment's growth. Greenberg and West argue that this suggests "it is not minorities in general, but blacks in particular, who are perceived as threatening." (2001:640). They conclude that their "results are consistent with the 'racial threat' hypothesis. Blacks – black males in particular – appear to have become 'symbolic assailants' whose presence in a city evokes fear of crime independent of the actual level of crime" (2001:640).[13] Using a very similar methodology, Jacobs and Carmichael find significant effects for growth in Hispanic populations (which grew more substantially over the period covered in their analysis than did black populations – 47.9 percent versus 4.6 percent), though they too conclude "that black threat has a more substantial influence on U.S. imprisonment rates" (Jacobs and Carmichael, 2001:81).

Punitiveness, Conservatism, and Religiosity

Greenberg and West (2001) found that states in which greater numbers of the population identify as conservative (based on pooled poll data) experienced higher levels of incarceration and faster growth in incarceration rates.[14] In other words, conservative states were more punitive to begin with and became increasingly punitive more rapidly over the period covered by their study. They also found some interesting regional effects related to conservatism. While by most accounts Southern states are more punitive than states in other regions, Greenberg and West demonstrate that including variables that capture characteristics of the South, such as political conservatism and religiosity, eliminates any independent regional effect.[15]

Although they find that the percentage of the population identifying as conservative was significantly related to imprisonment rates, they found that political party affiliation of state governors was unrelated to both conservatism of the population and growth in imprisonment. This finding is interesting because Jacobs and Carmichael (2001), measuring Republican strength by the political party affiliation of the governor *and* the percent of Republican state legislators, found that growth in Republican strength significantly predicted growth in imprisonment rates. Moreover, they find that this relationship remains strong and significant even after controlling for conservatism and religiosity. The distinction between the two studies is in the measurement of 'Republican strength' – with Jacobs and Carmichael using more than one measure of political party affiliation. Both sets of researchers also found that *growth* in religious fundamentalism significantly predicted growth in imprisonment rates.

Punitiveness, Unemployment, and Economic Inequality

Greenberg and West (2001) found that both the level of unemployment and growth in unemployment were related to variations in imprisonment across the states. Interestingly, they found that while economic inequality is strongly and positively correlated with imprisonment at the national level, it did not significantly predict state-level variations. Jacobs and Carmichael (2001) find no evidence of a relationship between either unemployment or income inequality and imprisonment. The contradictory unemployment findings between the Greenberg and West and Jacobs and Carmichael studies is somewhat inexplicable because both measured unemployment in the same years (1970, 1980, and 1990). A review of the means and standard deviations in each study suggests that they used slightly different unemployment numbers.

Punitiveness and Welfare

Like Beckett and Western (2001), Greenberg and West (2001) find that increased use of imprisonment is negatively related to welfare spending.[16] As imprisonment rates increased, per capita welfare expenditures decreased. Both sets of researchers describe welfare as an inclusionary method and imprisonment as an exclusionary method of dealing with the poor, with states situated at various places along the inclusion-exclusion continuum. According to the findings of both, states that have more inclusionary welfare programs do seem to be less punitive toward criminal offenders, at least in terms of imprisonment rates. Conversely, those that have more fully adopted the exclusionary policy of increasing imprisonment have, at the same time, cut welfare expenditures.

Summary

Broadly speaking, there are two types of empirical studies that assess state-level variations in imprisonment rates. While those engaged in sentencing policy studies specifically test the effect of various sentencing policy decisions on imprisonment outcomes, others attempt to explain variations in imprisonment rates across states over time using a myriad of potential explanatory variables. The sentencing policy studies, each of which examined the effect of sentencing guidelines on imprisonment rates and prison admission rates, demonstrate that sentencing guidelines appear to have reduced or stabilized these rates, but perhaps only in states where the guidelines are mandatory and linked to resources. Those doing empirical work seeking to explain variation in imprisonment rates across the states over time invariably find that a number of social, structural, political, and demographic indicators are important to any explanation.

All three sets of researchers discussed in this review (Beckett and Western 2001; Greenberg and West, 2001; and Jacobs and Carmichael, 2001), find that crime rates, particularly violent crime rates, explain some of the variation in imprisonment rates over time. All three also find that race can explain some of the variation, with percent of the population that is black significantly predicting imprisonment rates and growth in imprisonment rates across all three studies. Violent crime and the percent black appear most consistently as significant explanatory variables in studies of variations in imprisonment rates.[17]

Findings with regard to ethnicity, measured by the percent of the population that are Hispanic, and minority presence more generally were less consistent. Measures of political conservatism and religiosity also reliably predict variation in imprisonment rates across these three studies, with growth in conservative and religious ideologies leading to more rapid growth in imprisonment rates. Welfare spending was significantly and negatively related to imprisonment rates in both the Beckett and Western (2001) and Greenberg and West (2001) studies.[18] Findings with regard to unemployment rates, poverty rates, and income inequality measures varied across the three studies.[19]

In part because so many variables are significantly related to fluctuations in punitiveness as measured by imprisonment rates, researchers can to a certain extent pick and choose the variables that they prefer to emphasize. Greenberg and West conclude that imprisonment rates are primarily "responsive to crime rates, to a state's racial composition, and to its economic circumstances" (2001:641), but also note the importance of addressing the political and religious culture of states in any study of variations in punitiveness, adding that "punishment policy is part of a larger constellation of policies united by a consistent logic" (641). Jacobs and Carmichael focus their discussion almost exclusively on the political determinants of state-level variation arguing that Republican strength and minority threat (which they describe as "indirectly political") are the most significant predictors of state-level variation. Finally, Beckett and Western find empirical support for their hypothesis that punishment and welfare comprise "a single policy regime aimed at the governance of social marginality" (2001:55).

In the next chapter, I argue that when punitiveness is gauged by alternate measures, state-level variations in punitiveness may differ substantially. If so, those empirically exploring explanations for variations in punitiveness across places or over time might need to be more specific in their hypotheses about the nature and direction of expected relationships between the explanatory variables and the dependent (punitiveness) variable.

NOTES

[1] Admission rates per capita are also used frequently.

[2] I have focused here on three recent, longitudinal studies of the relationship between various factors and variations in imprisonment rates. Other studies that could have been included in the discussion were either not as recent or employed less sophisticated, cross-sectional methodologies to explore these relationships (Garofalo 1980, Joubert, Picou, & McIntosh, 1981; Carroll & Doubet, 1983; McGuire & Sheehan, 1983; Carroll & Cornell, 1985; Michalowski & Pearson, 1990; Arvanites, 1993; McGarrell, 1993; Arvanites & Asher, 1995; Selke & Andersson, 2003).

[3] The nine states with sentencing guidelines in 1990 included Delaware, Florida, Michigan, Minnesota, Oregon, Pennsylvania, Tennessee, Washington, and Wisconsin (Marvell, 1995).

[4] Sorenson and Stemen (2002:462) point out that every state has enacted mandatory sentencing provisions, and therefore, in the case of mandatory sentencing, they coded the adoption of more than three mandatory sentencing provisions as 1 and the adoption of three or less as 0.

[5] As suggested by Zimring, Hawkins, & Kamin (2001) in the case of three strikes, and Zimring (2001) in the case of sentencing policy more generally.

[6] Nicholson-Crotty (2004) lagged prison admission rates (which included new court commitments and parole re-commitments) by one year and imprisonment rates by two years.

[7] Population density is measured by the percent living in metropolitan areas. The crime prone population was measured as the population between the ages of 18 and 24, and imprisonment prone population between the ages of 25 and 34 (see discussion on crime vs. imprisonment prone populations in Chapter 7). The citizen ideology measure was developed by Berry, Ringquist, Fording, & Hanson (1998) and is used as the liberalism indicator in most of the studies of variation in punitiveness.

[8] Nicholson-Crotty's crime rate measure (the overall index crime rate) may have limited the potential explanatory power. As noted below, those who break the crime rate into its two components (violent and property crime rates) find that violent crime rates significantly predict imprisonment rate variations, while the property crime rate typically is unrelated (Greenberg & West) or negatively related (Beckett & Western, 2001) to imprisonment rate growth.

[9] Jacobs and Carmichael acknowledge that they borrowed much of their methodology from Greenberg and West who presented an early version of their 2001 paper at the annual meeting of the American Sociological Association in 1998.

[10] Jacobs and Carmichael's (2001) analysis covered the exact same period.

[11] The variation explained depends on the model. Variables in Jacobs and Carmichael's analysis also explained upwards of 80 percent of the variation in state imprisonment rates.

[12] Jacobs and Carmichael included only violent crime in their analysis and also found that it significantly predicted variation in imprisonment rates over time. They tested their models with other measures of crime – total crime rate, property crime rate, etc. – and found that the use of these other measures did not change the results, but did reduce the explanatory power.

[13] As noted by Jock Young upon reading an early draft of this Chapter, in asserting support for the racial threat hypothesis, Greenberg and West rely on an individual level explanation for their results (the perception of blacks as threatening) after having conducted a state-level analysis – a classic case of ecological fallacy.

[14] Both Greenberg and West (2001) and Jacobs and Carmichael (2001) use the measure of citizen ideology developed by Berry et al. (1998).

[15] Jacobs and Carmichael (2001) also found that region was unrelated to imprisonment rates when conservatism and religiosity were included in the model.

[16] Jacobs and Carmichael (2001) did not include a measure of welfare spending in their analysis.

[17] In addition to the studies discussed in detail here, many others (see Arvanites, 1993; Garafalo, 1980; Joubert, et al., 1981;; McGarrell, 1993; Selke & Andersson, 2003 to list but a few) find positive and significant relationships between crime (often violent crime), percent of the population that is black, and variations in imprisonment rates. While a significant race finding is one of the more consistent findings, some have not found such a relationship (Arvanites & Asher, 1998; Michalowski & Pearson, 1990).

[18] See also Western & Guetzkow (2002).

[19] Evidence for unemployment, poverty, and economic inequality has been inconsistent across studies. Some find a significant positive effect of unemployment on imprisonment rates (Box & Hale, 1982), while others (see Arvanites, 1993; Michalowski & Pearson, 1990) find no relationship (see Chapter 4 for a brief discussion of findings on the relationship between unemployment and imprisonment, and Chiricos & Delone (1992) for a thorough review). Similarly inconsistent evidence has been reported with regard to poverty (see Arvanites & Asher, 1995; Beckett & Western, 2001) and economic inequality (Arvanites & Asher, 1995, 1998; Jacobs & Helms, 1996, 1997, 2001; Melossi, 1993; Western, Kleykamp, & Rosenfeld, 2003).

CHAPTER 6

THE PROBLEM WITH PUNITIVENESS

I am guilty of using the word "punitiveness" carelessly in the first five chapters of this book. I have done so, in part, to demonstrate the inadequacy of the construct. The word "punitiveness" is all too often used as a convenient substitute for the word punishment, where greater punitiveness simply implies more punishment. Moreover, in the way it is currently used, the term punitiveness typically does not imply more punishment generally, but rather more imprisonment. The United States, for example, is often considered the most punitive nation not because it more readily punishes offenders through any one of a number of punishment options, but rather because it has the most prisoners per 100,000 residents. Individual states like Oklahoma, Louisiana, and Texas, are also frequently described as the most punitive simply by reference to their imprisonment rates.

Given the all too frequent failure to define punitiveness as anything more than the relative amount of punishment (and then generally only the relative amount of imprisonment), it should come as little surprise that those who measure the punitiveness (of either one place over time or of one place compared to another), do so simply by reference to the variations in imprisonment rates over time or across places. Although imprisonment rates indeed say something about the changing *scale* of punishment, in and of themselves, they say little about the changing *character* of punishment. Before we can allege that something about the character of American criminal justice policy has fundamentally changed in a more punitive direction, we ought to understand what we mean by "punitiveness".

CONCEPTUALIZING PUNITIVENESS

The debate over whether or not we, as a nation or as individual states, have become more punitive depends to a large extent on what we mean when we say a place is more or less punitive. Although there is a substantial literature devoted to documenting, discussing, debating, and explaining the changing nature of punishment over the past several decades, few take the time to explain exactly what they mean by punitiveness. In the field of social science research, a premium is placed on the explicit defining and operationalization of constructs, yet authors of studies of punishment have not given sufficient attention to detail in this regard. They have instead typically appealed to a broad, general understanding of punitiveness. Granted, by definition to be punitive is to punish, and therefore, if we are punishing more we are becoming more punitive and vice-versa. But this definition of punitiveness as "simply punishing" is too broad to be of much use. When those who claim that we have become more punitive use the term, they do so in a context that suggests that they mean much more than just that we are punishing. Take for example the following extracts:

> American punishment is comparatively *harsh*, comparatively *degrading*, comparatively *slow to show mercy*... Over the last quarter century, America has shown a systematic drive toward increased *harshness* by most measures, while continental Europe has not (Whitman, 2003: 19 & 38, emphasis added).

> All Western nations have witnessed an upsurge in both the rhetoric and practice of *severe punishment* for offenders; we refer to this as a rise in penal punitiveness... there is no escaping the fact that over the past decade, sentencing has become *harsher* in most Western nations, particularly the United States (Roberts, Stalans, Indermauer, and Hough, 2003: vii & 3, emphasis added).

> Crime control policies became unprecedentedly *harsh* during the early to mid-1990s. That was the time of three-strikes, truth-in-sentencing laws, and zero-tolerance policing, and of a striking increase in the *severity* of punishments and in the numbers of people in prisons and jails (Tonry, 2004:9, emphasis added).

Clearly, the common presence of words like 'severity' and 'harshness' in the works on the punitive turn clearly suggests that these writers are referring to more than just the presence of punishment or even simply the overall scale of imprisonment, but rather to the character of punishment.

Michael Tonry, one of the most prolific punishment scholars, routinely reflects upon the punitive turn and most frequently speaks about the increasing punitiveness of American penology in terms of harshness and severity (See Tonry, 1999a, 1999b, 2004a, 2004b for just a few examples). In the recent work, *Harsh Justice: Criminal Punishment and the Widening Divide Between America and Europe,* James Q. Whitman (2003) also argues that what makes the United States uniquely punitiveness is its harshness. Whitman distinguishes five types of harshness in criminalization and three types of harshness in punishment. Harshness in criminalization, while interesting, is not directly relevant to the study at hand. Harshness in punishment, however, directly relates to the discussion presented here. Interestingly all three of Whitman's harshness in punishment constructs (harshness in the law of punishment, in the application of punishment, and in the inflexibility of punishment) refer directly to the intensity of punishment, in terms of duration, conditions, and lack of individualization respectively, and say little about the propensity to punish more offenders (though harshness in criminalization certainly affects propensity).

Jonathan Simon has tried to get at the essential character of the new punitiveness recently arguing that we have become so punitive that we have become cruel. Simon describes as cruel "this trend toward penalties that are painful, vengeful, and destructive of the penitent in body as well as life chances," among which he includes "the death penalty, life-trashing prison sentences, and shame sanctions." (2001:126). Simon's 'life-trashing sentences' include not only actual life sentences, but also lengthy sentences of imprisonment.[1]

Moreover, when those in academia speak of increasing punitiveness, they frequently refer to the influx of particularly punitive legislative initiatives that focus more on sending people to prison for longer periods of time, than on sending more and more people to prison. For example, particularly punitive legislation that has been the focus of the most criticism over the past few decades includes the establishment of harsh mandatory sentences, mandatory minimums, three-strikes, truth-in-sentencing, and drug offense laws. New York's Rockefeller Drug Laws serve as a good example in that they are almost universally condemned for being particularly draconian and unnecessarily punitive. The Rockefeller Drug Laws are routinely condemned not simply because they *impose penalties of imprisonment* for drug offenses, but rather because they *impose particularly lengthy sentences* of imprisonment, specifying sentences of 15 years imprisonment for the possession or sale of small amounts (two and four ounces respectively) of narcotics (Mauer, 2001; Donziger, 1996; see also DiIulio, 1999a). Like the Rockefeller Drug Laws, each of the most widely criticized sentencing initiatives is expected to increase length of stay more than they increase admissions. The punitive sentencing laws, which were discussed in detail in Chapter 1, when combined with a truth-in-sentencing eighty-five percent minimum time-served requirement will almost certainly result in longer sentences for those sentenced under these laws.

EXPLICIT DEFINITIONS OF PUNITIVENESS IN THEORETICAL WORK

Although most scholars of the punitive turn appeal to their audiences' broad general understanding, there are some notable exceptions to the failure to define punitiveness. A few conscientious scholars have taken the time to either explicitly define punitiveness, or replace the term punitiveness with a more nuanced term that captures the essence of the construct they are attempting to explain. Clear (1994), for example, gets around the problem by substituting the notion of "penal harm" for that of punitiveness, and then explicitly defining penal harm as "that situation when law violators are restricted, hampered, or prevented from acting in their own legitimate… self-interest" (Clear, 1994:17). Clear then documents our increasing willingness to impose greater harm on our fellow citizens primarily through imprisonment emphasizing that in the decade between 1972 and 1982, "in one way or another, every state altered its penal policy in the direction of greater punitive severity" (Clear, 1994:50). As noted by Frank Cullen, "Clear's insistent use of 'penal harm' as his organizing concept strips away this comforting language, and forces us to confront the naked truth that corrections is, to a greater or lesser extent, a mean-spirited enterprise" (Cullen, 1995: 341).

In arguing that the currently popular crime policies in the United States and England serve both expressive and instrumental ends, Garland (2001) also provides a more refined definition of punitiveness. Garland explicitly refers to the 'punitive' aspects of current policies as those which appeal to the emotive desire for "condemnation and suffering." (2001:142). For Garland, penalties that are particularly punitive are those that are "explicitly retributive or deliberately harsh" (p.8) and express "vengeful sentiment" (p.9). Indicative of the punitive turn, in Garland's view are the "decidedly punitive measures such as the death penalty, chain gangs, and corporal punishment." (p.9) He emphasizes our increasing reliance on imprisonment suggesting that "punitive segregation – lengthy sentence terms in no frills prisons, and a marked, monitored existence for those who are eventually released – is increasingly the penal strategy of choice" (Garland, 2001:142). In Garland's use of the word punitive, it is clear that he too is referring to the character of punishment rather than just the existence of more or less punishment.

EXPLICIT DEFINITIONS OF PUNITIVENESS IN EMPIRICAL WORK

Some of the most explicit definitions can be found in empirical work of cross-national variations in punitiveness. Ken Pease (1994), in a study of cross-national variations, made forceful arguments against the use of imprisonment rates per population and for a more refined measure of punitiveness. Pease begins by noting that "at base, [punitiveness] refers to the calibration of diminished quality of life of those punished against another variable" adding that the other variable "depends upon the prevailing principles of sentencing" and might include crimes prevented, offense seriousness, or offender seriousness (1994:118). He then presents a table depicting the total prison populations and imprisonment rates of various European nations and makes a point that can easily be applied to similar tables depicting state-level variations in imprisonment rates:

> This sort of depiction [of imprisonment rates] conflates differences in crime with differences in responses to crime. It has meaning only in showing the effects of some combination of national differences on rates of crime, rates of clearance of crime, and identification of putative offenders, processing of those offenders, and choice of final sanction. Any of those variables, singly or in combination, will produce differences in indices of prison use. As saying anything about national differences in 'punitiveness', Table 1 is useless. (Pease, 1994:119).

It seems important to note that Pease is not persuaded that punitiveness can actually be empirically measured. He emphatically argues that "practicable measurement of the concept can never be more than a remote proxy for true punitiveness. Indeed there is every reason to believe that the criminal justice process incorporates only crude devices for ensuring a uniform method for converting distaste into sentence" (Pease, 1994:118). In spite of his reservations, Pease then goes on to identify measures that might serve as more suitable proxies for punitiveness than imprisonment rates. Pease first concedes that prison admissions or prison populations are likely the most reasonable numerators in punitiveness ratios, and then proceeds to discuss the variety of denominators that might allow for an approximation of actual punitiveness. He notes that the size of the resident population, used in calculations of imprisonment rates, "is an appropriate denominator only if people are imprisoned at random" (Pease, 1994:120), and then identifies three alternate ratios that more plausibly measure punitiveness. Pease argues that the prison admission/conviction ratio is likely the best measure of punitiveness in sentencing, the prison population/conviction ratio the best measure of punitiveness in sentencing *and* release practices, and concludes that "if one wishes a measure of system punitiveness... apprehensions (or arrests) is probably the closest one can get to an appropriate denominator" (1994:120).[2] I have quoted Ken Pease at length because of all of those doing empirical work addressing variations in punitiveness, he most fully articulated the many distinctions in types of punitiveness.

James Lynch, in a series of studies (1988; 1993; 1995; 2002), has also tried to refine the concept of punitiveness and through doing so has managed to demonstrate that while the United States is certainly somewhat more punitive than comparable nations, that punitiveness is often exaggerated largely due to the failure of most researchers to properly conceptualize punitiveness. In the earliest of these studies, Lynch noted that across cross-national studies "the concept of punitiveness is often vaguely defined, with the result that observed differences in incarceration rates are spuriously attributed to differences in punitiveness" (1988:182). It would be fair to critique national and state-level studies on the same grounds. For the purposes of his own study, Lynch explicitly defines punitiveness by arguing first that "differences in punitiveness imply more severe responses to similar acts" (1988:182), and second that there are numerous dimensions of punitiveness. Implicit in his definition of punitiveness is the notion that the extent of the 'crime problem' matters. Moreover, both overall levels of crime and specific types of crime matter. With regard to the dimensions of punitiveness, Lynch isolates three separate dimensions of severity: (1) propensity to impose severe sanctions (with custodial sanctions, such as imprisonment, distinguished as more severe sanctions than non-custodial sanctions); (2) severity in the duration of sanctions (with longer sentences representing more severe responses); and (3) severity in the degree of deprivation imposed by the sanction (where Lynch argues that a lengthy sentence in a maximum security institution is clearly more punitive than a sentence of the same length in a minimum security institution).

Because cross-national findings are of limited importance here, I will just briefly summarize Lynch's key findings across the three studies. In the 1988 study, Lynch examined variations in only the first of his dimensions, the propensity to incarcerate, across England, Canada, West Germany and the United States. In examining the propensity to incarcerate, Lynch controlled for distinctive experiences of crime by calculating stock, flow, arrest and population based incarceration rates and found that:

> when the range of crimes examined is made more comparable in terms of seriousness and when the rates are standardized for differences in the level of crime cross-nationally, the extreme differences in the use of incarceration between the United States and several other Western democracies are lessened considerably and, in some cases, disappear (1988:196).

Lynch is careful to note however that these varying experiences of crime cannot fully account for variations in the propensity to imprison.

In his later studies, Lynch (1993; 1995; 2002) again notes that "greater punitiveness requires that a more *severe* sanction be imposed in response to a similar provocation" (2002:27, emphasis added) and measures variations in punitiveness on more than one dimension. In 1993, Lynch explored variations in punitiveness across the same countries in his 1988 analysis (though here he adds Australia), and examines variations in sentence length and time served instead of the propensity to incarcerate. To oversimplify, Lynch found that while the average sentence imposed for comparable offenses was markedly longer in the U.S. in the other four nations, differences in the actual time served were not as pronounced. Lynch's similar findings in subsequent studies (1995, 2002) similarly lend support to his hypothesis that comparatively the United States is not as punitive as simple imprisonment rate analyses might suggest.

MEASURING PUNITIVENESS

As discussed in earlier chapters, there have been many empirical studies that explore increasing punitiveness in the United States generally and state-level variations in punitiveness more specifically. In the vast majority of those studies, the relative punitiveness of the states is measured by reference to their imprisonment rates. Few researchers doing this state-level work take the time to define exactly what they mean by increasing punitiveness, but by implication, they mean an increasing tendency to imprison.[3] The following comments, extracted from empirical studies of state-level variation in punitiveness, are typical:

> Because our analysis will control for reported levels of crime, we refer to states with high rates of [imprisonment] as more punitive than states with lower levels of [imprisonment] (Beckett & Western, 2001:55).[4]

> We analyze prisoners per hundred thousand because this outcome is a more comprehensive indicator of total punitive responses than admission rates or sentences... [imprisonment rates] capture the probability of imprisonment, time served, early releases, and the states provisions about parole violation reincarcerations (Jacobs & Carmichael, 2001:70).

Conceptually defining punitiveness as a propensity to imprison, and then measuring changes in punitiveness by reference to fluctuations in the relative size of prison populations, ignores the distinctiveness of the dual determinants of the size of prison population: admissions and length of stay. This is a potentially crucial failing because as noted by Lynch (1988) imprisonment rates fail to differentiate stock and flow. A state may appear to be more eager to use imprisonment because its imprisonment rate is high (even controlling for crime) but the stock is inflated because inmates serving long sentences (a different measure of punitiveness) are counted in that measure.

MODELING PUNITIVENESS

Those reflecting on the 'determinants' of imprisonment typically begin from a sociological perspective emphasizing the changing sociological conditions that contribute to fluctuations in the use of imprisonment. Speculation as to what might be related to, or potentially cause, the fluctuations in imprisonment would ideally follow rather than precede, an analysis of the engineering of imprisonment. The benefit of the engineering model is that it is relatively simplistic, describing the fluctuations in the size of prison populations as the result of a fairly straightforward input-output equation. An engineering model would suggest that the size of the prison population at any given time is ultimately a function of the number of admissions (input) and the number of releases (output).[5] When prison admissions outpace prison releases, prison populations increase. Similarly if releases outpace admission, those prison populations decrease. When admissions and releases are in a state of equilibrium, prison populations will fluctuate very little.

DUAL DETERMINANTS

While many who reflect upon rates of imprisonment recognize the dual determinants of those rates, few who do empirical work in this area actually examine the relative contribution of each determinant separately.[6] To state the obvious, admissions determine who goes in and length of stay when they come out. Together, over time, these two determinants produce prison populations of various sizes. A full accounting of the number of admissions and the length of stay would allow one to reasonably project the size of the prison population into the future.[7]

Prison populations increase both in times when increasing admissions are accompanied by increasing lengths of stay, and in times when increases in prison admissions outpace stable or declining lengths of stay. Conversely, prison populations will decrease in times when decreasing admissions are accompanied by decreasing lengths of stay or when decreasing admissions outpace stable or increasing lengths of stay. Moreover, prison populations might appear stable if increasing admissions are accompanied by decreasing lengths of stay, or conversely, if decreasing admissions are accompanied by increasing lengths of stay.[8] Yet taken as separate components of imprisonment, increases in admissions or length of stay each might suggest that we are becoming more punitive even though the imprisonment rate remains stable. While in the short term, the number of admissions to custody is a more important determinant of the growth of the prison population, in the long run length of stay becomes as important.

A series of hypotheticals might prove useful in working out the implications of the effect of fluctuations in the number of admissions and length of stay on the size of the prison population. The theoretical relationship between prison admissions, length of stay and prison population growth can be illustrated by exploring three hypothetical outcomes (see Table 6.1).

Table 6.1: Prison Populations, Admissions and Length of Stay: Incremental Increases

6.1a: Admissions and Length of Stay (LOS) Held Constant

Month	*Admissions*	*Length of Stay*	*Releases*	*Prison Population*
Jan	2	2	0	2
Feb	2	2	0	4
Mar	2	2	2	4
Apr	2	2	2	4
May	2	2	2	4
June	2	2	2	4
July	2	2	2	4
Aug	2	2	2	4
Sept	2	2	2	4
Oct	2	2	2	4
Nov	2	2	2	4
Dec	2	2	2	4

6.1b: Admissions Held Constant while LOS Increases Incrementally

Month	*Admissions*	*Length of Stay*	*Releases*	*Prison Population*
Jan	2	2	0	2
Feb	2	3	0	4
Mar	2	4	2	4
Apr	2	5	0	6
May	2	6	2	6
June	2	7	0	8
July	2	8	2	8
Aug	2	9	0	10
Sept	2	10	2	10
Oct	2	11	0	12
Nov	2	12	2	12
Dec	2	13	0	14

6.1c: Admissions Increase Incrementally while LOS is Held Constant

Month	*Admissions*	*Length of Stay*	*Releases*	*Prison Population*
Jan	2	2	0	2
Feb	3	2	0	5
Mar	4	2	2	7
Apr	5	2	3	9
May	6	2	4	11
June	7	2	5	13
July	8	2	6	15
Aug	9	2	7	17
Sept	10	2	8	19
Oct	11	2	9	21
Nov	12	2	10	23
Dec	13	2	11	25

Table 6.2: Prison Populations, Admissions, Length of Stay: Effect of a One-time Increase

6.2a:Admissions Double in the 6th Month; LOS Held Constant

Month	*Admissions*	*Length of Stay*	*Releases*	*Population*
Jan	2	2	0	2
Feb	2	2	0	4
Mar	2	2	2	4
Apr	2	2	2	4
May	2	2	2	4
June	4	2	2	6
July	4	2	2	8
Aug	4	2	4	8
Sept	4	2	4	8
Oct	4	2	4	8
Nov	4	2	4	8
Dec	4	2	4	8

6.2b: LOS Doubles in the 6th Month; Admissions Held Constant

Month	*Admissions*	*Length of Stay*	*Releases*	*Population*
Jan	2	2	0	2
Feb	2	2	0	4
Mar	2	2	2	4
Apr	2	2	2	4
May	2	2	2	4
June	2	4	2	4
July	2	4	2	4
Aug	2	4	0	6
Sept	2	4	0	8
Oct	2	4	2	8
Nov	2	4	2	8
Dec	2	4	2	8

Beginning with a zero prison population, if you hold both admissions and length of stay constant, at two offenders admitted for two months each month, the size of the prison population reaches a maximum of 4 inmates in the second month and remains stable through the rest of the year (Table 6.1a). If you hold admissions constant at 2 and increase length of stay by 1 month each month, the size of the prison population increases by two inmates every other month resulting in a year end prison population of 14 inmates (Table 6.1b). If you hold length of stay constant and incrementally increase admissions by one additional admission each month, the prison population increases most significantly, to a population of 25 inmates at year end (Table 6.1c). Of course, these hypotheticals hardly reflect reality. Neither admissions nor lengths of stay increase or decrease in consistent equal increments and therefore, prison population growth invariably occurs much more haphazardly than suggested by this first hypothetical. Still the hypothetical is illustrative in that it demonstrates that both admissions and length of stay contribute to the fluctuations in the overall size of prison populations.

The second set of hypotheticals, depicted in Table 6.2, demonstrate the long term effect of a one-time decision to either double admissions or length of stay and then return to a steady state. A decision to either double the number of admissions or double the length of stay would each eventually quadruple the prison population. While the one-time doubling of admissions would increase the prison population quite suddenly, the effect of a one time doubling of length of stay would take longer to manifest (both though would ultimately have the same effect).

FROM ADMISSIONS AND RELEASES TO PROPENSITY AND INTENSITY

In a study of punitiveness, a measure of imprisonment risk has advantages over a pure measure of admission rates. Admission rates are typically measured as the number of admissions per 100,000 population and, in and of themselves, say little about changes in punitiveness. Increasing prison admissions might afterall be a reasonable response to increasing crime. Imprisonment risk, measured as the ratio of prison commitments to arrests, controls for increases in crime.[9] If arrests and new court commitments to prison increase at the same time, the ratio stays the same. It is only when new court commitments increase as arrests remain stable that the risk of imprisonment per arrest increases. Conversely, when arrests increase and the number of new court commitments goes down, the risk of imprisonment per arrest decreases. A time-served measure has advantages over a simple count of prison releases in a study of punitiveness because, while release counts can isolate the number of inmates coming out, average time served allows for an assessment of their average length of stay.

IMPRISONMENT RATES AS THE SOLE MEASURE OF PUNITIVENESS

I contend that much of the research on variations in imprisonment relies on imprisonment rates for two reasons: first because these rates are clearly (to a certain extent) relevant to punitiveness and second because these rates are relatively uncomplicated and easy to acquire. With regard to the first reason, imprisonment rates do say something about punitiveness. Specifically imprisonment rates say something about the cumulative effect of various punishment policies on the overall size of prison populations, and therefore are not unreasonable measures. As James Lynch has noted these rates do provide "prima facie evidence of punitiveness" (2002:40). On account of the second, data on imprisonment rates are both easy to acquire and allow for the least complicated analysis. This is at once both a strength and limitation of imprisonment rate data. Imprisonment rate data are easiest to acquire because imprisonment rates are a fairly limited and rudimentary measure of punitiveness. Just about every place, whether it be a state or nation, reports on the number of prisoners in custody on a given day allowing for the calculation of rates standardized to account for the size of the population. Prison population and imprisonment rate data, as noted by many who use them, only speak to the end result, or cumulative total punitive response, and as I argue may mask important nuances in variations in punitiveness when this total punitive response is deconstructed. Imprisonment rate data allow for the least complex analysis because a simple count of the number of people in prison on any given day can be measured with a relatively high degree of consistency across places.[10] Analyzing relative punitiveness by reference to some of the other measures of punitiveness requires a much higher degree of consistency and specificity across not only measures of punishment but also definitions of crime. It requires that comparable data be collected in a similar way across the places in which relative punitiveness is to be determined.

A measure of imprisonment risk, for example, requires at the very least that arrests are reported as arrests consistently across places, that the offense definitions are consistent across places, that the arrest offense is recorded consistently across places, and that this data is suitably comprehensive in its scope (i.e. that this data is reported on a regular basis by most, if not all, of the jurisdictions that comprise the state or nation). A measure of actual time served requires that prison administrators not only report how many offenders were released from custody, but that they also routinely and accurately record and report the date of admission, the type of offense, and the date of first release for each inmate. These requirements complicate more refined cross-national measures of punitiveness because the consistency across nations is far from assured. Definitions of offenses vary greatly across nations as do understandings of what constitutes an arrest (see Lynch, 2002 for a description of the many complications of cross-national data). Across the states that comprise the United States however there are datasets that come close to meeting these requirements and thereby allow for state by state comparisons. Although there are limitations associated with these datasets, they can be used to produce relatively consistent and comprehensive estimates of imprisonment risk and time served across states.[11]

UNDERSTANDING PUNITIVENESS

Those who study punitive turn should not simply address whether imprisonment rates have increased and for what reasons, but should additionally identify the specific ways in which places might become more punitive. It seems fair to ask whether varying imprisonment rates reflect actual changes (and adequately capture fluctuations) in punitiveness. Have imprisonment rates increased because more and more offenders are being sentenced to prison for offenses for which they might have received either a shorter jail sentence or a non-custodial sentence in the past, or are the offenders that have always been sentenced to prison simply serving longer sentences for the same types of offenses that would have in the past put them in prison for significantly less time?

As was argued in the previous section, increasing imprisonment rates might reflect an increasing *propensity* to imprison offenders, or an increase in the *duration* (or *intensity*) of imprisonment for the offenders that are sentenced to prison. No doubt it is a combination of both, and just as imprisonment rates vary across states, so will the relative contribution of each determinant (propensity vs. intensity). Here it is argued that some states have likely increased the probability that an arrest will lead to an imprisonment, while others have likely increased the amount of time served per offense, and still more have potentially increased both. It seems reasonable to argue that those states that have increased both the risk of imprisonment and the duration of imprisonment are the most punitive by any definition. It is also likely that those states that have seen significant increases in both risk and duration of imprisonment will be those with the highest per capita imprisonment rates. That said, it seems equally fair to argue that states that have increased intensity, in terms of the duration of imprisonment, with or without a concomitant increase in the overall imprisonment rate, have also become more punitive. Similarly those states that have increased the probability of serving a prison sentence following an arrest, again with or without a concomitant increase in the imprisonment rate, have also become more punitive (simply in a different way). Changes in one punitive approach (intensity) could counterbalance changes in the other (propensity) or vice-versa. To summarize, a state could take on a punitive strategy in any number of ways, each of which might make the state more punitive, but which may or may not be captured as punitiveness if measured by the imprisonment rate. To the extent that increases in duration are met with decreases in imprisonment risk, the increasing punitive intensity will not necessarily be reflected in a simple imprisonment rate analysis.

Moreover, there may be reason to believe that the punitive strategy may have changed over time. One of the most frequent recent observations is that while crime has declined significantly over the past decade, imprisonment rates have continued to steadily rise. Prison populations might be continuing to rise in the face of declining crime because we are now seeing the effects of an increase in the intensity of punishment rather than continued increases in the propensity to punish. Zimring (2001) suggested this might be the case in his periodization of the growth in imprisonment. As noted in Chapter 2, Zimring argued that the early part of the imprisonment surge could be attributed to an increase in the risk of imprisonment of low-level offenders, the middle part to an increase in the commitment and length of sentence for drug offenders, and the most recent to an increase in the amount of time served more generally.

Others too have suggested that it is now harshness that is driving increases in imprisonment rates. Recall Tonry arguing that "imprisonment rates became unprecedentedly harsh *during the early and mid-1990s*," (2004a:9, emphasis added), Roberts et al. similarly arguing that "*over the past decade*, sentencing has become harsher… particularly in the United States" (2003:3, emphasis added) and Blumstein and Beck suggesting that on the national level "*in recent years*, only growth in time served is contributing to growth in incarceration" (1999:55, emphasis added). If the punitive strategy has changed, and if the different punitive strategies can be parsed and when analyzed separately seem to explain growth in imprisonment more powerfully at one period than at another, then those theorizing the punitive turn might need to revisit their theories and explain the change in emphasis from one of imprisonment en masse during the early part of the punitive turn to one of increasingly lengthy terms of imprisonment during the latter.

POTENTIAL THEORETICAL IMPLICATIONS

In Chapter 2, I described a number of theories that have been advanced to explain the punitive turn. Some of the theories described might be more readily tested if they were further specified based on a deeper understanding of the role of the dual determinants. Theories emphasizing the role of socially marginal populations, for example, might better explain fluctuations in the risk of imprisonment than they do changes in the length of stay. One could argue that during economic down-turns, the size of the threatening population grows quite rapidly and increasing the risk of imprisonment might be conceived of as an immediate response to that growing threat. Sudden increases in immigration or growing heterogeneity might similarly explain fluctuations in imprisonment risk. Alternately, the more politically oriented and populist theories might be advanced to explain the increasingly harsh or vindictive character of punishment. The escalation (and growing influence) of conservative political rhetoric, the concentration of fundamentalist religious affiliation, and the growing anxiety about (or fear of) the problem of serious and violent crime each might suggest greater punitiveness in terms of growth in the intensity in the duration of punishment.

Before trying to explain imprisonment variations across the fifty states, it seems imperative that one look beyond a simple calculation of the imprisonment rate to variations in the dual determinants of prison populations at the state level. Sociological models that do not fully account for the dual determinants of prison populations miss a potentially theoretically important distinction. The failure to incorporate separate analyses of the dual determinants of prison population size will likely problematize empirical tests of sociological theories because it is quite possible that the sociological, or socio-political, determinants of imprisonment risk differ from those of time-served. To that end, the central goal of analysis section of this study is to fill a void in the literature and ultimately offer a more comprehensive understanding of variations in punitiveness across the states that comprise what is frequently referred to as the most punitive nation in the Western world.

NOTES

[1] While Simon explicitly mentions sentences of upwards of forty years, he likely would argue that sentences need not be even that long to be considered life-trashing. In Simon's words, "What judge could realistically say, 'And I hope you come out a better person' to a twenty-year old receiving a fifty-year sentence for drug trafficking? They might as well say, 'You have forfeited your right to live among us'' (2001:129).

[2] Pease (1994) does not directly address punitiveness in the duration of imprisonment.

[3] Very few of those doing empirical work use the 'incarceration rate' (including those incarcerated in both prisons and jails).

[4] I replaced the word "incarceration" with "imprisonment" in the extract because Beckett and Western exclude inmates housed in jails (which they call the "state prison incarceration rate", and I have called the "imprisonment rate") (2001:49).

[5] A more fully developed engineering model would take into account not only the existence of dual determinants, but the multiple determinants of admissions and releases. As persuasively argued by Langan (1991) and Cohen and Canela-Cacho (1994), prison admissions may increase (1) because felony crime is increasing and therefore the pool from which we draw offenders is larger than in previous times, (2) because reported felonies are more likely to result in arrests, (3) because felony arrests are more likely to result in felony convictions, or (4) because felony convictions are more likely to result in imprisonments. In other words changes at virtually any stage of the process may ultimately impact prison admissions. Likewise there are numerous determinants of prison releases. Prison releases fluctuate based on (1) length of sentences, (2) nature of sentences (determinate, indeterminate, mandatory, etc.) (3) mechanisms for early release (parole, good time credits, etc.), and (4) court orders to reduce prison populations. These determinants can all be captured in an analysis of length of stay, or time served on admission, which represents an important constraint on the pacing of prison output.

[6] Notable exceptions include Blumstein and Beck (1999; 2005) on a national level, Lynch (1988, 1995, 2002) and Pease (1994) in cross-national studies, and to a certain extent Sorenson and Stemen (2002) in a sentencing policy outcome study.

[7] There are, of course, limits to the accuracy of prison population forecasts because of the numerous back-end adjustments that affect length of stay, and other unpredictable system adjustments, for example, legislative changes that affect sentencing outcomes and court orders that require states to fairly quickly reduce prison populations, etc.

[8] Some of those doing empirical work explicitly recognize this distinction and then rely on imprisonment rates as the sole measure of punitiveness anyway. Jacobs and Carmichael (2001), for example, note that "prison admissions or sentence length… could expand even when total imprisonments stay constant or decline," but then "analyze prisoners per hundred thousand because this outcome is a more comprehensive indicator of *total punitive responses* than admission rates or sentences" (p. 70, emphasis added).

[9] This is the measure identified by Pease (1994) as the most plausible measure of "system punitiveness".

[10] This consistency is not nearly as straightforward as is sometimes assumed. As noted earlier, imprisonment rates in a handful of states include jail populations, while in the majority of others they do not, thereby overestimating the imprisonment rates of some.

[11] The deficiencies of state-level data on these two measures are discussed in Chapter 7 and the Appendix A.

CHAPTER 7

MEASURING PUNITIVENESS

It is important to note once again at the outset of the analysis that the empirical portion of this study is intended to lend some empirical support to the conceptual argument made in Chapter 6. Two primary research questions can be derived from that argument: (1) in determining state-level variations in punitiveness, does the way in which you measure punitiveness matter?, and (2) Has the relative punitiveness of the states changed over time and if so, in what ways? Have states that were once relatively less punitive by one or more of the measures become more so (and vice versa).

With regard to the first research question, I have argued that measuring punitiveness by reference to the imprisonment rate alone will not fully capture the notion of punitiveness. Punitiveness in the use of imprisonment is, therefore, measured first in terms of traditional imprisonment rates and then by reference to the dual determinants - imprisonment risk and time served. As a measure of the propensity to imprison, imprisonment risk is the probability that an arrest will result in an imprisonment. The time served measure captures one aspect of the intensity of imprisonment (duration). I intend to demonstrate that measures of imprisonment risk and time served produce punitiveness rankings that differ from each other and from the imprisonment rate rankings, suggesting that there is more than one way to respond punitively.

To address this first research question, I measure the punitiveness of the fifty states in several different ways to determine whether the different ways of measuring punitiveness produce different state level punitiveness rankings.[1] If the various ways of measuring punitiveness produce significantly different rankings, it would seem that one would need to theoretically justify the use of one measure of punitiveness over another. Moreover, if different ways of measuring punitiveness produce different state-level rankings, then studies that have tried to explain variations in punitiveness need to be re-assessed in light of the different ways of responding punitively. If the punitiveness measures produce similar rankings, then presumably it does not matter which measure is used because any one could serve as a proxy for the others.

The analysis of punitiveness across measures need only be done at one point in time. The states are ranked using each of the measures and rank order correlations are calculated to determine the strength of the association between them. The imprisonment risk and time served analyses are then repeated on data disaggregated to the offense type (violent, property, and drug offenses) in Chapter 9. Even if time-served and imprisonment risk produce different rankings, the punitiveness of the state on a particular measure might not be unreasonable depending upon the types of offenders it is imprisoning. An average time served of 40 months might be extremely punitive if a large proportion of offenders are property and drug offenders, but markedly lenient if the majority of offenders are violent offenders. It is difficult to argue that a state is unreasonably punitive without knowing the types of offenses that offenders are being imprisoned for. Variations in imprisonment risk and time served might also suggest that states are employing different punitive strategies. It is possible that states low on imprisonment risk and high on time served are pursuing an incapacitation strategy, reserving imprisonment for the most serious or violent offenders. Similarly, states with a higher than average propensity to imprison and lower than average time served might be pursuing a general deterrence strategy.[2]

The second primary research question asks whether the relative punitiveness of states has varied over time and in what ways. As discussed in Chapter 4, in a study of variations in punitiveness across the fifty states, Zimring and Hawkins, find that "while rates of imprisonment change dramatically in almost all states, there is a pronounced tendency for a particular state to maintain the same position relative to other states in imprisonment rate over time."

(1991:151) To reach this conclusion, they rank-ordered all fifty states on the basis of their imprisonment rate in 1950 and again in 1980, and found that the rank order correlation between the two time periods was .68. When they compared 1980 rank ordered imprisonment rates to those of 1987, they found an even stronger correlation of .77. They conclude that a state's imprisonment rate relative to other states predicts its position in the punitiveness continuum in a later time period relatively well. It remains to be seen whether this 'stability of relative position of the states' has held as the use of imprisonment has continued to grow over the past decade and whether it will hold when punitiveness is measured by reference to the dual determinants of prison populations.

The years 1990, 1995, and 2000 will be used to track changes in state-level variations over time. It was during this time period that some of the more punitive sentencing initiatives (three-strikes and truth-in-sentencing) were passed in most states. The separation of time points by 5 years allows for observations that are far enough apart for legislative change to impact the states' observed punitiveness. Once ranked, I then calculate the rate of change in punitiveness of each state from point A (1990), to point B (1995), to point C (2000). While I predict that all of the states will have become more punitive regardless of the measure of punitiveness ultimately employed, it is predicted that some states will have become substantially more punitive between 1990 and 2000 than others. For example, state A may have been very punitive in 1990 (near the top end of the scale) and still be high on the punitiveness scale in the latter two time periods. This state would be considered consistently over-punitive – even though it may have become increasingly punitive over the period of study. State B, may have been fairly low on the punitiveness scale in 1990 and remained low through the subsequent periods. This state would be considered consistently under-punitive even though it too may have become more punitive over time. In other words, while it will have increased in punitiveness, State B, like State A, will have retained a similar relative position in the punitiveness rankings. State C, on the other hand, may have been fairly low on one of the punitiveness measures in 1990 and soared to near the top of the rankings in one or both of the latter time periods.

I contend that, for purposes of a study of the determinants of punitiveness, it is both those states that rank very differently depending upon the measure employed and those that have experienced significant shifts in punitiveness relative to other states based on these measures that are of the most interest. In this study, the states that moved in their relative rankings dramatically in favor of greater punitiveness on one or more of the measures are especially interesting because presumably something other than the national trend towards punitiveness has taken place in those jurisdictions.

ADDRESSING THE RESEARCH QUESTIONS

Addressing the research questions requires an analysis across measures, offense types, and time. To perform such an analysis, I had to identify data that would cover as many states as possible across each of the measures at three distinct points in time. Additionally I needed to identify state-level data that could be disaggregated to the offense type.

The data and methodology employed to conduct the empirical analyses are described in six sections: these include (1) the data sources used in this study, (2) the limitations of the data and important data caveats, (3) the methodology used to isolate relevant data for subsequent analyses, (4) the methodology used in constructing the imprisonment rate, imprisonment risk and time-served measures, (5) the disaggregation of the data to the offense type, and (6) the methodology used to classify the states in terms of punitiveness. Finally, I briefly outline the format of the presentation of the findings in the analysis chapters.

DATA

Population Data

Where needed, state population data for each relevant year is drawn from the United States Census Bureau population counts and estimates

(U.S. Census Bureau, 2002). Census data allows for the parsing of population by age groups and, where necessary, these parsed data were used.

Crime and Arrest Data

While the strength of the relationship between crime and punishment is frequently debated, there can be no doubt that the imprisonment rate depends to a certain extent on the crime rate. It should go without saying that with no criminal offenders to treat punitively, there would be no measurable punitive criminal justice response. Therefore across portions of the analyses various Uniform Crime Report (UCR) measures of reported crime and arrests are included in the calculations. While UCR data are not necessarily the most accurate for purposes of constructing a realistic portrait of crime, they are the most appropriate data for a study of punitiveness. The only crimes that actors in the criminal justice system can impose punishment for are those that they are aware of. Many of those who commit crimes are not eligible for punishment simply because the crimes they commit are never reported, the offenders are never identified, or because an arrest is never made. Except where noted, all crime and arrest data are drawn from the Uniform Crime Report data files for 1989, 1994, and 1999 allowing for a one-year lag between the crime and arrest and the imprisonment data (U.S. Department of Justice, Federal Bureau of Investigation, 2000, 2001, & 2002).

Imprisonment Data: Imprisonment Rates

Prison population counts and imprisonment rates for every state are released bi-annually by the Bureau of Justice Statistics (BJS) in the series of reports "Prison and Jail Inmates at Mid-Year YYYY" and "Prisoners in YYYY". The reports distinguish prisoners serving sentences of more than one year in prison from the total number incarcerated overall (in prisons and jails). Imprisonment rates were derived from this report series for the year 2000 (Beck & Harrison, 2001) and from a BJS data spreadsheet for the years 1990 and 1995

(Harrison, 2000). Where imprisonment rates were calculated, prison population counts were derived from these BJS publications and only those serving prison sentences more than one year were included in the ratio calculations.

Imprisonment Data: Imprisonment Risk and Time Served

Additional data for the imprisonment risk analyses, and all of the data for the time-served analyses, were drawn from the annual Bureau of Justice Statistic's data collection effort referred to as the National Corrections Reporting Program (NCRP). The NCRP is an annual survey of state prison and parole admissions and releases. Data from three NCRP data files were used in the analyses of imprisonment risk and time served (U.S. Department of Justice, Bureau of Justice Statistics, 1997, 1998, & 2003). Although not all states participate in the NCRP data collection effort, the states that do participate report on all offenders admitted or released over the calendar year. The coverage of the NCRP datasets is impressive. The 2000 NCRP datasets cover three-quarters of the states, representing almost 93 percent of the U.S. population. Moreover, the 529,416 prison admission files and 502,494 release files represent approximately 93 and 86 percent of all state prison admissions and releases respectively.[3]
Each NCRP dataset is divided into three separate datafiles: (1) prison admissions, (2) prison releases, and (3) parole releases. Data from the first two of these sections, prison admissions and prison releases, were included in this analysis. The prison admissions and releases sections cover the entire population of offenders admitted to and released from prison in each participating state over a calendar year. Between 35 and 38 states participated in the NCRP data collection effort in 1990, 1995, and 2000.[4] Because state participation varied by year, states that participated in one year may or may not have participated in other years. There is, however, some consistency in participation with thirty-four states participating in all three years included in the analysis over time (1990, 1995, and 2000). Table 7.1 indicates state participation in the NCRP data collection effort for the years 1990, 1995, and 2000.

Table 7.1: State Participation in the National Corrections Reporting Program (NCRP) Data Collection Initiative

	1990	*1995*	*2000*
Alabama	X	X	X
Alaska			X
Arizona			
Arkansas	X	X	X
California	X	X	X
Colorado	X	X	X
Connecticut			
Delaware			
Florida	X	X	X
Georgia	X	X	X
Hawaii	X	X	X
Idaho			
Illinois	X	X	X
Indiana			
Iowa	X	X	X
Kansas			
Kentucky	X	X	X
Louisiana		X	X
Maine		X	X
Maryland	X	X	X
Massachusetts	X	X	
Michigan	X	X	X
Minnesota	X	X	X
Mississippi	X	X	X
Missouri	X	X	X
Montana			
Nebraska	X	X	X
Nevada	X	X	X
New Hampshire	X	X	X

	1990	*1995*	*2000*
New Jersey	X	X	X
New Mexico			
New York	X	X	X
North Carolina	X	X	X
North Dakota	X	X	X
Ohio	X	X	X
Oklahoma	X	X	X
Oregon	X	X	X
Pennsylvania	X	X	X
Rhode Island			
South Carolina	X	X	X
South Dakota		X	X
Tennessee	X	X	X
Texas	X	X	X
Utah	X	X	X
Vermont			
Virginia	X	X	X
Washington	X	X	X
West Virginia	X	X	X
Wisconsin	X	X	X
Wyoming			

DATA LIMITATIONS

As with any empirical study relying on large national data sources, there are numerous data limitations and caveats that need to be noted at the outset.

Crime and Arrest Data

While the UCR data provides impressive coverage, not all jurisdictions report full crime and arrest data to the FBI and therefore, the data do not always reflect the precise number of offenses reported and crimes cleared by arrest per state.[5] Where possible, the UCR provides estimates of offenses and arrests based on either partial year reporting or the reports of similar jurisdictions.[6] Beginning in 1994, the UCR datafiles include a coverage indicator that allows the user to distinguish estimates from actual reports and true zeros from missing values. The coverage indicator enables an assessment of the reliability of the estimates. The coverage indicator for the 1999 UCR data revealed, for example, that Illinois' arrest data (compiled based on the complete report of only one jurisdiction – Chicago) dramatically undercounted arrests and were insufficient for inclusion. The coverage indicator is not available for UCR data prior to 1994, so the 1989 data may be somewhat less reliable than the data for the latter two periods. The researcher can however, compare state data from years prior to 1994 with data in the years that followed to isolate particularly troubling data.[7]

The UCR datafiles include no data (or extremely limited data) for several states (Illinois, Florida, Kansas, Montana and Wisconsin in 1999; Kansas and Montana in 1994; Florida and South Dakota in 1989). With the exception of Florida in 1999, these states were excluded from the analysis.[8] Florida, while not included in the 1999 UCR datafile, did report comparable crime and arrest figures to the Federal Bureau of Investigation that were included in the annual report *Crime in the United States, 1999* (USDOJ, FBI, 2000). Florida crime and arrest data for 1999 were extracted from this report.

Imprisonment Data

Six states (Alaska, Connecticut, Delaware, Hawaii, Rhode Island, and Vermont) have mixed systems and include jail populations in their average daily population, admissions, and release counts. The imprisonment rates reported in the BJS prisoner series include inmates sentenced to less than one year for these states, and therefore overestimate their imprisonment rates. To minimize the impact of this potentially confounding problem, the NCRP data was filtered to include only those sentenced to more than one year for the imprisonment risk and time served analyses. Filtering in this manner should exclude most, if not all, of those who were actually sentenced to a term of incarceration in jail rather than prison.

There are numerous other data anomalies in the NCRP datafiles, but these tend to be limited to individual states and relevant to only specific parts of the analyses. Describing each of these anomalies here would be cumbersome and distracting; therefore, individual state anomalies are footnoted in the analysis section for which they are relevant. In instances where these anomalies might distort the analysis, the state is excluded and a footnote explains the exclusion. A more thorough description of data anomalies by state is included in the Appendix.

METHODOLOGY: DATA REDUCTION

NCRP Prison Admissions and Releases

Preparing the NCRP data for analysis required that I perform numerous data manipulations. Although here I describe the data reduction technique using the 2000 NCRP data, relevant data for each of the years in the analysis were isolated in the same manner. Data reduction methods common to both admission and release files are summarized here. The section that follows distinguishes one additional manipulation that was required for the prison releases.

The initial prison admission and release datafiles, which included data from 38 states, contained an individual case file for 529,416 offenders admitted to prison and 502,494 offenders released from prison in the year 2000. The NCRP datasets include two possible state-level grouping variables: 'state,' which refers to the state where the inmate is actually imprisoned, and 'jurisdiction at time of admission,' in recognition that offenders in state custody are not always sentenced in the state where they serve their sentences. Additionally, several other jurisdictions (Washington DC, California Youth Authority, Guam, etc.) not relevant to this study were identified as having authority over some inmates admitted to or released from state prisons. For both the admission and release analyses of NCRP data, 'state' was the selection variable, and the data were filtered on the 'jurisdiction at time of admission' so that the data include only those offenders actually imprisoned in a state *and* under that state's jurisdiction. Filtering the data in this manner left 526,660 admissions and 501,999 releases for inclusion in the analysis.[9]

The NCRP datasets also allow for the identification of the type of commitment to prison. Possible commitment types included court commitments, suspended sentences imposed, probation revocation commitments, transfers, various types of parole revocation, and escapees returned to prison. Both the admission and release data were filtered to include only those offenders admitted or released following new court commitments, probation commitments and the imposition of suspended sentences – each of these were designated as 'court commitments.'[10] 343,618 (or 65 percent) of the 526,660 admissions and 312,796 (or 62 percent) of the 501,999 releases followed court commitments.[11] Finally, because offenders sentenced to less than one year usually serve their sentences in jails rather than prisons, it was necessary to filter based on sentence length so that only inmates sentenced to more than one year were included. [12] 291,136 (or 85 percent) of the 343,618 offenders admitted to prison and 276,013 (or 88 percent) of the 312,796 offenders released from prison following a new court commitment were sentenced to more than one year. After data reduction, the final sample sizes for prison admissions were 291,136 for the 2000 data, 301,368 for the 1995 data, and 279,478 for the 1990 data.

Prison Releases

Although the data reduction strategy was the same for the prison admission and release files, one additional filter was required for the prison releases. The NCRP prison release data file distinguishes nineteen different release types. Among the types of release are: various conditional (parole) and unconditional releases, 'releases' due to death (homicide, suicide, execution, natural causes, etc.), releases to custody, and escapes. Release types had to be sorted so that only valid releases, conditional and unconditional releases from custody, were included in time-served calculations.[13] The vast majority of those released were released conditionally or unconditionally from custody. In the year 2000, for example, 267,235 (or 97%) of the 276,013 offenders committed by courts to serve a sentence of more than one year, were released via a relevant mechanism. The final sample sizes for prison releases after all data reductions were: 267,235 for the 2000 data, 241,408 for the 1995 data, and 224,573 for the 1990 data. Table 7.2 presents the data reduction and final sample size for prison admissions and releases in each of the years covered in the analysis. Tables B1 through B3 in Appendix B document the beginning and final sample size *for each state* in each of the years included in the analysis over time.

Excluded States

As noted above, not all states participate in the NCRP data collection effort, so a varying number of states are excluded from the propensity to imprison and duration in imprisonment analyses due to lack of comparable data.[14] While the analyses is provided to lend credence to the argument put forth in Chapter 6 rather than to unequivocally characterize any particular state as punitive or not punitive, it seems important to make sure that the states included represent a spectrum of states on the imprisonment rate continuum. An examination of the imprisonment rates of the states excluded in 2000 (see Table 7.3), demonstrates that the excluded states are fairly evenly distributed with regard to their imprisonment rates – some are among the most punitive by reference to their imprisonment rate, some are among the least punitive, and the majority are in the middle.

To ensure that the excluded states were not fundamentally different from the included states, I ran a comparison of mean imprisonment rates for the two groups in 2000. The mean imprisonment rate for the states included in the analyses was somewhat higher than, but not significantly different from, the mean imprisonment rate for states that were excluded (398 vs. 337 per 100,000, $t = -1.22$, $p = 0.23$).

Table 7.2: Data Reduction for NCRP Admissions and Releases (1990, 1995, 2000)

	1990	
	Admissions	*Releases*
Beginning N	470,353	382,276
Valid Jurisdictions	433,576	346,175
Court Commitments	310,357	261,100
Sentence > 1 Year	279,478	233,768
Valid Release Types	n/a	224,573
Final Sample Size	**279,478**	**224,573**
	1995	
	Admissions	*Releases*
Beginning N	504,815	420,949
Valid Jurisdictions	503,347	419,268
Court Commitments	333,507	284,850
Sentence > 1 Year	301,368	250,369
Valid Release Types	n/a	241,408
Final Sample Size	**301,368**	**241,408**
	2000	
	Admissions	*Releases*
Beginning N	529,416	502,494
Valid Jurisdictions	526,660	501,999
Court Commitments	343,618	312,796
Sentence > 1 Year	291,136	276,013
Valid Release Types	n/a	267,235
Final Sample Size	**291,136**	**267,235**

Table 7.3: Imprisonment Rates of States Excluded from the 2000 Analysis of Imprisonment Propensity and Intensity

	Imprisonment Rate	*Rank*
Arizona	515	9
Connecticut	398	22
Delaware	513	10
Idaho	430	16
Indiana	335	33
Kansas	312	35
Massachusetts	152	48
Montana	348	30
New Mexico	279	38
Rhode Island	197	45
Vermont	218	43
Wyoming	349	29

Varying Sample Sizes

In part due to the varying state participation in the NCRP, the sample sizes also vary across measures and time. The measurement of imprisonment risk uses both UCR and NCRP data and therefore states with missing or unreliable data in either one of these datasets had to be excluded from the imprisonment risk analyses.[15] Similarly, some states provided reliable NCRP admissions data, but unreliable release data and had to be excluded from the time served portion of the analyses.[16] Additionally, as noted above, some states did not participate in the NCRP in all three time periods and are therefore excluded from portions of the analysis across time. The sample size for each analysis is clearly indicated in the text and tables associated with that analysis. Additionally lists of excluded states, and the reasons for exclusion, are provided in footnotes that accompany that portion of the analysis.

METHODOLOGY: CONSTRUCTING THE IMPRISONMENT RATE, PROPENSITY AND INTENSITY MEASURES

Numerous different ways of modeling the punitiveness measures were assessed using empirical data drawn primarily from 1999 and 2000 data sources for as many states as possible. Identifying measures that would best represent the imprisonment rate, the propensity to imprison, and intensity in the duration of imprisonment involved assessing numerous measures across each of the constructs to tease out all of the various measurement issues. The methodology for the construction of the measures and the assessment of measures ultimately discarded are documented in some detail here. The analyses in the chapters that follow use only the measures that were ultimately selected. As the construction of those measures is described in detail in this chapter, the results are presented in a more direct manner in the analysis chapters that follow.

Imprisonment: Calculating Imprisonment Rates

The seemingly straightforward matter of determining the number of offenders in state custody (and standardizing across states to allow for comparisons) becomes increasingly complex as one tries to identify the most appropriate way to calculate the rates. Table 7.4 presents the variety of numerators and denominators that might go into the calculation of custody rates.

The most frequently used method of measuring the relative punitiveness of the states is to compare their imprisonment or incarceration rates per 100,000 residents. Imprisonment rates are generally calculated by dividing the number of inmates currently serving prison sentences of more than one year by the size of the resident population. Incarceration rates, on the other hand, tend to include inmates serving custodial sentences regardless of whether they are serving them in prison or jail (and these incarceration rates occasionally also include those incarcerated in juvenile detention centers). Austin and colleagues (Austin & Tillman,1988; Austin and Brown, 1989) expand the measure further still by calculating "total control rates" that include not only those serving custodial sentences in prison, jail or juvenile facilities, but also adults on probation or parole. In that series of studies, Austin and colleagues found that varying the numerator in calculations of punitiveness produces even more variation in state level analysis.

Table 7.4: Calculating Custody Rates

Numerator

Denominator	***Prison Population***	***Prison & Jail Population***	***Jail, Prison, Probation & Parole Population***
Population*	Imprisonment Rate per 100,000 residents	Incarceration rate per 100,000 residents	Control rate per 100,000 residents
Adult Population	Imprisonment Rate per 100,000 adults	Incarceration rate per 100,000 adults	Control rate per 100,000 adults
Crime Prone Population (Aged 18-44)	Imprisonment rate per 100,000 at-risk adults	Incarceration rate per 100,000 at-risk adults	Control rate per 100,000 at-risk adults

As depicted in Table 7.4, the calculation of custody rates might be affected not only by the choice of numerator, but also by the choice of denominator. Most calculate the rates by counting the number of persons in custody, dividing by the number of state residents, and multiplying by 100,000 to arrive at a rate per 100,000 residents.[17] Calculating the imprisonment, incarceration, or control rate using the entire population in the denominator fails to account for the fact that not everyone in the population is eligible for punishment via imprisonment, incarceration, probation or parole. Only those who commit crimes (and more specifically felonies) are 'eligible' for punishment, and the vast majority of felonies processed through the criminal courts are those committed by individuals over the age of 18. Although part of the get-tough movement included the drafting of laws that facilitated juvenile transfer to adult court, the vast majority of convicted juvenile offenders continue to be processed through the juvenile justice system and therefore can be considered 'ineligible' for adult punishment. Harrison and Karberg (2004), for example, reported that in 2003 only 0.2% of inmates in state prisons were under the age of eighteen. It therefore seems more appropriate to calculate the imprisonment, incarceration, or control rate based on the size of the *adult* resident population, rather than the overall resident population.

One might also want to consider that even among eligible adults not everyone is equally 'at-risk' for imprisonment. In fact, much of the population is not 'at-risk.' Desistance literature suggests that people 'age out' of crime, and therefore, those in the population over the age of 45 are far less likely to commit crime and at less risk for imprisonment.[18] Several scholars have noted that the at-risk age for crime, and the at-risk age for imprisonment differ. The peak age for adult offending (measured by arrests) is somewhere in the late-teens or early twenties. Arrest rates fall dramatically and quickly as the age range increases. Blumstein (2002), for example, reports that those in their early twenties (for property crimes) and in their early thirties (for personal crimes) have arrest rates approximately half of the rate of those in their late teens. According to Blumstein, the peak age for imprisonment, however, is quite a bit higher than the peak age for arrests, with imprisonment peaking almost ten years after arrest (when offenders are in their late twenties and early thirties). Nicholson-Crotty (2004) also notes that adults between the ages of 18 and 24 have the highest arrest rates and adults between the ages of 25 and 34 have the highest imprisonment rates. To account for this, one might want to calculate custody rates using only the 'at-risk' adult population within a state.[19]

I calculated imprisonment rates using each of the three possible denominators.[20] The rank order correlations between the rankings based on various denominators (resident population, adult population, and 'at-risk' population) were extremely high (.99 and above), suggesting that the choice of denominator makes little difference to punitiveness rankings based on imprisonment rates.

Table 7.5: Rank-Order Correlations of Imprisonment Rates Varying the Denominator

	Imprisonment Rate per 100,000 Adults	Imprisonment Rate per 100,000 At-Risk Adults
Imprisonment Rate per 100,000 Residents	.996*	.994*
Imprisonment Rate per 100,000 Adults		.993*

* p = .00

Although it might be more reasonable or methodologically sound to calculate imprisonment rates using either the adult or at-risk populations in the denominator, the remaining analyses use the total resident population to allow for greater comparability between this and other studies of state-level variations in imprisonment.

Propensity to Imprison: Constructing the Imprisonment Risk Measure

As a measure of the propensity to imprison, imprisonment risk should capture the probability of an imprisonment following an adult arrest.[21] One of the more difficult tasks involved determining how to best measure imprisonment risk. The numerator in such an equation is fairly straightforward: the number of court commitments to prison. Only new court commitments to prison are included because parole revocation admissions often do not follow an arrest for a new offense.

The denominator is slightly more tricky and one is forced to make a choice. Clearly only adult arrests should be included in the calculation of imprisonment risk, but which of the adult arrests are most relevant? Using total adult arrests underestimates imprisonment risk because the vast majority of arrests are for non-felony offenses (offenses typically not eligible for imprisonment to begin with). Using total index offense arrests overestimates imprisonment risk because the new court commitments used to calculate risk are new commitments to prison for *any* offense, not just index offenses. Using index arrests results in the seemingly incongruous finding that in most states imprisonment risk overall is higher than imprisonment risk for violent offenses when the data are disaggregated. Additionally, because drug offenses are not counted as index offenses, using only index offense arrests to calculate imprisonment risk leaves out a large class of imprisonment eligible offenders. Scholars frequently contend that the driving force behind the punitive turn has been increasing use of (and duration of) imprisonment for drug offenders (see for example, Blumstein, 2000; Currie, 1998; Fagan, 2004). Using total index offense arrests plus drug offense arrests, while not traditional, seems the most prudent of the methods. For this initial analysis, I calculated imprisonment risk in all three ways using court commitments in 2000 and arrests in 1999. Table 7.6 presents the rank order correlations between imprisonment risk measured using each method.

Table 7.6: Rank-Order Correlations between Imprisonment Risk Measures

	Adult Index Offense Arrests	Adult Index and Drug Offense Arrests
All Adult Arrests	.65*	.67*
Adult Index Offense Arrests		.92*

* p = .00

Although the choice of denominator made little difference to the calculation of imprisonment rates, it appears to make a fairly substantial difference to the measure of imprisonment risk. The correlation between imprisonment risk using 'index offense arrests' versus using 'index plus drug offense arrests' in the denominator is fairly high (+0.92). Since drug offense commitments have presumably played a crucial role in increasing punitiveness over the past several decades, the latter measure will be used in calculations of imprisonment risk. It is also important to note that regardless of the choice of denominator, the imprisonment risk figures in aggregate form overestimate imprisonment risk (as noted above, new court commitments are commitments for any offense). This overestimate is somewhat tempered because the vast majority of prison admissions are for index offenses. Cohen and Canela-Cacho (1994) note that approximately 74 percent of prison admissions result from a conviction for one of the seven index offenses (excluding arson) or a drug offense. In a more recent study, Blumstein and Beck (1999) also note that five of the index offenses combined with drug offenses "account for three-quarters of state prison populations" (1999:20).[22] When the data are disaggregated to the offense type, the estimates are more precise because admission offenses are more specifically isolated.

In all analyses that follow, imprisonment risk (or the propensity to imprison) will be operationalized as the probability of a court commitment to prison, for a term of more than one year, following an index or drug offense arrest.

Intensity of Imprisonment: Constructing the Time Served Measure

In constructing a measure of time-served, three important methodological issues emerge: (1) whether to calculate actual time-served using a release cohort or to estimate time served using a stock-flow ratio, (2) whether to calculate time served on the current admission or total time served (including jail time credited to the admission), and (3) whether to use the mean or median as the measure of average.

Actual Time-Served or Stock-Flow Estimate?

As a measure of the intensity in the duration of imprisonment, time served can be determined in one of two ways: it can be calculated based on data from a release cohort or estimated using a stock-flow ratio.

Cohen and Canela-Cacho (1994) argue that stock-flow time-served estimates are superior to the actual time-served figures derived from release cohorts because stock-flow ratios take into account time-served by those serving exceptionally long sentences and those who will never be released (see also, Blumstein & Beck, 1999). While those serving exceptionally long sentences (say for example, 20 years or more) will not be reflected in time-served release cohort figures for some time, those serving life sentences without the possibility of parole or under sentence of death will, without some intervention, never show up in a release cohort.

While it is true that time served calculations based on release cohorts fail to capture those who will never be released, this shortcoming becomes less problematic when you disaggregate the data and calculate time served based on either offense type or specific offenses (see Chapter 9). The underestimate of time served is most likely to be reflected in time served for violent offenses, and more specifically time served for a conviction of murder or non-negligent manslaughter where a sentence of life without parole or death is more likely. It is very unusual for someone whose most serious conviction offense is a violent offense other than homicide/non-negligent manslaughter (rape, robbery, aggravated assault), a property offense (burglary, larceny, arson), or a drug offense (distribution/sale or possession of drugs) to be sentenced to life in prison without the possibility of parole.[23] Of those in prison on January 1st, 2001, across the states an average of 2.5 percent of all inmates were sentenced to life without parole and an average of just 0.09 percent were sentenced to death (Camp & Camp, 2002). While the vast majority of all offenders admitted to prison will eventually be eligible for release, an actual time-served analysis estimate might underestimate the punitiveness of those states with larger proportions of inmates serving either life sentences or death sentences as neither of these groups of inmates would be reflected in release cohorts. Using data from the *2001 Corrections Yearbook* (Camp & Camp, 2002), Table B5 in the Appendix lists the number of inmates serving such sentences in each state.

Cohen and Canela-Cacho acknowledge that stock-flow time-served estimates are "very sensitive to large year to year variations in the rate of new commitments to prison," (1994:363) and are most accurate during times of steady admissions. Determining the stock-flow ratio based on either type of offense or specific offense requires prison population breakdowns by offense type and specific offenses and while these breakdowns are available nationally, they are not readily available disaggregated to the state level. Appendix Table B6, which provides a side-by-side comparison of the two methods of determining average time served, indicates that the stock-flow estimate of time served, at least for 2000, produces substantially different estimates of length of stay than the actual time served of a release cohort. In half of the states (18 of 36), the difference between actual time served and estimated time served is less than one year (which in and of itself is considerable). In the other eighteen states, the stock/flow estimate is more than one year greater than the actual time served, and in seven of those states it is close to or more than two years. The stock-flow ratio for Michigan suggests that the average time served in that state is 74.84 months, when the actual time served of the offenders released in Michigan in 2000 was 36.66 months (a difference of over three years).

Overall the stock-flow ratio overestimates the average time served for 32 of the states and underestimates time served for the remaining 4 states (See Appendix Table B6). The rank order correlation between actual time served rankings and stock-flow estimate rankings was only moderate ($r^s = .43$, $p = .01$) suggesting that the two measures produce quite different state-level rankings. In all analyses that follow, actual time served of release cohorts in 1990, 1995, and 2000 are used.

Time Served on Current Admission or Total Time Served?

Time served on current admission reflects only the time served in prison at first release, whereas total time served adds the time served in jail that was credited to the current release. Appendix Table B7 provides a comparison of time served on current admission and total time served by state. The rank-order correlation between the two measures was strong, positive and significant ($r^s = .86$, $p = .00$). In most states, adding the credited time served prior to the current admission increases the time served estimate by between one and eight months.[24] Using total time served, however, would eliminate between three and six states from the analysis (depending upon the year) because not all states provide data on time served prior to the current admission.[25] The interest in retaining a reasonable sample size outweighs the benefit of capturing those additional months of imprisonment, particularly because a substantial proportion of inmates in all states likely served some of their sentence prior to the current admission. The time served on current admission will be used for the remaining analyses.

Mean or Median as the Measure of Average?

The final methodological consideration for the time served analyses involved deciding whether to measure average time served on the basis of the mean or the median. As a measure of average, the mean is sensitive to extreme outliers in the data while the median is not. To determine whether use of the mean would result in substantial distortions in the rankings, average time served for the 2000 release cohort was calculated using both measures (see Table B8 in Appendix B). While in all instances median time served is lower than mean time served, the rank ordering of states in terms of average time served are not substantially affected by the choice of mean or median. The rank order correlation between the two measures is strong, positive, and significant ($r^s = 0.91$, $p = .00$). Because use of the mean permits more advanced statistical analyses, the mean is used as the measure of average in all time served analyses.

DISAGGREGATING DATA TO THE OFFENSE TYPE

For the analysis presented in Chapter 9, the NCRP prison admission and release data were disaggregated to the offense type for the imprisonment risk and time-served analyses. The NCRP offense codes are grouped into seventy-nine offense categories with multiple codes within each of those categories. The 'murder' offense category, for example, distinguishes fourteen types of murder categorized into three subgroups: (1) actual murders (including murder, felony murder, accessory to murder, etc.), (2) attempts (attempted murders, including various types of assault and battery with intent to kill), and (3) conspiracy to commit murder. For each offense type, the NCRP divides offenses into subgroups.

Although the NCRP offense codes do not match up perfectly with the UCR offense categories, it is possible to isolate offenses similar to those used in the UCR indexes.[26] Initially I isolated the offense types most representative of the UCR index offenses and grouped these individual offenses as violent, property, drug, or other. When isolated to this level of specificity, the majority of offenses are classified as 'other' and a lot of cases that fall into the categories of interest are excluded. I therefore re-grouped into broader categories where all admissions and releases for each category of offense were grouped together. The broader categories allowed for more cases to be included without losing distinction in the variations across states; therefore, for the analysis across offense types, NCRP admission and release data were grouped into the four broad categories: (1) violent offenses; (2) property offenses; (3) drug offenses; and (4) all other offenses (weapons, public order, etc.).[27]

METHODOLOGY: CLASSIFYING STATES

The classification tables presented in subsequent chapters assess relationships on two or more of the measures simultaneously. To allow for the classification of states, data values for each state on each measure were transformed into standard scores (z-scores). The states were then classified based on the distribution of those standard scores. States with a standard score between -1 and +1 (e.g. within one standard deviation of the mean for all states included in the analysis) were classified as average in terms of their punitiveness by that measure, while states with standard scores greater or less than 1 or -1 were classified as over-punitive and under-punitive respectively.

PRESENTATION OF FINDINGS

In all instances, when the states are ranked, they are ranked in descending order – in other words, the state with the highest imprisonment rate, imprisonment risk, or average time served is ranked one. Correlations between measures are Spearman rank order correlations, and across measures Pearson correlations. To distinguish the two, in the text and tables, rank order correlations are clearly identified. To provide a measure of consistency in presentation, each portion of the analyses includes results presented in three ways: (1) data tables present the actual data values and rank orders of each state on each essential of the measures, (2) correlation matrices identify the strength and direction of relationships between measures, and (3) scatterplots (that identify under and over-punitive states by their state abbreviation) are included to provide a visual aid. In addition to these standard methods of presentation, in some of portions of the analyses, additional figures and classification tables are included to further assist the reader in the interpretation of the findings.

NOTES

[1] The District of Columbia will not be included for two reasons. I am conducting a state-level analysis and not only is D.C. not a state, but the federal prison system recently assumed jurisdiction over D.C.'s prison population. The transfer of DC's inmates to the federal system was completed in 2001 (Harrison & Karberg, 2003).

[2] This potential strategy distinction is discussed in more detail in Chapter 11.

[3] Camp and Camp (2002: at pages 55 and 70-71) report that in the year 2000, there were a total of 571,779 state prison admissions and 584,302 state prison releases.

[4] 35 states participated in 1990 and 38 states participated in 1995 & 2000 (See Table 7.1).

[5] Additionally, the conversion to NIBRS (National Incident Based Reporting System) in some states required that the FBI convert NIBRS data to UCR formats.

[6] For a description of the methodology used to compile these estimates, see Section VII, Appendix I of the 1999 report *Crime in the United States* (U.S. Department of Justice, Federal Bureau of Investigation, 2000).

[7] A comparison of the arrest figures between the three time periods suggested there were no glaring anomalies in the 1989 crime and arrest data.

[8] Two of the states excluded on this basis (Kansas and Montana) also did not participate in the NCRP data collection effort, and so they would have been excluded anyway (Illinois and Wisconsin were excluded in 1999 due to insufficient arrest data).

[9] The sample drops significantly in terms of valid jurisdictions in 1990, because in that year the NCRP data file included more than 30,000 federal prisoners admitted and released that year.

[10] These are the commitment categories designated as 'court commitments' in Bureau of Justice Statistic's reports and publications.

[11] As per BJS filtering instructions, unknown admission types for Louisiana, Missouri, Oklahoma, Oregon, Tennessee, and Texas were reset to 'new court commitment.' While this will obviously over-count court commitments in these states, these recodes are used by BJS in calculating the national averages.

[12] As discussed below, including only those sentenced to more than one year also limited the effect of inflating the numbers for states which have mixed prison/jail systems and therefore do not distinguish jail and prison sentences when reporting to NCRP.

[13] The release codes included were: (1) parole board decision, (2) mandatory parole release, (3) probation release, (4) other conditional release, (5) expiration of sentence, (6) commutation/pardon, and (8) other unconditional release.

[14] For most of the analyses, fourteen states were excluded in the 2000, twelve were excluded in 1995, and fifteen were excluded in 1990.

[15] Illinois and Wisconsin participated in the 2000 NCRP data collection effort but 1999 UCR arrest data were unreliable (Illinois) or unavailable (Wisconsin). These two states are included in the intensity (time served) analysis, but are excluded from the propensity (imprisonment risk) analysis.

[16] Florida participated in the 1990 NCRP but reported admissions only in that year, and is therefore excluded from the 1990 time-served analyses. Tennesee was excluded from the time served analyses in all years due to unusual

anomalies in their release data (for a full description of these anomalies, see Appendix A).

[17] Even this simple calculation is affected by the choice of population size measure. Each year the U.S. Census Bureau estimates state populations in thousands. Following the 2000 decennial census, the Census Bureau undertook a time-series analysis to more precisely estimate the size of the resident population in each state in the years between the 1990 and 2000 decennial censuses. These two state population counts produce slightly different imprisonment rates (more precise population estimates produce slightly lower imprisonment rates), and slightly different state-level rate rankings. Most of the differences appear in the middle of the punitiveness rankings where the imprisonment rates cluster. Interestingly, both of these produce slightly different rates than those provided in the BJS publications.

[18] The desistance literature is expansive, see, for example, Bushway, Piquero, Broidy, Cauffman, & Mazerolle (2001); Farrington (1986); Sampson & Laub (2003).

[19] In this analysis, the population between the ages of 18 and 44 are considered 'at risk'.

[20] The analysis of imprisonment rates varying the denominator was the earliest analysis performed and relied on 1998 data because that was the most recent year for which data were available at the time. Because the calculation of rates varying the denominator made virtually no difference to the rankings, this analyses was not performed using more recent data.

[21] The per capita commitment admission rate (or the number of new court commitments per 100,000 population) allows one to look at the independent contribution the flow each year has made to the cumulative prison population. While useful as an indicator of annual fluctuations in flow, admission rates do not control for crime, and therefore say little about the propensity to imprison. A measure of imprisonment risk is superior in that regard.

[22] The five index offenses include murder, rape, robbery, aggravated assault and burglary (this excludes the other three index offenses: larceny, motor vehicle theft, and arson).

[23] In three-strikes states, you may see property offenders sentenced to 20 or 25 years to life upon the third felony conviction, but research suggests that, with the exception of California, these laws have rarely been invoked (see Zimring, 2001, and Zimring, Hawkins, and Kamin, 2001 at page 20-21). Even in

California, due to uneven implementation and notable attempts to circumvent the policy, the three-strikes law has had a much smaller impact than initially projected (see Zimring, Hawkins, and Kamin, 2001).

[24] In Georgia and Louisiana, using total time served would have increased the average time served by 13 and 11 months respectively.

[25] In 2000, for example, Arkansas, Pennsylvania, and Utah provided no data on total time served. Additionally, total time-served in a number of states could be calculated for only some of the offenders, so there were far more missing cases for this measure than there were for 'time served on current admission.' This increased the standard error of the estimates and for one state (Tennessee) resulted in the incongruous finding that the total time served was actually less than the time served on current admission.

[26] To construct offense types similar to those used in the UCR crime and arrest reports, the following offense codes can be isolated (the offense codes reported here represent the offense codes as they appear in the NCRP codebook). For homicide and non-negligent manslaughter, codes 010, 013, and 015 (murder, unspecified homicide, and voluntary non-negligent manslaughter); for rape/sexual assault, codes 050, 060, 070 (rape-force, rape-statutory, sexual assault-other); for robbery, codes 090 and 100 (armed and unarmed robbery); for aggravated assault, codes 120 and 140 (aggravated assault and assaulting public officer); for burglary, code 190 (burglary); for arson and motor vehicle theft, codes 200 and 210 respectively (arson and auto theft); for larceny, code 230 (grand larceny-theft over $200); for drug offenses – drug trafficking, codes 340, 345, 350, 360, and 370 (trafficking heroin, cocaine or crack, other controlled substances, marijuana, and drug unspecified respectively) – drug possession, codes 380, 385, 390, 400, 410 (possession/use heroin, cocaine or crack, other controlled substances, marijuana, and drug unspecified respectively).

[27] Offense types were grouped using the following NCRP offense codes: for violent offenses (010 through 180), for property offenses (190 through 335), for drug offenses (340 through 450); and for other offenses (all other codes).

CHAPTER 8

PUNITIVENESS ACROSS MEASURES

In Chapter 6, I developed the conceptual argument that the way in which criminologists have operationalized 'punitiveness' in empirical studies of state-level variations to date fails to capture the complex nature of punitiveness as a construct. I argued that the use of imprisonment rates as often the sole measure by which punitiveness is gauged might confound results, particularly when using various extralegal variables to predict punitiveness in empirical work. I additionally argued that states may have adopted varying strategies, with some preferring to increase their reliance on imprisonment (which I have called propensity), others preferring to increase the duration of imprisonment (which I have called intensity), some doing both, and others perhaps doing neither. Furthermore, I have argued that a state could become notably more punitive over time by either a propensity or intensity change with little or no discernable change in their imprisonment rate (particularly relative to other states).

VARIATION IN IMPRISONMENT RATES

As studies have shown time and time again, when measured by imprisonment rates, some states appear to be quite substantially more punitive than others, imprisoning far more offenders per 100,000 population than other states. Figure 9.1 graphically depicts the imprisonment rates of all 50 states for the year 2000.

FIGURE 9.1: State Imprisonment Rates, 2000 (per 100,000 population)

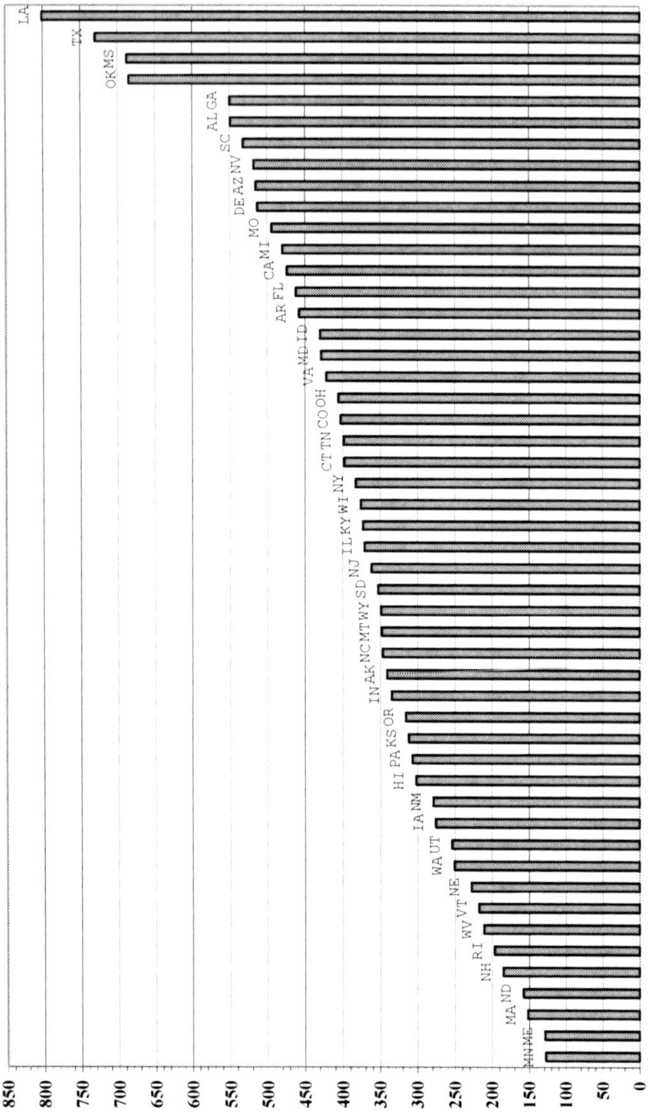

Southern states tend to have much higher rates of imprisonment than Northern States. The five most punitive states (Louisiana, Texas, Mississippi, Oklahoma, and Georgia) are all Southern states and each has an imprisonment rate of at least 550 prisoners per 100,000 population.[1] The five least punitive states (Minnesota, Maine, Massachusetts, North Dakota and New Hampshire) are all Northern states and each has an imprisonment rate of less than 200 prisoners per 100,000 population.[2] It has typically been on the basis of this imprisonment rate variation across states that scholars have tried to explain state-level variations in punitiveness.

Can Variations in Crime Rates Explain Variations in Imprisonment Rates?

The imprisonment rate per 100,000 measures imprisonment relative to the size of the resident population with no reference to the amount of crime. When one ignores the size of the crime rate, a state with a 'reasonably punitive' imprisonment policy based on its level of crime may appear to have an unreasonably high imprisonment rate relative to other states. A cursory look at imprisonment rate rankings from 2000 and crime rate rankings from 1999, allowing for a one-year lag between crime and imprisonment, demonstrates the less than perfect relationship between crime rates and imprisonment rates (Table 8.1).

The index crime rate includes all UCR index crimes while the violent and property crime rates split the index crimes into two parts (murder, rape, robbery, and aggravated assault comprise the violent crime rate, and burglary, larceny, motor-vehicle theft, and arson comprise the property crime rate). The correlations between the imprisonment rate and the index crime rate ($r = .48$), violent crime rate ($r = .53$), and property crime rate ($r = .43$) are not as strong as one might expect.[3] The index crime rate rankings explain approximately 23% of the variation in imprisonment rate rankings (when broken down, the violent crime rate explains 28% of the variation and the property crime rate 18%).[4]

Table 8.1: Imprisonment Rates (2000) and UCR Index (ICR), Violent (VCR), and Property (PCR) Crime Rates

	IR	ICR	VCR	PCR
LA	801	5747 (4)	733 (6)	5014 (4)
TX	730	5032 (9)	560 (14)	4472 (12)
MS	688	4270 (24)	349 (31)	3921 (21)
OK	685	4684 (16)	508 (19)	4176 (14)
GA	550	5149 (8)	534 (18)	4615 (9)
AL	549	4412 (21)	490 (21)	3922 (20)
SC	532	5324 (5)	847 (2)	4477 (11)
NV	518	4654 (17)	570 (13)	4084 (16)
AZ	515	5897 (3)	551 (15)	5345 (2)
DE	513	4835 (14)	734 (5)	4101 (15)
MO	494	4579 (18)	500 (20)	4079 (17)
MI	480	4325 (23)	575 (12)	3750 (23)
CA	474	3805 (29)	627 (10)	3178 (33)
FL	462	6206 (1)	854 (1)	5352 (1)
AR	458	4043 (27)	425 (23)	3618 (28)
ID	430	3149 (42)	245 (43)	2904 (40)
MD	429	4919 (12)	743 (4)	4176 (13)
VA	422	3374 (37)	315 (35)	3059 (35)
OH	406	3996 (28)	316 (34)	3680 (26)
CO	403	4063 (26)	341 (33)	3723 (25)
TN	399	4694 (15)	695 (7)	3999 (19)
CT	398	3389 (36)	346 (32)	3044 (37)
NY	383	3279 (39)	589 (11)	2691 (45)
WI	376	3296 (38)	246 (42)	3051 (36)
KY	373	2953 (44)	308 (36)	2645 (46)
IL	371	4515 (19)	690 (8)	3825 (22)
NJ	362	3400 (34)	412 (25)	2988 (38)
SD	353	2645 (48)	167 (46)	2477 (47)
WY	349	3393 (35)	274 (40)	3119 (34)
MT	348	3533 (33)	237 (44)	3296 (31)
NC	347	5175 (7)	542 (17)	4633 (7)

	IR	ICR	VCR	PCR
AL	341	4363 (22)	632 (9)	3732 (24)
IN	335	3766 (30)	375 (29)	3391 (29)
OR	316	5002 (10)	375 (28)	4627 (8)
KS	312	4439 (20)	383 (26)	4056 (18)
PA	307	3114 (43)	421 (24)	2693 (44)
HI	302	4838 (13)	235 (45)	4602 (10)
NM	279	5962 (2)	835 (3)	5128 (3)
IA	276	3224 (41)	280 (38)	2944 (39)
UT	254	4977 (11)	276 (39)	4701 (6)
WA	251	5256 (6)	377 (27)	4878 (5)
NE	228	4108 (25)	430 (22)	3678 (27)
VT	218	2817 (46)	114 (47)	2704 (43)
WV	211	2721 (47)	351 (30)	2370 (48)
RI	197	3582 (32)	287 (37)	3295 (32)
NH	185	2282 (50)	97 (49)	2185 (50)
ND	158	2393 (49)	67 (50)	2326 (49)
MA	152	3263 (40)	551 (16)	2712 (42)
ME	129	2875 (45)	112 (48)	2763 (41)
MN	128	3597 (31)	274 (41)	3323 (30)

Note: Ranked by imprisonment rate rank; for ICR, VCR, and PCR (ranks in parentheses)

Five of the states with the highest imprisonment rates are also in the top ten in terms of index crime rates (Louisiana, Texas, South Carolina, Arizona, and Georgia). Likewise six of the states that have the lowest imprisonment rates have correspondingly low crime rates (Maine, Massachusetts, New Hampshire, North Dakota, West Virginia, and Vermont). A close look at Table 8.1, however, reveals some interesting anomalies. The two states with the highest crime rates, Florida ranked 1st and New Mexico ranked 2nd are not even among the top 10 in terms of imprisonment rates (ranked 14th and 38th respectively). Mississippi is extremely punitive in terms of its imprisonment rate (ranked 3rd) yet has a relatively low crime rate (with 4270 crimes per 100,000 residents, Mississippi ranks 24th in terms of its crime rate). Alabama, Arkansas, California, Michigan, Idaho, and

Virginia also appear to be imprisoning at a higher rate than their crime rate would suggest. At the other end of the continuum, Washington ranks 41st in terms of it imprisonment rate, yet has the 6th highest crime rate. Utah, Hawaii, and North Carolina also stand out in this regard – each has a relatively high crime rate yet comparatively low imprisonment rate relative to other states.

Table 8.2: Rank-Order Correlations between Imprisonment and Crime Rates

	Index Crime Rate, 1999	Violent Crime Rate, 1999	Property Crime Rate, 1999
Imprisonment Rate, 2000	.475	.533	.433
Index Crime Rate, 1999		.681	.987
Violent Crime Rate, 1999			.581

The relationship between crime and imprisonment might be so attenuated for any one of three reasons. Crime can be considered an input of imprisonment, an output of imprisonment, or a disconnected phenomenon. Crime can clearly be an input of imprisonment, but can also, somewhat less obviously, be an output of imprisonment. Rose and Clear (1998) have argued that imprisonment may actually increase social disorganization, contribute to the development of crimogenic social conditions, and as a result increase crime (see also Clear, 1996, 2002; Clear et al., 2003; Fagan, 2004; Sabol and Lynch, 2004). In this sense, crime might be considered an output of imprisonment. If crime is at once both an input and an output of imprisonment, one would expect to see a rather strong positive correlation between the two phenomena: afterall, whether crime is an input or an output, one would expect that as crime increased imprisonment would also increase.[5]

Few have argued persuasively that crime is completely disconnected from imprisonment. Imprisonment, to a certain extent, depends upon the commission of crime. Many, however, have suggested that crime and punishment might best be conceived as largely disconnected phenomena, related to each other to the extent that they are each related to other more important structural variables (economic structure, unemployment, the size of socially marginal populations, etc.). As noted in Chapter 1, in a series of works, Blumstein and colleagues (Blumstein & Cohen, 1974; Blumstein, Cohen & Nagin, 1977) argued that, at least for its part, imprisonment might be a self-regulating phenomena (and therefore, would be rather insensitive to fluctuations in the separate phenomena of crime). Crime and imprisonment trend data clearly demonstrate that the two phenomena do not always fluctuate in the same direction at the same time. While crime has fluctuated over the past thirty years, sometimes increasing and sometimes decreasing, imprisonment has taken on a life of its own, increasing every year until the year 2001 when imprisonment decreased slightly before resuming its upward trend.

Examining variations in states' imprisonment rates is a cumulative way assessing punitiveness. As argued earlier, the level of imprisonment in any given state is ultimately a function of the number of admissions and the length of stay. Snapshot views of imprisonment rates tell us little about variations in punitiveness because imprisonment is additive (many of the prisoners reflected in the 2000 imprisonment rates were sentenced years ago and are simply contributing to the imprisonment rate because of their lengthy stays). The analyses that follow disaggregate punitiveness in terms of propensity to imprison (imprisonment risk) and intensity in the duration of imprisonment (length of stay).

PROPENSITY TO IMPRISON: IMPRISONMENT RISK

I have argued that a state may become more punitive over time by increasing its propensity to imprison, or by increasing the duration of the imprisonment sentence. Imprisonment risk, or the probability that an index or drug offense arrest will result in a prison commitment, is a way of assessing a state's propensity to imprison apprehended criminal offenders. On average across the sample, the propensity to imprison was .118, or approximately 12 imprisonments for every 100 index or drug offense arrests. The propensity to imprison, like the imprisonment rate, varies greatly across states, from a low of less than .06 in New York to a high of over .20 in Alaska. In other words, in Alaska for every 100 index/drug offense arrests, there are twenty new court commitments to prison, while in New York there are just six.

Table 8.3: Descriptives: Imprisonment Risk, 2000

	N	Minimum	Maximum	Average
Imprisonment Risk 2000	36	.055	.204	.118

Imprisonment Risk and Imprisonment Rates

Imprisonment risk, state level rankings of imprisonment risk, and imprisonment rate rankings are presented in Table 8.4.[6] As is made evident in the table, the rank-order correlation between the propensity to imprison rankings and the imprisonment rate rankings is moderate and non-significant ($r = .29$, $p = .09$).[7]

A state's punitiveness in terms of its imprisonment rate tells you little about the risk of actually going to prison following a felony arrest. The states at the upper end of the imprisonment risk continuum (Alaska, North Dakota, and Oklahoma) have propensities that are at least three times higher than states at the lower end (Maine, New York and Pennsylvania). Few could deny that a state that imprisons a larger portion of arrested felony offenders compared to other states could be characterized as punitive; yet North Dakota, considered a non-punitive state in many studies of punitiveness because it has one of the lowest imprisonment rates in the country, actually ranked 2nd in punitiveness when measured by overall propensity to imprison in 2000. Louisiana, the state that had the absolute highest imprisonment rate in the country in 2000, has a below average propensity to imprison in that same year (ranked 25th of 36).

Table 8.4: Imprisonment Risk and Imprisonment Rates, 2000

	Imp. Risk	*Rank*	*Imp. Rate*	*Rank*
North Dakota	0.196	2	158	47
Oklahoma	0.187	3	685	4
Iowa	0.166	4	276	39
Nevada	0.156	5	518	8
South Carolina	0.153	6	532	7
Mississippi	0.148	7	688	3
Missouri	0.146	8	494	11
South Dakota	0.143	9	353	28
Tennessee	0.141	10	399	21
Texas	0.139	11	730	2
Arkansas	0.139	12	458	15
Hawaii	0.139	13	302	37
Virginia	0.135	14	422	18
Alabama	0.132	15	549	6
Oregon	0.116	16	316	34
NewHampshire	0.111	17	185	46
Georgia	0.110	18	550	5
New Jersey	0.108	19	362	27
West Virginia	0.106	20	211	44
Michigan	0.104	21	480	12
Kentucky	0.102	22	373	25
Ohio	0.101	23	406	19
Colorado	0.100	24	403	20
Louisiana	0.097	25	801	1
Maryland	0.096	26	429	17
Washington	0.096	27	251	41
North Carolina	0.092	28	347	31
Nebraska	0.090	29	228	42
California	0.089	30	474	13
Florida	0.088	31	462	14
Minnesota	0.082	32	128	50
Utah	0.078	33	254	40
Maine	0.066	34	129	49
Pennsylvania	0.066	35	307	36
New York	0.055	36	383	23

Some states have both a low imprisonment rate and a low propensity to imprison (Maine and Minnesota), while others (Oklahoma, Texas, and Mississippi) have a high imprisonment rate and a high propensity to imprison. Alaska, North Dakota and Iowa are particularly interesting in that these three states have relatively low imprisonment rates, yet exceptionally high propensities to imprison. Louisiana is the most notable outlier in the other direction with a high imprisonment rate, and a relatively low propensity to imprison. Other states, including Colorado, Ohio, and Kentucky, have moderate imprisonment rates and an average propensity to imprison.

It is difficult to say what this means at this point in the analysis because, to a certain extent, figuring out what is going on requires an analysis over time (presented in Chapter 10). It may be that Louisiana's prisons had reached or exceeded their capacity in 2000 and the ability to sentence to imprisonment was markedly reduced. It may mean that Louisiana, even though it has the highest imprisonment rate, still has a much bigger crime problem than other states, and therefore simply cannot imprison an equivalent proportion of arrested offenders in any given year. It almost certainly means, however, that measured by the propensity to imprison, Louisiana was not particularly punitive toward apprehended serious offenders in 2000 and is therefore potentially mischaracterized as overly punitive in the vast majority of empirical work. In contrast, North Dakota, always characterized as a non-punitive state in empirical work, is actually markedly punitive in its propensity to imprison. North Dakota may not have many prisoners per 100,000 residents, but it certainly imprisons a large proportion of its serious offenders relative to other states.

INTENSITY IN IMPRISONMENT: TIME SERVED

The preceding imprisonment risk analysis demonstrated that states vary not only in their imprisonment rates, but also in their propensities to imprison those arrested for serious felonies. I have argued that propensity to imprison is only one of the ways a state could become more punitive and that, if Blumstein and Beck (1999) and Zimring (2001) are correct, then it is potentially not the more important way in which states have become more punitive in recent years. The analysis of actual time served for offenders released in 2000 demonstrates that, just as there is substantial variation in imprisonment rates and imprisonment risk, there is also substantial variation in average time-served.[8]

Table 8.5: Descriptives: Average Time Served at First Release, 2000

	N	Minimum	Maximum	Average
Time Served 2000	35	16.70	49.60	28.55

Average time served at first release aggregated across all offenses (28.55 months) varies from a low of just under 18 months in Missouri, North Dakota, and West Virginia to a high of close to 50 months in Maine. Inmates in the most punitive states serve almost three times as many months in prison before first release than those in least punitive states.

Time Served and Imprisonment Rates

Table 8.6 presents the actual time served of the 2000 release cohort and the state-level rankings of the 36 states included in the analysis according to both time-served and imprisonment rates. The moderate rank-order correlation between time-served and imprisonment rates (r^s = .278, p = .10) is essentially the same as the rank-order correlation between imprisonment risk and imprisonment rates. States with the highest imprisonment rates are not necessarily those that are the most punitive in terms of time served. Although Texas has both a high imprisonment rate (ranked 3rd) and a lengthy average time served (ranked 2nd), Maine has the second *lowest* imprisonment rate in the country, yet is ranked 2nd in terms of average time served. At the other end of the continuum, several states (Minnesota, North Dakota, and

Table 8.6: Average Time Served and Imprisonment Rates, 2000

	Time Served	*Rank*	*Imp. Rate*	*Rank*
Ohio	72.97	1	406	19
Maine	49.60	2	129	49
Texas	45.09	3	730	2
Pennsylvania	41.46	4	307	36
Maryland	40.42	5	429	17
Oklahoma	39.49	6	685	4
Florida	36.90	7	462	14
Michigan	36.66	8	480	12
North Carolina	34.12	9	347	31
New York	31.33	10	383	23
Mississippi	30.43	11	688	3
Hawaii	29.93	12	302	37
South Carolina	29.61	13	532	7
New Hampshire	29.57	14	185	46
Nevada	28.48	15	518	8
Georgia	28.20	16	550	5
Virginia	27.76	17	422	18
Colorado	27.53	18	403	20
Iowa	27.44	19	276	39
Utah	26.85	20	254	40
Louisiana	26.58	21	801	1
Alabama	26.35	22	549	6
Oregon	26.29	23	316	34
Washington	25.74	24	251	41
New Jersey	25.64	25	362	27
Nebraska	25.24	26	228	42
Wisconsin	24.64	27	376	24
California	24.19	28	474	13
Kentucky	22.47	29	373	25
Arkansas	21.12	30	458	15
South Dakota	20.35	31	353	28
Illinois	19.91	32	371	26
Minnesota	18.23	33	128	50
North Dakota	17.97	34	158	47
West Virginia	17.75	35	211	44
Missouri	16.70	36	494	11

West Virginia) have both low imprisonment rates and comparatively low time-served figures, but others (Arkansas, California, and Missouri) have relatively high imprisonment rates and low time-served figures.

IMPRISONMENT RATES, IMPRISONMENT RISK AND TIME SERVED

Relationship between the Propensity to Imprison and Intensity in the Duration of Imprisonment

The relationships between imprisonment rates and the propensity to imprison and intensity of imprisonment were discussed individually and in relation to imprisonment rates in the previous sections. What is the relationship between these two alternate measures of punitiveness? While the correlation between imprisonment risk and time-served (r^s = -.18, p = .31) is slightly negative, it is non-significant (in part due to the low N for states with data on both measures, N=34).

Relationship between Propensity, Intensity, & Imprisonment Rates

In Chapter 6, I argued that the dual determinants of imprisonment (imprisonment risk and time served) and imprisonment rates are related to one another in important ways. I argued that imprisonment rates represent the cumulative effect of variations in the two other types of punitiveness: propensity and intensity. I further argued that states might have adopted varying punitive strategies with some notably increasing (or decreasing) propensity, others increasing intensity in duration, some doing both, and others doing neither.

Table 8.7, which presents the rank-order correlations between the three measures of punitiveness, suggests that the propensity to imprison and intensity in the duration of imprisonment were related to the overall imprisonment rate in similar ways. Both were moderately positively correlated with imprisonment rate rankings (though neither correlation reached significance at the .05 level).[9] Although propensity and intensity were slightly negatively correlated, this correlation was non-significant, suggesting that the two measures of punitiveness are largely unrelated to each other (in the sample there is a slight tendency for states with a low propensity to imprison for longer durations and vice-versa).

Table 8.7: Rank-Order Correlations between Imprisonment Rates, Imprisonment Risk, and Time Served, 2000

	Imprisonment Risk	Time Served
Imprisonment Rate	.291	.278
Imprisonment Risk		- .178

Classifying States

To assist in interpretation, I constructed Table 8.8 to classify states on all the measures simultaneously. In this table, states are classified as under-punitive, average, or over-punitive on two axes (time-served and imprisonment risk), and states with under-punitive or over-punitive imprisonment rates are identified in italics and bold italics respectively.[10]

The most interesting cells are the four corners (shaded in gray). Only Minnesota (top left cell) is under-punitive and only Oklahoma (bottom right cell) is over-punitive on all three measures of punitiveness. Maine and Pennsylvania (top right cell) are both under-punitive with regard to risk and over-punitive in terms of time served. North Dakota (bottom left cell) is over-punitive with regard to risk and under-punitive in terms of time served. Each of the states that are over-punitive in terms of imprisonment are either average or over-punitive across the other two measures (in other words, none are under-punitive on any of the measures of punitiveness). Two of the six states with over-punitive imprisonment rates are over-punitive with regard to intensity (Oklahoma and Texas), while the remaining four are average on each of the other two measures. Similarly, with the exception of Maine, all the states that have under-punitive imprisonment rates are either average or under-punitive with regard to time-served, and only one (North Dakota) is over-punitive with regard to imprisonment risk. Maine and North Dakota are especially interesting because each has an imprisonment rate that is among the lowest in the country, each is over-punitive by one of the other punitiveness measures, and each displays a precisely opposite pattern with regard to punitiveness on those other measures.

Table 8.8: Classifying States: All Three Measures of Punitiveness, 2000 (N=34)

Imprisonment Risk	Time Served: ***Under Punitive***	Time Served: ***Average***	Time Served: ***Over Punitive***
Under Punitive	*Minnesota*	New York Utah	*Maine* Pennsylvania
Average	Missouri South Dakota *West Virginia*	17 States[11]	Florida Maryland Michigan Ohio ***Texas***
Over Punitive	*North Dakota*	Iowa Nevada	***Oklahoma***

SUMMARY

While these findings are interesting in and of themselves, they beg the questions of crime and of changes over time. Are Maine and Pennsylvania so over-punitive in time-served yet under-punitive in imprisonment risk, because they reserve prison space for those who commit only the most serious of offenses? If so, one might expect either that the prisons in these states primarily house serious violent offenders or that the time-served across offense types might vary considerably, with time-served for serious violent offenses pushing up the average time-served overall. If this were the case, one could conceivably argue that these states have adopted 'reasonable' punitive strategies. Or alternately, do these states simply have a smaller pool of offenders across all offense types and sentence offenders to lengthy terms of imprisonment regardless of offense? If this were the case, one could argue that they are indeed over-punitive in the duration of imprisonment relative to other states.

Similarly, is North Dakota under-punitive in its average time-served and over-punitive in its imprisonment risk because it has a less serious crime problem and therefore are more able to pursue a general deterrence strategy, or because it sees less value in the long term incapacitation of offenders including violent offenders? One might expect that either its prison population is comprised of less serious offenders, or that it simply imprison a large proportion of felony offenders to shorter terms of imprisonment.

As has been argued in earlier chapters, the imprisonment rate reflects the cumulative effect of these two types of punitiveness and so a cross-sectional comparison of outcomes on each measure cannot tell us much about the process by which the states ultimately ended up with exceptionally high or low imprisonment rates. In the chapter that follows, I disaggregate admission and release data to the offense type, and in Chapter 10, I examine this relationship at several points in time to more closely examine these relationships.

NOTES

[1] Imprisonment rates are Louisiana (801), Texas (730), Mississippi (688), Oklahoma (685), and Georgia (550).

[2] Imprisonment rates are Minnesota (128), Maine (129), Massachusetts (152), North Dakota (158), and New Hampshire (185).

[3] In this portion of the analysis, the significance tests matter far less than the correlations themselves. Significance tests simply report whether the relationship found in the data (the sample) are strong enough to say that the relationship exists in the population. This portion of the study includes the entire population of states and therefore significance is irrelevant. Moreover, we are interested in how closely related the *measures* are, and therefore the correlations themselves are particularly important.

[4] It should come as little surprise that imprisonment is more strongly correlated with violent crime than it is with property crime. Violent crimes are generally considered more serious, and would therefore be expected to result in a sentence of imprisonment more frequently than property crimes.

[5] If crime were consistently both an input and output of imprisonment, the system would eventually spiral out of control. Rose and Clear (1998) argue that imprisonment likely produces increase in crime only after reaching a tipping point.

[6] Twelve states are excluded from the imprisonment risk analysis because they did not participate in the National Corrections Reporting Program data collection effort in 2000, and therefore, it was not possible to isolate new court commitments from total prison admissions. The excluded states are: Arizona, Connecticut, Delaware, Idaho, Indiana, Kansas, Massachusetts, Montana, New Mexico, Rhode Island, Vermont, and Wyoming. In addition, Illinois and Wisconsin are also excluded from this portion of the analysis because accurate arrest data for these two states was unavailable in 1999. The N for the imprisonment risk in 2000 analysis is therefore 36. Supplementary tables, documenting imprisonment risk and imprisonment rates in 1990 and 1995 can be obtained from the author.

[7] Here the significance test is relevant because the sample (N=36) does not comprise all fifty states.

[8] Ohio's average time-served at first release in 2000 was a clear outlier, 20 months longer than any other state, and so Ohio was removed from all time-served calculations that assume a normal distribution.

[9] Both were significant at the .10 level.

[10] As explained in the data and methodology chapter (Chapter 8), states are classified on the basis of their distribution from the mean for the sample. States more than one standard deviation below and above the mean are classified as under-punitive and over-punitive respectively.

[11] The seventeen states that are average on both measures in 2000 include: ***Alabama,*** Arkansas, California, Colorado, ***Georgia***, Hawaii, Kentucky, ***Louisiana***, ***Mississippi,*** *Nebraska*, *New Hampshire*, New Jersey, North Carolina, Oregon, South Carolina, Virginia, and Washington.

CHAPTER 9

PUNITIVENESS ACROSS OFFENSE TYPES

As punitiveness rankings vary quite notably across measures, it seems reasonable to suspect that there might also be variation across states in terms of imprisonment risk and time served for different offense types. Admissions and releases from prison need to be disaggregated to the offense type to fully appreciate the variations in punitiveness across the measures. Two of the states with the lowest imprisonment rates in the country (Maine ranked 49th and North Dakota ranked 47th) exhibited exactly opposite punitiveness patterns on the other two measures. Maine was under-punitive in its propensity to imprison yet particularly punitive in its intensity and North Dakota was under-punitive in intensity yet particularly punitive in terms of propensity. Unless the imprisonment risk and time served analyses are disaggregated to offense type, it is difficult to interpret these findings.

The analysis across offense types again uses 1999 UCR and 2000 NCRP data. In this chapter, I assess state-level variations in the propensity to imprison and the intensity in the duration of imprisonment across violent, property, and drug offenses.

DISTRIBUTION OF OFFENSE TYPES FOR NCRP ADMISSIONS AND RELEASES

On average across the sample, prison admissions and releases in 2000 were approximately evenly distributed across the three primary offense types (with a slightly higher percentage of admissions and releases for drug offenses than for violent or property offenses (see Table 9.1)).

Table 9.1: Distribution of Offense Types, Admissions and Releases 2000

	Violent	*Property*	*Drug*	*Other*
2000 Admissions	29.1%	26.3%	31.3%	13.3%
2000 Releases	27.2%	28.1%	32.5%	12.2%

These averages mask substantial state-level variation in the distribution of admissions and releases across offense types. The percent of admissions that were for violent offenses ranges from a low of 17.4 percent in Louisiana to a high of 45.0 percent in Oregon, and for property offenses from a low of 17.4 percent in New York to a high of 39.8 percent in Alabama. The most substantial variation in the distribution of admission offense types is in admissions for drug offenses. While only 10 percent of Maine's prison admissions in 2000 were for drug offenses, close to half of all of New Jersey's (49.2%) and New York's (44.1%) new court commitment admissions were for drug offenses.

As the percent distributions for admission offenses varies substantially across the states, one can expect that either these states experience comparable variations in arrest patterns or that state-level variations in imprisonment risk across offense types will also be substantial. If the latter is the case, it appears that some states may be reserving imprisonment for certain types of offenders. Unless Maine has a far smaller drug crime problem than New Jersey or New York, it seems reasonable to argue that Maine has a lower propensity to use imprisonment as punishment for drug offenders. The imprisonment risk analysis that follows facilitates interpretation of the state-level variation in admission offenses.

The percent break down of releases by admission offense also masks substantial state-level variation in the distribution of releases across offense types, and, as would be expected, the release patterns mirror the admission patterns. The percent of releases that followed admissions for violent offenses ranges from a low of 12.5 percent in Louisiana to a high of 55.1 percent in Ohio and for property offenses from a low of 16.1 percent in New York and to a high of 43.7 percent in Alabama. Again the most substantial variation is in the distribution of releases for drug offenses where just over 10 percent of Maine's prison releases in 2000 were releases following an admission for a drug offense and close to half of all of New Jersey's and New York's releases were for drug offenses.

Even though those being released from prison in 2000 were admitted an average of two and a half years ago, the symmetry between admission and release offense types is notable. Alabama both admitted and released a larger proportion of property offenders than any other state. Similarly, New Jersey and New York admitted and released larger proportions of drug offenders than any other states. Very few of Maine's admissions in 2000 were for drug offenses, as were very few of its releases. The correlations between the percentage of admissions and releases by offense types are all above +0.85 and all are significant at the .00 level.

As the percent distributions for release offenses varies substantially across the states, one can expect that either these states experience comparable variations in time served (e.g. states that released a lot of violent offenders should have the highest overall time served and vice-versa) or that state-level variations in time-served across offense types will also be substantial, with some states being particularly punitive to certain classes of offenders while others are not. If the latter is true, then one can reasonably argue that states that exhibit higher average time served patterns relative to other states are indeed over-punitive on this measure of punitiveness. The time-served by offense type analysis facilitates interpretation of state-level variation in time-served overall.

PROPENSITY TO IMPRISON ACROSS OFFENSE TYPES

In the previous chapter, 'imprisonment risk' was operationalized as the probability of an index or drug offense arrest resulting in a term of imprisonment of more than one year. For the analysis across offense types, both 1999 UCR arrest and 2000 NCRP prison admission data were disaggregated to the offense type to allow for a more comprehensive assessment of the variations in the propensity to imprison across states.[1] Here imprisonment risk is operationalized in a similar, but more offense specific, manner: imprisonment risk for violent offenses is the probability of an arrest for a violent index offense resulting in a new court commitment to prison for more than one year for a violent offense, property offense arrests are paired with property offense admissions, and so on.

The analysis across offense types will help distinguish the offenses that are targeted by states that exhibit a high propensity to imprison overall. While a state with a high propensity to imprison may exhibit that propensity across all offenses, it is possible that the overall propensity to imprison masks variations in propensities across offense types. If a state's propensity to imprison property and drug offenders was relatively low, while its propensity to imprison violent offenders exceptionally high, its overall imprisonment risk might be unduly affected by that unusually high propensity to imprison violent offenders. Were that the case, one might be less inclined to consider the state over-punitive. Similarly, states with a low overall propensity might exhibit high propensities for certain classes of offenders but extremely low propensities for others bringing down the average propensity overall. These states might be mistakenly classified as under-punitive.

Table 9.2 presents the descriptive statistics for imprisonment risk across offense types and Table 9.3 breaks down the propensity to imprison by offense type by state - with the states sorted by reference to their propensity to imprison violent offenders (the two far right columns of the table indicate the states overall imprisonment risk and overall rank on imprisonment risk from the previous chapter).

The least surprising finding is that across all of the states the propensity to imprison violent offenders is higher than the propensity to imprison either property or drug offenders, indeed it would be odd if this were not the case. There is, however, variation in propensities on more than one dimension: the propensity to imprison across offense types *between* states varies substantially, as does the magnitude of the differences in propensity across offense types *within* states.

Table 9.2: Descriptives: Propensity to Imprison by Offense Types, 2000[2]

	N	*Min*	*Max*	*Average*
Violent Offenses	34	.09	.63	.24
Property Offenses	35	.03	.18	.08
Drug Offenses	35	.02	.14	.08

With regard to the variation *between* states, the greatest variation in the propensity to imprison is across violent offenses. While the average propensity to imprison violent offenders across the sample is 0.24 (or 24 violent prison admissions for every 100 violent arrests), the propensities vary from a low of 0.09 in Louisiana to a high of 0.63 in Oregon.[3] In other words, Oregon's propensity to imprison violent offenders is seven times higher than is Louisiana's. The variation across propensities is quite a bit lower for property offenses, where the propensities vary from a low of .03 in Pennsylvania to a high of 0.18 in South Carolina, and lowest for drug offenses, where they vary from a low of 0.02 in Maine to a high of 0.14 in Oklahoma.

The magnitude of differences in propensities *within* states is also notable and suggests that some states have fairly consistent propensities to imprison across offense types, while others have much higher propensities to imprison some classes of offenders than they do others. The average propensities to imprison property and drug offenders across the sample are both .08 (or 8 imprisonments for every 100 arrests). Although across most of the states the propensities to imprison property and drug offenders are roughly proportional (e.g. the

Table 9.3: Propensity to Imprison across Offense Types, 2000

	Violent Offenses	*Property Offenses*	*Drug Offenses*	*Overall*	*Rank*
N. Dakota	1.04	0.13	0.13	0.20	2
Oregon	0.63	0.05	0.05	0.12	16
NH	0.48	0.10	0.04	0.11	17
Maine	0.42	0.04	0.02	0.07	34
Texas	0.37	0.07	0.09	0.14	11
Nebraska	0.33	0.06	0.05	0.09	29
Hawaii	0.32	0.06	0.10	0.14	13
S. Dakota	0.31	0.11	0.07	0.14	9
Nevada	0.31	0.09	0.13	0.16	5
Utah	0.27	0.04	0.08	0.08	33
Colorado	0.26	0.06	0.07	0.10	24
Ohio	0.26	0.06	0.05	0.10	23
Oklahoma	0.26	0.15	0.14	0.19	3
Mississippi	0.25	0.13	0.10	0.15	7
Virginia	0.24	0.10	0.09	0.13	14
Minnesota	0.24	0.06	0.05	0.08	32
Maryland	0.23	0.05	0.09	0.10	26
Tennessee	0.22	0.12	0.10	0.14	10
Washington	0.22	0.04	0.09	0.10	27
Missouri	0.19	0.10	0.10	0.15	8
S. Carolina	0.19	0.18	0.09	0.15	6
Iowa	0.19	0.13	0.11	0.17	4
Georgia	0.18	0.09	0.08	0.11	18
Arkansas	0.17	0.11	0.12	0.14	12
New Jersey	0.17	0.06	0.10	0.11	19
Florida	0.16	0.07	0.05	0.09	31
Alabama	0.16	0.12	0.10	0.13	15
Michigan	0.16	0.09	0.04	0.10	21
N. Carolina	0.15	0.04	0.05	0.09	28
W. Virginia	0.13	0.09	0.04	0.11	20
Pennsylvana	0.11	0.03	0.05	0.07	35
California	0.11	0.08	0.06	0.09	30
New York	0.10	0.04	0.04	0.06	36
Kentucky	0.10	0.06	0.08	0.10	22
Louisiana	0.09	0.07	0.09	0.10	25

propensities are within .02 of each other), there are handful of notable exceptions. In Michigan, New Hampshire, South Carolina, and West Virginia imprisonment risk for property offenders is at least double the imprisonment risk for drug offenders. In Maryland and Washington the relationship is reversed and the imprisonment risk is twice as high for drug offenders as it is for property offenders.

Although the propensities are roughly equivalent between property and drug offenses, the propensity to imprison these two types of offenders and violent offenders vary much more substantially within states. The average propensity to imprison violent offenders (.24) is three times higher than the average propensities to imprison either property or drug offenders. Those states that have a low propensity to imprison violent offenders tend to have the smallest difference in magnitude between the propensity to imprison property/drug offenders versus violent offenders, and those with the highest propensities to imprison violent offenders tend to have a far more substantial gap between these propensities. While the propensity to imprison violent offenders is only one to three times higher in some states (e.g., most of the states at the lower end of the continuum), it is six to eight times higher among some of the states with the highest imprisonment risk for violent offenders (e.g. the states at the upper end).

The correlations between the various types of imprisonment risk are all positive but vary in strength (Table 9.4). The strongest correlations are those between the overall imprisonment risk and the imprisonment risk for property and for drug offenses. The latter are also significantly related to each other. While overall imprisonment risk is also significantly related to imprisonment risk for violent offenders, the correlation between the two is not as strong largely because the variation in imprisonment risk for these offenders varies so greatly across the states. The most loosely coupled of the relationships are those between imprisonment risk for violent offenses and imprisonment risk for property and for drug offenses (where the correlations are actually quite weak and non-significant). In some states the propensity to imprison violent offenders is different enough in magnitude from the other propensities to suggest that these states possibly do reserve the penalty of imprisonment for those arrested for the most serious offenses.

Table 9.4: Correlation Matrix, Propensity to Imprison by Offense Types

	Imprisonment Risk Violent Offenses	*Imprisonment Risk Property Offenses*	*Imprisonment Risk Drug Offenses*
Overall	.33*	.65**	.61**
Violent Offenses		.16	.16
Property Offenses			.58**

* p > .05, ** p = .00

Classifying States on Imprisonment Risk across Offense Types

Table 9.5 classifies states in terms of imprisonment risk across offense types. The states are classified on the two primary axes according to their relative propensities to imprison for violent and property offenses. Punitiveness in the propensity to imprison drug offenders is indicated by the italics: states in plain italics are under-punitive and states in bold italics over-punitive in their propensities to imprison drug offenders. As indicated in the classification table, only New York is under-punitive and only North Dakota is over-punitive across all three offense types. Maine and New Hampshire are each over-punitive in their propensities to imprison violent offenders and under-punitive in their propensities to imprison drug offenders (Maine is additionally under-punitive in its propensity to imprison property offenders). A number of states are under or over-punitive in their propensities to imprison just one class of offender. Oregon and Texas are over-punitive and California, Kentucky, and Louisiana under-punitive in imprisonment risk for only violent offenders. Both Arkansas and Nevada are exclusively over-punitive and Michigan, Minnesota, and West Virginia exclusively under-punitive in their propensities to imprison drug offenders.

Table 9.5: Classifying States on the Propensity to Imprison across Offense Types (n=34)

Imprisonment Risk for Property Offenses	Imprisonment Risk for Violent Offenses: ***Under Punitive***	***Average***	***Over Punitive***
Under Punitive	*New York* Pennsylvania	North Carolina Utah Washington	*Maine*
Average	California Kentucky Louisiana	15 States[4]	*New Hampshire* Oregon Texas
Over Punitive		Alabama Iowa Mississippi ***Oklahoma*** South Carolina Tennessee	***North Dakota***

One of the most valuable insights that can be gleaned from this classification table is that simply knowing the percentage of inmates who were admitted to prison for a certain type of offense is not enough to say that the state is under or over punitive to a particular class of offenders. For example, the states that are over-punitive in imprisonment risk for drug offenders are not necessarily those that have the largest percentage of drug admissions in a given year. Despite admitting a below average percentage of drug offenders, North Dakota is over-punitive in its propensity to imprison drug offenders. The two states with the largest percentage of admissions of drug offenders (New Jersey, 49% and New York, 44%) are actually average (New Jersey, .10) and under-punitive (New York, .04) in terms of imprisonment risk for drug offenders relative to other states. The same phenomenon can be observed for violent offenses, where North Dakota has an exceptionally high imprisonment risk for violent offenders (1.04) yet its percent of admissions for violent offenses (26.54%) is lower than the average across the sample. This finding underscores the importance of utilizing a more nuanced measure of punitiveness when assessing variations in imprisonment across offense types. An imprisonment risk measure controls for the number of arrests thereby allowing for an assessment of punitiveness given the size of the eligible offender pool.

INTENSITY IN IMPRISONMENT ACROSS OFFENSE TYPES

In the previous chapter, 'intensity in the duration of imprisonment' was operationalized as actual time served at first release following a new court commitment admission to prison of more than one year. For the analysis across offense types, 2000 NCRP prison release data were disaggregated to the offense type to allow for a more comprehensive assessment of the variations in the intensity of imprisonment across states and offenses. Table 9.6 presents the descriptive statistics for average time served across offense type and Table 9.7 disaggregates time served in prison to the offense type by state – with the states sorted by reference to their average time served for violent offenders (the two far right columns indicate the average time served overall and the state's rank in overall time served from the previous chapter).

As was the case for imprisonment risk, the least surprising finding in the offense specific time served analysis is that across all of the states the average time served for violent offenders is higher than for either property or drug offenders, again it would be odd if this were not the case. There is again variation on two dimensions: intensity in the duration of imprisonment across offense types *between* states varies substantially, as does the magnitude of the differences in intensity across offense types *within* states.

Table 9.6: Descriptives: Intensity in Imprisonment by Offense Type, 2000[5]

	N	*Minimum*	*Maximum*	*Average*
Violent Offenses	35	24.33	64.08	46.05
Property Offenses	35	11.70	50.76	24.47
Drug Offenses	35	12.53	38.75	22.20

With regard to the variation *between* states, the greatest variation in time served is again across violent offenses.[6] While the average time served for violent offenses across the sample is 46 months, the average time served varies from a low of 24 months in North Dakota to a high of 64 months in Michigan. In other words, the average time served for violent offenders released in Michigan is close to three times higher than in North Dakota. The variation is somewhat lower for property offenses, where the average time served is 24.5 months but varies from a low of 12 months in Minnesota to a high of 51 months in Maine, and lowest for drug offenses where the average time served is 22 months but varies from a low of less than 13 months in Minnesota and West Virginia to a high of approximately 38 months in Maine and Texas.

The magnitude of differences in intensity *within* states suggests that some states have fairly consistent intensity in imprisonment across offense types, while others require some classes of offenders to serve far more time prior to release than they do others. In more than a third of the states, the time served at first release for property and drug offenders is roughly equivalent (e.g. the time served averages are within two months of each other). While in sixteen states the time served by property offenders is higher than the time served by drug offenders, in the remaining five states drug offenders on average served more time than property offenders.[7] In most states the difference in

Table 9.7: Intensity in Imprisonment across Offense Types, 2000

	Violent	*Property*	*Drug*	*Overall*	*Rank*
Ohio	85.75	63.57	46.74	72.97	1
Michigan	64.08	26.14	29.34	36.66	8
Texas	61.76	45.60	38.75	45.09	3
Pennsylvania	61.14	33.18	28.21	41.46	4
Maryland	59.98	30.39	30.68	40.42	5
Oklahoma	58.29	41.16	31.73	39.49	6
Mississippi	55.98	21.64	24.61	30.43	11
Louisiana	54.41	22.50	22.80	26.58	21
Utah	54.03	19.11	14.79	26.85	20
Hawaii	52.85	27.59	24.48	29.93	12
Maine	52.47	50.76	37.92	49.60	2
New York	51.35	24.88	23.28	31.33	10
Nevada	51.32	24.56	23.48	28.48	15
South Carolina	50.41	23.47	26.12	29.61	13
Florida	49.04	33.82	27.95	36.90	7
Virginia	48.55	22.78	21.80	27.76	17
Alabama	46.81	21.22	22.85	26.35	22
Georgia	46.20	20.75	18.67	28.20	16
New Jersey	44.09	20.48	20.59	25.64	25
North Carolina	43.88	39.71	28.42	34.12	9
New Hampshire	43.36	23.42	20.55	29.57	14
Arkansas	42.88	15.05	15.91	21.12	30
Iowa	42.44	24.57	27.77	27.44	19
South Dakota	41.89	21.38	13.18	20.35	31
Washington	41.76	17.86	20.35	25.74	24
Wisconsin	41.31	25.79	20.20	24.64	27
Missouri	41.11	14.63	13.56	16.70	36
Colorado	40.89	23.40	22.35	27.53	18
Oregon	38.51	20.27	16.42	26.29	23
Kentucky	38.01	18.70	15.52	22.47	29
Illinois	37.55	15.83	15.08	19.91	32
Nebraska	36.68	21.10	20.78	25.24	26
California	36.32	22.56	18.46	24.19	28
West Virginia	29.45	14.32	12.53	17.75	35
Minnesota	28.52	11.70	12.94	18.23	33
North Dakota	24.33	16.08	14.91	17.97	34

time served between property and drug offenders is small (e.g. less than six months), though notable exceptions include Maine, North Carolina, Ohio, and Oklahoma where the difference was more than 10 months.

The difference in magnitude of time served for violent offenses versus property/drug offenses is more substantial. In twenty-one states, time served for violent offenders was double that for property or drug offenders. Violent offenders in Arkansas served almost three times as many months as did property or drug offenders. In all but three states, the average time served for violent offenses was at least one year longer than for property or drug offenses, and in half of the states it was at least two years longer. In only three states was the difference between time served for violent and for property/drug offenses quite small: in Maine those released for violent offenses served only 2 months more than those released for property offenses, in North Carolina only 4 months more, and in North Dakota only 8 months more.

Table 9.8 presents the correlations of average time served across offense types.

Table 9.8: Correlation Matrix, Time Served across Offense Types

	Time Served Violent Offenses	*Time Served Property Offenses*	*Time Served Drug Offenses*
Time Served, Overall	.79*	.92*	.94*
Time Served, Violent Offenses		.61*	.74*
Time Served, Property Offenses			.90*

* p = .00

The correlations all strong, positive, and significant at the .00 level. The strongest correlations are those between the overall time served and time served for property and drug offenses. The latter are also significantly correlated with each other. Again, the most loosely coupled of the relationships are those between time served for violent offenses and time served for property and for drug offenses (though these are still quite strong and significant). A classification table will help further clarify these relationships.

Classifying States on Time Served across Offense Types

Table 9.9 classifies states' in terms of time served across offense types. The states are classified on the two primary axes according to the punitiveness of their average time served for violent and property offenses. Punitiveness in time served for drug offenders is indicated by the italics: states in plain italics are under-punitive and states in bold italics over-punitive relative to other states in the amount of time served by drug offenders.

As indicated in the classification table, Minnesota and West Virginia are under-punitive and Ohio, Oklahoma, and Texas are over-punitive in terms of time-served regardless of the type of offense. These states were also identified as under and over punitive in the analysis of time-served overall. With the exception of Mississippi and Pennsylvania, which are over-punitive to violent offenders only, all of the states that are over-punitive in time-served overall are over-punitive in time served for at least two classes of offenders.[8] Maine is over-punitive in time served for property and drug offenders, but average in its punitiveness toward violent offenders. Maryland and Michigan, on the other hand, are over-punitive toward violent and drug offenders, but average in their punitiveness toward property offenders. North Dakota exhibits a pattern exactly opposite to that of Maryland and Michigan, with an under-punitive intensity for violent and drug offenders, and an average intensity for property offenders. The remaining states are average on at least two of the three time served measures and were all classified as average in punitive intensity overall in the previous chapter.

Table 9.9: Classifying States, Time Served across Offense Types

	Time Served for Violent Offenses		
Time Served for Property Offenses	***Under Punitive***	***Average***	***Over Punitive***
Under Punitive	*Minnesota* *West Virginia*	Arkansas *Missouri*	
Average	California *North Dakota*	20 States[9]	***Maryland*** ***Michigan*** Mississippi Pennsylvania
Over Punitive		Florida ***Maine*** North Carolina	***Ohio*** ***Oklahoma*** ***Texas***

THE IMPORTANCE OF DISAGGREGATING PROPENSITY AND INTENSITY DATA TO THE OFFENSE TYPE

What has been gained by the analysis of the propensity to imprison and intensity in imprisonment disaggregated to the offense type? Clearly, the analyses of the disaggregated data allow for a more nuanced assessment of these two types of punitiveness. The analyses demonstrated that in terms of imprisonment risk, North Dakota, one of the most punitive overall by this measure, is punitive in its propensity to imprison regardless of offense. Maine, one of the most punitive states in terms of time served overall, is indeed quite punitive in that regard but only to property and drug offenders. Pennsylvania is over-punitive in overall time served, but when its data are disaggregated it is actually only over-punitive toward violent offenders.

Disaggregating also allows for a clearer understanding of the relationship between the two determinants. Maine and North Dakota both have exceptionally low imprisonment rates relative to other states, yet they are each among the most punitive when punitiveness is gauged by one of the other measures of punitiveness. North Dakota is particularly punitive in terms of its propensity to imprison across all offenses but balances that punitiveness by being under-punitive in terms of average time served for violent and drug offenders. Maine is particularly interesting because its average time served overall was exceptionally high and its overall imprisonment risk exceptionally low. This finding can best be interpreted through simultaneously considering the offense specific imprisonment risk and time served analyses. Maine was identified as over-punitive in imprisonment risk and average in time served for violent offenders. Maine, however, has an exceptionally low propensity to imprison both property and drug offenders (imprisoning only 2 in 100 and 1 in 100 respectively) and exceptionally high average time served for those offenders. In other words, in the few instances in which Maine imprisons property and drug offenders, the duration of imprisonment is exceptionally lengthy relative to other states. Although this analysis cannot distinguish varying levels of offense seriousness, this low propensity-high intensity finding suggests that perhaps only the most serious or repeat property and drug offenders are sentenced to prison in Maine.

A comparison of the overall imprisonment risk and time served classification table (Table 8.8 in the previous chapter) and the imprisonment risk and time served by offense type classification tables (9.5 and 9.9 respectively), suggests that the analysis by offense type, while helpful in interpreting the nature of these relationships is not necessarily essential for capturing variations in the punitiveness of the states on these dimensions. Five of the nine states classified in Table 8.8 as the most and least punitive states in terms of imprisonment risk are actually more and less punitive generally (across at least two of the offense types on that dimension).[10] In the remaining four states it appears that an exceptionally high or low risk for just one class of offender is influencing the average risk overall.[11]

Ten of the thirteen states classified as either under- or over-punitive in the intensity of imprisonment overall are actually less or more punitive generally (across at least two offense types).[12] The three exceptions are Florida and Pennsylvania, which were both classified as over-punitive overall, and South Dakota, which was classified as under-punitive overall. Florida and Pennsylvania are over-punitive in time served only for property or violent offenders respectively, and South Dakota is under-punitive only in its time served for drug offenses. While these distinctions allow for a more nuanced interpretation, they do not seem substantial enough to require that the propensity to imprison and duration in the intensity of imprisonment be disaggregated to the offense type. In most cases, the aggregate propensity and intensity is suggestive of a trend across multiple offense types.

NOTES

1 As in the previous chapter, Illinois and Wisconsin are excluded from imprisonment risk analyses due to unreliable or unavailable UCR arrest data for 1999. While included in the imprisonment risk overall analysis, Alaska was excluded from the analysis of imprisonment risk across offense types because the vast majority of their admission offenses (67%) were coded as 'other.'

2 North Dakota was a clear outlier in its exceptionally high imprisonment risk for violent offenders and was therefore removed from the calculation of the mean on this particular measure.

3 Again, North Dakota's imprisonment risk for violent offenders (1.04) is notably higher than any other state – almost sixteen times higher than Louisiana's. While North Dakota is classified as an over-punitive state in this regard, its imprisonment risk for violent offenders was excluded from all calculations that rely on a normal distribution.

[4] The fifteen states that exhibit average intensities to imprison violent and property offenders include ***Arkansas***, Colorado, Florida, Georgia, Hawaii, Maryland, *Michigan*, *Minnesota*, Missouri, Nebraska, ***Nevada***, New Jersey, Ohio, Virginia, *West Virginia*. As indicated by the italics three of these states (Michigan, Minnesota, and West Virginia) are under-punitive in imprisonment risk for drug offenders and two (Arkansas and Nevada) are over-punitive.

[5] As noted earlier, Ohio is an outlier in terms of average time served overall, and across each of the offense types. While classified as over-punitive on each of these measures in Table 9.9, Ohio was excluded from calculations that assume a normal distribution.

[6] Across all offense types, Ohio's average time served at first release greatly exceeded that of any other state. Due to the potential anomalous distortions in Ohio's data (see Appendix A), time served comparisons will be drawn omitting Ohio.

[7] In Iowa, Michigan, Mississippi, South Carolina, and Washington the average time served for drug offenders was longer than average time served for property offenders.

[8] The states that were over-punitive in the overall time served analysis in the previous chapter included Louisiana, Maine, Maryland, Ohio, Oklahoma, Pennsylvania and Texas.

[9] The twenty states that exhibit average punitiveness in time served for violent and property offenders include Alabama, Colorado, Georgia, Hawaii, *Illinois*, Iowa, Kentucky, Louisiana, Nebraska, Nevada, New Hampshire, New Jersey, New York, Oregon, South Carolina, *South Dakota*, *Utah*, Virginia, Washington, and Wisconsin. As indicated by the italics two of these states (Illinois, South Dakota, and Utah) are under-punitive in average time served for drug offenders.

[10] New York is under-punitive and North Dakota over-punitive in imprisonment risk for all three classes of offenders. Maine is under-punitive in its imprisonment risk for property and drug offenders but over-punitive in its imprisonment risk for violent offenders. Pennsylvania is under-punitive in its imprisonment risk for violent and property offenders but average in its imprisonment risk for drug offenders, and Oklahoma is over-punitive in its imprisonment risk for both property and drug offenders and average in its imprisonment risk for violent offenders.

[11] Minnesota is classified as under-punitive in its propensity to imprison in Table 9.8 but appears to be under-punitive only in its propensity to imprison drug offenders. Conversely, Nevada as identified as over-punitive because of its exceptionally high risk of imprisonment for drug offenders. Utah and Iowa are under- and over-punitive only in their imprisonment risk for property offenders.

[12] Minnesota and Virginia are under-punitive and Ohio, Oklahoma, and Texas are over-punitive in average time served for all three classes of offenders. Missouri is under-punitive and Maine is over-punitive toward both property and drug offenders, but average in imprisonment risk for violent offenders. North Dakota is under-punitive and Maryland and Michigan are over-punitive toward both violent and drug offenders, but average in imprisonment risk for property offenders.

CHAPTER 10

PUNITIVENESS OVER TIME, 1990-2000

Having established that imprisonment rates, imprisonment risk, and time served analyses each say something different about variations in punitiveness, it might be instructive to examine what has happened over time across each of these measures. In the analysis over time, I first present some general trends across each of the measures from 1990 to 2000, and then describe some of the interactions between imprisonment risk and time served on the one hand and changes in imprisonment rates on the other. For the analysis over time, data were gathered for as many states as possible, on as many of the measures as possible, going back one decade in five year increments to 1990. Five year increments allow enough time to pass for changes to manifest in each of the measures.

IMPRISONMENT RATE TRENDS, 1990-2000

The trends in imprisonment rates across the states over the past few decades have been the focus of much empirical work. The discussion in Chapter 5 described the significant variation in imprisonment rates across the states. This pattern of variation holds across each time period under study. In all three periods, states at the upper end of the continuum had imprisonment rates five to six times those of states at the lower end. Between 1990 and 2000, there were numerous imprisonment rate rank changes and no one state held the top rank across the three periods. In 1990, South Carolina was the most punitive state by reference to imprisonment rates and its imprisonment rate of

451 was almost seven times that of North Dakota. Three states had imprisonment rates of over 400 (Louisiana, South Carolina, and Nevada) and three had rates of less than 100 (North Dakota, Minnesota, and West Virginia). By 1995, sixteen states had imprisonment rates over 400 (three were over 500 and one over 600) and only one (North Dakota) still had an imprisonment rate of less than 100. Texas more than doubled its imprisonment rate in just five years climbing from a rank of 16th in 1990 to 1st in 1995. With an imprisonment rate of 677, Texas imprisoned almost eight times as many convicted felons per 100,000 residents as North Dakota. By 2000, North Dakota, which had the lowest imprisonment rate in 1990 and 1995, had become notably more punitive climbing three ranks with an imprisonment rate in 2000 more than double its 1990 rate. Louisiana held the top rank in 2000 with an imprisonment rate of just over 800, and again its rate was more than six times that of the state at the lower end of the continuum (Minnesota).

When measured by imprisonment rates, all states have become more punitive over the past several decades. Moreover, as initially demonstrated by Zimring and Hawkins (1991), the states have, for the most part, maintained their relative position over time. Zimring and Hawkins analyzed changes in imprisonment rates between 1950 and 1980, and between 1980 and 1987, and found that most states had become significantly more punitive over the period of study and that the rank order correlations between the ranks at time 1 and time 2 were in both instances strong, positive, and significant (.68 and .77 respectively). This analysis of imprisonment rates between 1990 and 2000 adds support to Zimring and Hawkin's thesis that while there may be shifts in punitiveness, these shifts are indicative of a trend that manifests across all states. As all the states move in the same direction at the same time (albeit with different magnitudes of change), they generally maintain their relative punitiveness ranking. Table 10.1 presents the rank order correlations of imprisonment rate rankings over the three time periods.

Although the rank order correlations between imprisonment rates at the various times are all strong, positive, and significant, as time passes the correlation appears to weaken slightly. So, although the states rank very similarly when the span of time between the rankings is only five years, when that time is expanded to ten years the rank ordering has shifted more notably. So for instance, while Maryland and Alaska were both in the top ten in terms of imprisonment rates in 1990, by 2000 each had fallen fairly significantly (to 17th and 32nd respectively). Just as some states fell in imprisonment rate rankings, other states climbed. Wisconsin, ranked 40th in 1990, had moved notably to 24th in 2000.

Table 10.1: Rank Order Correlations: Imprisonment Rates 1990, 1995, 2000

	Imprisonment Rate 1995	*Imprisonment Rate 2000*
Imprisonment Rate 1990	.96*	.88*
Imprisonment Rate 1995		.94*

p = .00

There is also a high degree of consistency in the states that hold relative ranks among the top and bottom ten in terms of imprisonment rates. As depicted in Table 10.2, six states (Alabama, Arizona, Louisiana, Nevada, Oklahoma, and South Carolina) were among the ten most punitive by reference to imprisonment rates across all three periods. An additional four states (Florida, Georgia, Mississippi, and Texas) were among the most punitive across at least two of the three periods. Only four states (Alaska, Delaware, Maryland, and Michigan) appear among the ten most punitive in only one period. The consistency is even more impressive for the least punitive states. Eight of the states identified as among the least punitive in 1990 (Maine, Massachusetts, Minnesota, Nebraska, New Hampshire, North Dakota, and West Virginia), were also among the least punitive in 1995 and 2000. Two additional states (Rhode Island and Utah) were among the least punitive in at least two of the three periods, and only two states (Iowa and Washington) appear only once.

Table 10.2: Ten States with the Highest and Lowest Imprisonment Rates in 1990, 1995, and 2000

	1990	*1995*	*2000*
Ten Highest	***South Carolina***	**Texas**	***Louisiana***
	Nevada	***Louisiana***	**Texas**
	Louisiana	***Oklahoma***	**Mississippi**
	Oklahoma	***South Carolina***	***Oklahoma***
	Arizona	***Nevada***	**Georgia**
	Alabama	***Arizona***	***Alabama***
	Michigan	***Alabama***	***South Carolina***
	Maryland	**Georgia**	***Nevada***
	Alaska	**Mississippi**	***Arizona***
	Florida	**Florida**	Delaware
Ten Lowest	**Utah**	**Rhode Island**	Washington
	Nebraska	***Nebraska***	***Nebraska***
	Iowa	***Vermont***	***Vermont***
	Massachusetts	**Utah**	***West Virginia***
	Maine	***New Hampshire***	**Rhode Island**
	Vermont	***Massachusetts***	***NewHampshire***
	New Hampshire	***West Virginia***	***North Dakota***
	West Virginia	***Maine***	***Massachusetts***
	Minnesota	***Minnesota***	***Maine***
	North Dakota	***North Dakota***	***Minnesota***

Note: States in bold appear among the highest or lowest in average time served in two of the three periods. States in bold italics appear in all three.

Table 10.3 presents the percent change in imprisonment rates for the ten states with the largest and smallest growth between 1990 and 2000. As indicated in Table 10.3, those states with the highest imprisonment rates in 1990 were not those with the largest growth over the decade; in fact, five of the states with the highest imprisonment rates in 1990 are among the states with the least growth. Each of these states fell in the imprisonment rate rankings with only two (Nevada and South Carolina) remaining in the top ten in 2000. States with the most growth over the period tend to be states that had either average or low imprisonment rates in 1990. With the exceptions of Mississippi and Texas, each of the states experiencing the greatest growth had rankings of 30th or above in 1990. While each of these states climbed in its imprisonment rate ranking, all but two remained low to average in their imprisonment rates relative to other states.

Table 10.3: Percent Change in Imprisonment Rates, 1990-2000

	Imprisonment Rate (Rank) 1990		*Imprisonment Rate (Rank) 2000*		*% Change*
Ten Largest					
Wisconsin	149	(40)	376	(24)	152.35%
Texas	290	(16)	730	(2)	151.72%
West Virginia	85	(48)	211	(44)	148.24%
North Dakota	67	(50)	158	(47)	135.82%
Idaho	190	(33)	430	(16)	126.32%
Mississippi	307	(14)	688	(3)	124.10%
Hawaii	150	(39)	302	(37)	101.33%
Iowa	139	(43)	276	(39)	98.56%
Montana	176	(36)	348	(30)	97.73%
Colorado	209	(30)	403	(20)	92.82%
Ten Smallest					
Michigan	366	(7)	480	(12)	31.15%
North Carolina	265	(22)	347	(31)	30.94%
New York	304	(15)	383	(23)	25.99%
Rhode Island	157	(38)	197	(45)	25.48%
Maryland	348	(9)	429	(17)	23.28%
South Carolina	451	(1)	532	(7)	17.96%
Nevada	444	(2)	518	(8)	16.67%
Massachusetts	132	(44)	152	(48)	15.15%
Maine	118	(45)	129	(49)	9.32%
Alaska	348	(9)	341	(32)	-2.01%
Average					64.47%

This examination of imprisonment rates over time suggests that indeed, in keeping with the national trend, almost all states have become progressively more punitive over time when punitiveness is measured by imprisonment rates. Across all states, with only one exception, the states' imprisonment rates have increased as time has passed. Alaska was the only state to avoid growth and actually experienced a slight decrease in its imprisonment rate between 1990 and 2000. The decrease in Alaska's imprisonment rate explains how it fell from among the ten most punitive states in 1990, to 32nd in 2000. The magnitude of the increases in imprisonment rates for most states is substantial. In the ten years between 1990 and 2000, imprisonment rates in seven states have more than doubled and in an additional seven states the rates have almost doubled. The argument made thus far has suggested that the analysis of variations in imprisonment rates, while interesting, does not tell us enough about how punitive a state is, was, or has become because there is more than one way to respond punitively and imprisonment rates may or may not reflect changes on those other dimensions. In the next section, I examine changes in imprisonment risk over time.

IMPRISONMENT RISK TRENDS, 1990-2000

The average imprisonment risk across the sample has remained remarkably stable between 1990 and 2000 (see Table 10.4), leading some (Blumstein and Beck, 1999) to note that the risk of imprisonment following an arrest has not increased appreciably over the period. In 1990, imprisonment risk ranged from a low of .03 in Massachusetts to a high of .18 in Hawaii, with an average across the sample of .09 (or 9 imprisonments for every 100 index or drug offense arrests).[1] In 1995 and 2000, the average imprisonment risk across the sample was .11 and .12 respectively. Although not as stable as imprisonment rates, the rank order correlations between imprisonment risk rankings across the three periods are strong, positive, and significant. Again there is some consistency in states appearing among the ten most and ten least punitive by this measure (see Table 10.6).

Table 10.4: Descriptives: Imprisonment Risk, 1990, 1995, 2000

	N	*Minimum*	*Maximum*	*Average*
Imprisonment Risk 1990	33	.03	.18	.09
Imprisonment Risk 1995	38	.05	.19	.11
Imprisonment Risk 2000	36	.06	.20	.12

As depicted in Table 10.6, three states (Oklahoma, South Carolina, and Texas) were among the ten most punitive and four states (Minnesota, New York, Pennsylvania, and Utah) were among the ten least punitive by reference to imprisonment risk across all three periods. An additional seven states (Iowa, Mississippi, Nevada, North Carolina, Ohio, Tennessee, and Virginia) were among the most punitive and four states (California, Colorado, Maine, Washington, and Wisconsin) among the least punitive across at least two of the three periods. Seven states rank among the ten most punitive and eight states among the ten least punitive in only one period.

Table 10.5: Rank Order Correlations: Imprisonment Risk 1990, 1995, 2000

	Imp. Risk 1995	*Imp. Risk 2000*
Imprisonment Risk 1990	.64*	.58*
Imprisonment Risk 1995		.68*

p = .00

Table 10.6: Ten States with the Highest and Lowest Imprisonment Risk in 1990, 1995, and 2000

	1990	1995	2000
Ten Highest			
	Tennessee	***Texas***	North Dakota
	Hawaii	Illinois	***Oklahoma***
	North Carolina	**Iowa**	**Iowa**
	South Carolina	***Oklahoma***	**Nevada**
	Ohio	Arkansas	***South Carolina***
	Texas	***South Carolina***	**Mississippi**
	Oklahoma	**Ohio**	Missouri
	Georgia	**North Carolina**	South Dakota
	Virginia	**Virginia**	**Tennessee**
	Nevada	**Mississippi**	***Texas***
Ten Lowest			
	New York	**Wisconsin**	**Washington**
	New Jersey	**Maine**	North Carolina
	Colorado	Hawaii	Nebraska
	Minnesota	**Colorado**	**California**
	Pennsylvania	**Washington**	Florida
	New Hampshire	***New York***	***Minnesota***
	Wisconsin	***Minnesota***	***Utah***
	California	***Utah***	**Maine**
	West Virginia	***Pennsylvania***	***Pennsylvania***
	Utah	Oregon	***New York***

Note: States in bold appear among the highest or lowest in average time served in two of the three periods. States in bold italics appear in all three.

The stability in the average propensity to imprison across the states (depicted in Table 10.4) masks substantial shifts in propensity within individual states. Table 10.7 presents variations in imprisonment risk among the states experiencing the largest increases and decreases in imprisonment risk between 1990 and 2000.

Table 10.7: Ten States with the Highest and Lowest Percent Change in Imprisonment Risk, 1990-2000

	Imp. Risk 1990	*Imp. Risk 2000*	*% Change 1990-2000*
Highest Increases			
North Dakota	0.10	0.20	93.48
Utah	0.04	0.08	77.42
New Hampshire	0.06	0.11	74.62
West Virginia	0.06	0.11	67.81
Mississippi	0.09	0.15	57.25
Iowa	0.11	0.17	54.26
New Jersey	0.07	0.11	53.08
Colorado	0.07	0.10	51.99
Missouri	0.10	0.15	43.04
California	0.06	0.09	40.92
Ten Lowest			
Maryland	0.09	0.10	2.49
Michigan	0.11	0.10	-1.38
Texas	0.14	0.14	-2.85
South Carolina	0.16	0.15	-3.72
Georgia	0.13	0.11	-16.87
Hawaii	0.18	0.14	-23.96
New York	0.08	0.06	-29.02
Ohio	0.15	0.10	-34.37
North Carolina	0.18	0.09	-49.65
Tennessee	0.33	0.14	-57.57

Between 1990 and 2000, the risk of imprisonment following an index or drug offense arrest either stayed substantially the same or increased in all but nine of the states included in the analysis. Because the percent change is based on each state's own imprisonment risk in 1990 and 2000, some of those states that experienced the most change were not the most punitive by the imprisonment risk measure (a state with a very low imprisonment risk would experience a large percent change if its imprisonment risk moved slightly). So, for example, Utah despite having experienced one of the largest percent changes in imprisonment risk (77.42%) between 1990 and 2000 is still under-punitive relative to other states because its imprisonment risk of .08 is still substantially below the average across the sample of 0.12.

The classification table (Table 10.8) presented below assists in the interpretation of changes in imprisonment risk over time. Using the classification method described in Chapter 7, Table 10.8 classifies states as average, under or over-punitive on the imprisonment risk measure across all three periods simultaneously. As this table relies on the distribution from the mean to classify the states, a state may be among the ten most punitive by the imprisonment risk measure (in Table 10.6) and not be over-punitive relative to other states (in Table 10.8).

As indicated in Tables 10.7 and 10.8, only six states experienced substantial decreases in imprisonment risk over the period, and three of those states were over-punitive in terms of imprisonment risk in the earliest period. Notably, only Utah was under-punitive in terms of imprisonment risk across all three periods. No state was over-punitive across all three periods, nor did a state that was under-punitive in 1990 become over-punitive by 2000 and vice-versa. Minnesota, New York, and Pennsylvania were average in terms of imprisonment risk in 1990, but had become under-punitive by 1995 and remained so in 2000. Conversely, Iowa and Oklahoma were average in 1990, had become over-punitive by 1995, and remained so in 2000. Although no state was under-punitive in just one of the three periods, a number of states were average across two of the periods, but over-punitive in just one. Nevada and North Dakota were over-punitive only in 2000. Four states, Arkansas, Ohio, South Carolina, and Texas, were over-punitive in 1995 but average in the period preceding (1990) and following (2000).

Table 10.8: Classification Table: Imprisonment Risk Over Time

Imprisonment Risk 1990 \ Imprisonment Risk 2000	*Under Punitive*	*Average*	*Over Punitive*	*Excluded*
Under Punitive	*Utah*			*MA*
Average	*Minnesota* *New York* *PA*	20 States[2]	***Iowa*** Nevada ND ***Oklahoma***	***Illinois*** Wisconsin
Over Punitive		Hawaii NC Tennessee		
Excluded	Maine	Florida Louisiana South Dakota		

TIME-SERVED TRENDS, 1990-2000

Although imprisonment risk remained stable on average across the sample, the average time served across the sample increased slightly between 1990 and 1995 and substantially between 1995 and 2000.[3]

Table 10.9: Descriptives: Average Time Served: 1990, 1995, 2000

	N	Minimum	Maximum	Average
Time Served 1990	32	13.49	33.48	22.56
Time Served 1995	36	14.93	35.72	23.56
Time Served 2000	35	16.70	49.60	28.55

As indicated by the range of time served averages, there was substantial variation in average time served across states in each of the periods. In 1990, average time served ranged from a low of 13.49 months in North Carolina to a high of 33.48 months in Oregon. In 1995, the average time served ranged from a low of 14.93 months in North Dakota to a high of 35.72 months in Pennsylvania and in 2000, it ranged from a low of 16.70 months in Missouri to a high of 49.60 months in Maine.

Table 10.10: Rank Order Correlations: Time Served 1990, 1995, 2000

	Time Served 1995	Time Served 2000
Time Served 1990	.58*	.27
Time Served 1995		.71*

p = .00

When the time increment is ten years, the rank order correlation between average time served rankings is fairly weak (+.27) and non-significant. When the increment is five years, the correlations are notably stronger and significant. As indicated by the correlations, the rank order of states in terms of average time served shifted fairly significantly between 1990 and 2000. There was however again some consistency in states identified as among the ten most and ten least punitive by this measure (see Table 10.11).

Table 10.11: Ten States with the Highest and Lowest Average Time Served in 1990, 1995, 2000

	1990	1995	2000
Ten Highest			
	Hawaii	***Pennsylvania***	**Ohio**
	Oregon	***Michigan***	**Maine**
	Nevada	**Texas**	**Texas**
	Maryland	**Florida**	***Pennsylvania***
	New York	***Maryland***	***Maryland***
	Missouri	**Nevada**	**Oklahoma**
	Pennsylvania	Alabama	**Florida**
	Ohio	**Maine**	***Michigan***
	New Hampshire	***New York***	North Carolina
	Michigan	**Oklahoma**	***New York***
Ten Lowest			
	Kentucky	Nebraska	Wisconsin
	Virginia	**Georgia**	***California***
	North Dakota	***Arkansas***	**Kentucky**
	Minnesota	***Minnesota***	***Arkansas***
	Iowa	**North Carolina**	South Dakota
	California	**West Virginia**	**Illinois**
	Arkansas	**Virginia**	***Minnesota***
	Oklahoma	**Illinois**	***North Dakota***
	Georgia	***California***	**West Virginia**
	North Carolina	***North Dakota***	Missouri

Note: States in bold appear among the highest or lowest in average time served in two of the three periods. States in bold italics appear in all three.

Four states (Maryland, Michigan, New York, and Pennsylvania) were among the most punitive and four (Arkansas, California, Minnesota, and North Dakota) among the least punitive in terms of average time served across all three periods. An additional six states were among the most punitive and an additional six among the least punitive across at least two of the periods. Six of the states appeared among the most punitive and six among the least punitive in only one period. Perhaps the most interesting states in these rankings are Missouri, North Carolina, and Oklahoma each of which went from being among the least punitive in terms of average time served in one period to being among the most punitive in another. Oklahoma had been among the ten least punitive in 1990 and was among the most punitive in 2000. North Carolina was among the least punitive in 1990 and 1995 and also among the most punitive in 2000. Missouri moved in the opposite direction going from among the most punitive in 1990 to among the least punitive in 2000.

Table 10.12 presents the percent change in time served of the ten states experiencing the greatest increases and the ten states experiencing either the smallest increases (or decreases) in average time served between 1990 and 2000. Perhaps not surprisingly, the two states that went from being among the least punitive to among the most punitive experienced the greatest percent change in average time served between 1990 and 2000 (North Carolina's average time served increased 153 percent and Oklahoma's 146 percent). Similarly, Missouri experienced the largest decrease in average time served (decreasing by 44 percent) and moved from being among the most punitive to being among the least punitive.

In thirty-one states, average time served either remained substantially the same or increased between 1990 and 2000. In six of the eight states with a reduction in average time served between 1990 and 2000, a substantial decrease in time served between 1990 and 1995 offset an increase in average time served between 1995 and 2000.

As depicted in the classification table (10.13), twelve states were average in terms of time-served across all three periods. Only one state (Minnesota) was under-punitive and only one (Maryland) was over-

Table 10.12: Ten States with the Highest and Lowest Percent Change in Time Served, 1990-2000

	Time Served 1990	Time Served 2000	Percent Change
Ten Highest			
North Carolina	13.49	34.12	152.98
Oklahoma	16.07	39.49	145.76
Texas	19.58	45.09	130.31
Georgia	14.32	28.20	96.99
Iowa	16.40	27.44	67.33
Virginia	18.50	27.76	50.04
California	16.23	24.19	49.08
Pennsylvania	29.03	41.46	42.84
Michigan	26.76	36.66	36.98
Mississippi	22.57	30.43	34.86
Ten Lowest			
Utah	26.05	26.85	3.09
Wisconsin	24.44	24.64	0.85
New York	31.50	31.33	-0.54
Illinois	20.20	19.91	-1.46
Nebraska	25.87	25.24	-2.44
West Virginia	19.49	17.75	-8.89
Nevada	33.20	28.48	-14.21
Oregon	33.48	26.29	-21.49
Hawaii	40.55	29.93	-26.19
Missouri	30.03	16.70	-44.39

punitive across all three periods. Of the eight states that were over-punitive in 2000, five had also been over-punitive in an earlier period. Florida, Maryland, Michigan, Pennsylvania and Texas were each over-punitive in 1995 and remained so in 2000. Illinois and North Dakota, which were both average in terms of overall time served in 1990, had become under-punitive by 1995 and remained so in 2000. California had been under-punitive in both 1990 and 1995 but was average by 2000. Time served declined appreciably in only four states between 1990 and 2000 (Nevada, Oregon, Hawaii, and Missouri) and, as indicated in Table 10.13, each of these states was over-punitive in its average time-served in 1990.

Table 10.13: Classification Table, Average Time Served Over Time

Time Served 1990	Time Served 2000: ***Under Punitive***	***Average***	***Over Punitive***
Under Punitive	*Minnesota*	Arkansas *California* Georgia Iowa North Carolina	Oklahoma
Average	*Illinois* *North Dakota* West Virginia	12 States[4]	***Michigan*** ***Pennsylvania*** ***Texas*** Ohio
Over Punitive	Missouri	Hawaii Nevada New York Oregon	***Maryland***
Excluded	South Dakota	Louisiana	***Florida*** Maine

INTERACTION OF IMPRISONMENT RISK, TIME SERVED, AND IMPRISONMENT RATES

To the extent that shifts in the propensity to imprison and intensity in the duration of imprisonment have contributed to growing punitiveness in imprisonment rates over the period of study, they will have done so relative to the percent change in imprisonment rates over the period (rather than to the absolute imprisonment rate). It would be reasonable to expect that changes in imprisonment risk or time served could eventually explain why some states have dramatically increased their imprisonment rate in the past decade. Table 10.2 identified the states with the highest and lowest percent change in imprisonment rates between 1990 and 2000. Five of those states, two with the greatest percent change and three with the lowest percent change, were excluded from the imprisonment risk and time served analyses due to a lack of data on one or more of the measures. The interaction between imprisonment risk and time served among the remaining eight states experiencing the highest percent change and seven states experiencing the lowest percent change is described in the next few paragraphs.

Among those states with the largest percent change in imprisonment rates, five were among the states with the greatest percent change in imprisonment risk between 1990 and 2000 (Colorado, Iowa, Mississippi, North Dakota, and West Virginia). Texas demonstrated no appreciable change in imprisonment risk, but a dramatic increase in time served (130%). Hawaii's imprisonment risk and time served both decreased overall between 1990 and 2000 (-24% and -26% respectively), but Hawaii was substantially over punitive on both measures in 1990 (see Tables 11.5 and 11.8) and its imprisonment risk increased substantially between 1995 and 2000 (74%).[5] Due to a lack of arrest data for Wisconsin in 1999, imprisonment risk over the period 1990 to 2000 could not be calculated; Wisconsin did, however, experience an increase in imprisonment risk of 29% between 1990 and 1995.

Conversely, among those states with the smallest percent change in imprisonment rates, five experienced either no appreciable change (Maryland, Michigan, and South Carolina) or a notable decrease (North

Carolina and New York) in imprisonment risk. Nevada and New York also both saw slight decreases in time served between 1990 and 2000. It seems North Carolina's decrease in imprisonment risk (-58%) might have largely offset its substantial increase in time served (153%). While data on imprisonment risk and time served were not available for Maine in 1990, Maine experienced a decrease in imprisonment risk and a substantial increase in time served between 1995 and 2000.

Though there are a few notable exceptions, changes in imprisonment risk and time served do seem to be fairly good indicators of percent change increases in imprisonment rates. Those states that increased or decreased imprisonment risk most substantially tend to be the states experiencing the greatest and lowest percent increases in imprisonment rates. Across most of the states, imprisonment risk seems to be the stronger of the two indicators, though that may be in part because increases and decreases in imprisonment risk have a more immediate effect on imprisonment rates (as noted in Chapter 6, changes in time served have a delayed effect and will take longer to manifest in an increase in the imprisonment rate). As dramatic increases in average time-served begin to manifest, this analysis suggests that, given the time served averages remain high, states such as Florida, Michigan, Maine, and Pennsylvania will begin to see substantial increases in imprisonment rates.

NOTES

[1] Tennessee's imprisonment risk in 1990 was .33 – remarkably higher than any other state and almost double that of the next highest state. Because including Tennessee would inflate the average overall, it was removed from the calculation of average imprisonment risk in 1990.

[2] Alabama, ***Arkansas***, California, Colorado, Georgia, Kentucky, Maryland, Michigan, Mississippi, Missouri, Nebraska, New Hampshire, New Jersey, ***Ohio***, Oregon, ***South Carolina, Texas***, Virginia, Washington, and West Virginia.

[3] Hawaii's time-served in 1990 was 40.55, substantially higher than any other state. As a clear outlier that might distort the average, it was removed from the calculation of the mean time served in 1990. With Hawaii included, the mean in 1990 would have been 23.11 months. Ohio, as noted earlier, was removed from the calculation of the mean in 2000. With Ohio included, the mean in 2000 would have been 29.81 months.

[4] Alabama, Colorado, Kentucky, Mississippi, Nebraska, New Hampshire, New Jersey, South Carolina, Utah, Virginia, Washington, and Wisconsin. One state (Tennessee) is excluded due to data irregularities (see Appendix A).

[5] Hawaii's increase between 1995 and 2000 was offset by a decrease in imprisonment risk between 1990 and 1995.

CHAPTER 11

UNDERSTANDING VARIATIONS IN PUNITIVENESS

Addressing the question of whether prison works as a strategy for reducing crime, John DiIulio (1996) asked "If incarceration is not the answer, then what precisely is the question?" In 1997, Murray echoed that sentiment, asking:

> If the question is: "How can we restore the fabric of family life and socialize a new generation of young males to civilized behavior? then prison is not the answer. If the question is, "How can we make unemployable youths employable? then prison is not the answer. If the question is "How can we rehabilitate habitual criminals so that they become law-abiding citizens?" prison is only rarely the answer. But, if the question is "How can we deter people from committing crimes?" then prison is an indispensable part of the answer" (1997:20).

To borrow their rhetorical approach (though not their "prison works" orientation), if the question is "Which states are the most punitive?" then 'an indispensable part of the answer' should be "what, exactly, do you mean by punitive?"

The analyses in this study demonstrate that the way in which punitiveness is defined and measured makes a substantial difference to the answer to the question of which states are the most punitive. Virtually all previous studies of state-level fluctuations in punitiveness have relied on the imprisonment rate as the sole measure of punitiveness, and when punitiveness is measured by reference to imprisonment rates, some states stand out as particularly punitive relative to other states. The variation in imprisonment rates across states is indeed substantial enough that it seems there are nearly as many varying imprisonment policies as there are states. As Cullen et al. (1996:21) have noted, it takes a "fair measure of hubris" to speak of the punitiveness of the United States as though it can reasonably be described as one entity.

When measured by one of the other two punitiveness measures – the propensity to imprison and the intensity in the duration of imprisonment – not only do the state level puntiveness rankings shift significantly, but some of the least punitive states, as measured by reference to imprisonment rates, soar to the top of the punitiveness rankings on one or both of the other two punitiveness measures. Similarly some states that are the most punitive by reference to imprisonment rates, fall in the rankings and are situated among the least punitive states on one or both alternative measures.

The distinction between punitiveness measures is important because many of those that have built their careers on studying and theorizing fluctuations in punitiveness, speak of the increasing punitiveness of recent decades in a way that implies something more than just an increase in the number of offenders punished through imprisonment (though clearly many are dismayed by that increase). The common presence of words like "harsh," "cruel," "degrading," and "vindictive" in descriptions of the punitive turn clearly implies that many of these scholars believe that something about the *character* of punishment has changed (see Tonry, 2001c, 2004b; Simon, 2001; Whitman, 2003; Young, 2003b). Moreover, many of the most frequently criticized punishment policies of the past few decades (three-strikes, truth-in-sentencing, mandatory sentences, and mandatory minimums) are those that, if fully implemented, will result in substantial increases in the average time served per offense (particularly for certain types of offenders – see Chapter 1).

As a cumulative punitiveness measure, imprisonment rates are not particularly well-suited to capture fluctuations in the other two measures. As argued in Chapter 6, imprisonment rates confound stock prison populations and flow into and out of prison, and, therefore, do not permit for a nuanced assessment of the precise ways in which punitiveness has increased. Moreover, as demonstrated in Chapter 7, changes in length of stay take longer to manifest in an increase in the overall size of a prison population, and so states that increase punitiveness on this dimension may appear relatively non-punitive in their imprisonment rates for some time.

I do not contend that I am the first to note the importance of recognizing the dual determinants of punitiveness in imprisonment. Chapters 1 through 6 note numerous instances where scholars have noted these distinctions in their discussions of punitiveness. Some have gone further and analyzed increasing punitiveness by reference to variation in imprisonment risk and time served on the national and cross-national levels. Blumstein and Beck (1999; 2005) have demonstrated that, on a national level, only these two measures (commitments per arrest and average time served) have contributed to the escalating prison population. They note that changes in crime and in police effectiveness over the period between 1980 and 2001 explain virtually none of the growth in prison populations, and that the growth can be attributed wholly to, and is partitioned almost equally between, changes in what I have called the propensity to imprison and intensity in the duration of imprisonment.[1] In the more recent analysis, Blumstein and Beck (2005) partition the period into two separate periods, and find that increases in the propensity to imprison contributed more to growth in the early period (1980-1992), and increases in the duration of imprisonment contributed more to growth in the later period (1992-2001).

In a series of cross-national studies, James Lynch has demonstrated that the United States, while clearly more punitive than most nations when punitiveness is measured by the imprisonment rate, does not appear to be such an outlier when the measure of punitiveness used to make the comparisons is either the propensity to imprison or intensity in the duration of imprisonment. While these scholars have confronted these issues, to the best of my knowledge, the analyses contained in this study are the first to confront distinctions in the state-level patterns of variation across all three measures of punitiveness.

The additional punitiveness measures tested in this study allow for a more nuanced assessment of variations in punitiveness between states and fluctuations in punitiveness over time.

PUNITIVE BY ANY MEASURE?

Across most empirical work, states like Louisiana, Oklahoma, South Carolina, and Texas are described as among the most punitive because each currently has an exceptionally high imprisonment rate and typically ranks among the ten most punitive states by that measure each year. In the year 2000, only two states, Oklahoma and Texas, rank among the ten most punitive states regardless of the measure of punitiveness employed. Using the classification scheme employed in this study, both states can also be classified as *over-punitive* relative to other states in terms of imprisonment rates and time served (though only Oklahoma was also classified as 'over-punitive' in imprisonment risk). Despite having the highest imprisonment rate in the country in the year 2000, Louisiana was average on each of the other two measures, as was South Carolina.

Among the states most frequently depicted as the least punitive, a similar pattern emerges. States like Minnesota, Maine, North Dakota, and New Hampshire tend to rank among the least punitive by reference to their imprisonment rates, yet only Minnesota is among the least punitive states regardless of which punitiveness measure is employed. New Hampshire is average on each of the other two measures, and Maine and North Dakota are each among the least punitive by one of the other measures and the most punitive by the other. Not only were these two states among the ten most and ten least punitive by one of the other two measures, but they were additionally classified as *over-* and *under-punitive* relative to the distribution of states. Moreover, Maine and North Dakota exhibit precisely opposite punitiveness patterns. Maine is under-punitive in its propensity to imprison (and as the analysis across offense types demonstrated, particularly under-punitive in its propensity to imprison drug and property offenders), and markedly over-punitive in its average time served (again particularly for drug and property offenders). North Dakota, on the other hand, is the most punitive state in its propensity to imprison (across all offense types), and among the least punitive in average time served (particularly in time served for violent and drug offenses).

As to whether the states have become more punitive over time, the findings again depend on how punitiveness is measured. When punitiveness is measured by reference to imprisonment rates, all states but one (Alaska) have become more punitive over the past decade (from 1990 to 2000). When measured by the propensity to imprison, most – but certainly not all – states have become more punitive over the same period. The average propensity across the sample of states had not changed substantially between 1990 and 2000. There were variations within states over time, however, that were masked by this overall average. Nine states had lower propensities to imprison in 2000 than they had in 1990, five states had propensities that were roughly equivalent, and the remaining twenty-one states had propensities that were substantially higher in 2000 than they had been in 1990.[2]

A similar pattern emerges when punitiveness is measured by reference to the intensity in the duration of imprisonment (or average time served) over time. While the average time served across the sample increased substantially between 1990 and 2000 (from 22.56 to 28.55 months) and most states experienced fairly substantial increases in average time served, in some states average time served actually declined over the period. In other words, not all states have become more punitive by this measure. In some states, most notably Texas, a dramatic increase in average time served between 1990 and 2000 seems to have potentially propelled the increase in the imprisonment rate, and in others, such as Maine, a high average time served suggests that substantial imprisonment rate growth might loom in the coming years.

DIFFERENT PUNITIVE STRATEGIES?

The findings reported in the analyses beg the question of whether it might be inferred that various states are pursuing differing punitive strategies. While the analysis is not sophisticated enough to adequately address the question, it does seem that the interplay of imprisonment risk and time served across some of the states lends tentative credence to what could certainly be a testable hypothesis. To the extent that increasing imprisonment risk might be understood as a 'deterrence' strategy and increasing length of stay an 'incapacitation' strategy, there is some evidence that states tend to pursue one over the other.[3] While some of states were under or over-punitive on both measures, others tended to demonstrate a tendency toward punitiveness on just one.

Maine, for example, has an exceptionally low propensity to imprison drug and property offenders and an exceptionally high average time served for these offenders. North Dakota, on the other hand, has an exceptionally high propensity to imprison across all offenses, and an exceptionally low average time served (particularly for violent and drug offenders). Both states have maintained exceptionally low imprisonment rates relative to other states. These findings lend plausibility to the hypothesis that states might be pursuing different strategies. Maine might be described as emphasizing incapacitation, and North Dakota general deterrence.[4] Single state studies enable greater depth in the exploration of these differences, allowing one to add context and detail that cannot be captured in an analysis of large national datasets (Nicholson-Crotty & Meier, 2002) and might be a suitable direction for future research.[5]

IS THERE A 'BEST MEASURE'?

Although the analyses presented in this study confirmed that the way in which punitiveness is measured indeed makes a difference to state-level punitiveness rankings, the question remains whether the alternate measures can or should be deemed superior to the traditional imprisonment rate measure. While some are quite equivocal in their condemnation of the use of imprisonment rates as measures of punitiveness (see Pease, 1994; Lynch, 1988, 1993, 2002), I am more guarded.

Although I have argued that imprisonment rates cannot adequately capture all of the various ways in which a place can become more punitive, I hesitate to formally endorse any particular measure as superior because, while there are certainly limitations to the utility of an imprisonment rate analysis, the other measures raise problems of their own. There are important limitations to the propensity and intensity analyses, particularly as applied to state-level variation, not the least of which is the exclusion of a number of states due to a lack of comparable data on one or more of the measures. Additionally, as is always the case, the quality of the analysis and the reliability of the findings each depend on the quality of the underlying data. As noted throughout the analysis and in the accompanying appendices, despite the impressive coverage and comprehensiveness of the NCRP data, there are instances where the accuracy of the data are questionable.[6] There are also instances where data selection choices make a substantial difference to the measures and ultimately to the findings.[7] The accuracy of the arrest data derived from the Uniform Crime Reports is also at times questionable, particularly in the latter part of the 1990s when a number of states either made, or were in the process of making, the transition to NIBRS (the National Incident Based Reporting System).

THEORETICAL AND EMPIRICAL IMPLICATIONS

I have made the argument that if we further refine our understanding of punitiveness, we might develop more nuanced theories of the conditions under which punitiveness grows or declines, and might be better equipped to empirically explain variations in punitiveness across places. Data imperfections aside, it seems fair to argue that when the purpose of theoretical or empirical work is to simply explain or explore the overall growth of the use of imprisonment as a sanction, then the imprisonment rate might serve that purpose fairly well. The imprisonment rate does after all capture the cumulative effect of various punitive responses on the final 'punitive' outcome. When, however, the purpose of that work is to demonstrate: (1) that the character of punishment has changed in some fundamental way (become more degrading, more cruel, more harsh, or more vindictive), (2) that particular sentencing policies have resulted in increasing punitiveness, or (3) that as a punitive response imprisonment serves some larger sociological purpose or resonates with some deeper cultural or religious ideology, then theorists and researchers ought to be more specific in their articulation of the meaning of 'punitiveness' and in their specifications of the nature and direction of anticipated relationships. In such instances, one or both of the other "punitiveness" measures might be more appropriate dependent variables than the overall imprisonment rate.

Truth-in-sentencing laws, for instance, were enacted to ensure that certain classes of offenders – particularly violent offenders – serve a substantial portion of their court imposed sentences. Those seeking to explore the effects of the implementation of this legislation in practice might choose to isolate actual average time served among those offenders targeted by the legislation both before and after its enactment. A similar argument might be made for some of the other punitive sentencing policies (three-strikes, mandatory sentences, etc.). Those seeking to isolate the effect of the war on drugs on imprisonment populations might, on the other hand, explore variations in the propensities to imprison and intensity in imprisonment for just this offense type. If interested in empirically testing Zimring's hypothesis that the imprisonment binge can be parsed into three separate eras, a researcher could do so through imprisonment risk and average time served analyses using UCR and NCRP data covering the entire period. Each of these potential research projects calls for a more nuanced assessment of variations in punitiveness that an overall imprisonment rate analysis will almost certainly not capture.

LIMITATIONS

In addition to the aforementioned data limitations, there are other limitations of this study worth noting. First and foremost, the analyses in this study were largely descriptive – exploring variations in punitiveness and state-level rankings using various measures at three distinct points in time. The analysis certainly did not cover the entire period most frequently depicted as representing the punitive turn (approximately 1973 to the present), nor did it measure each of the variables in each year.[8] Doing so would allow for a comprehensive assessment of the relative contribution of the dual determinants to the cumulative imprisonment rate. Some of the states included in the analysis had exceptionally high imprisonment rates prior to 1990 – and therefore, despite having increased levels of imprisonment over the limited period of study – their overall punitiveness would not have been fully explained by changes in the other measures.

Additionally, there are two important limitations to the intensity of imprisonment measure (average time served). The first inherent limitation of an analysis of average time served is that, when that average is derived from a release cohort, it will not capture punitiveness toward those serving exceptionally lengthy sentences for some time, and cannot capture the time served of those who will never be released (Table B6 in Appendix B lists the percent of all inmates serving such sentences by state). Because those targeted by the particularly punitive sentencing laws tend to be serious, repeat or violent offenders, if these laws actually do enhance punitiveness in the duration of imprisonment (and they almost certainly will), this increased punitiveness will likely not be reflected in average time served figures for some time to come.[9]

The second inherent limitation is that intensity in the duration of imprisonment, as measured here, addresses only one of many aspects of intensity in imprisonment, and then only in a limited way. Although clearly longer terms of imprisonment are experienced as 'more punishing,' Spelman notes that "a two-year prison term is worse, but not twice as bad, as a one-year prison term" (2000b:472). Moreover, the intensity in the experience of imprisonment might depend on a number of other factors.[10] The experience of imprisonment might most obviously depend on the classification of the institution (super-maximum, maximum, medium, or minimum) and the classification of the offender. A prisoner classified as a security risk, serving time in a maximum or super-maximum security institution clearly might have a more painful experience of imprisonment than one classified as low risk in a medium or minimum security institution. Even across institutions of the same classification, varying conditions likely impact the experience of imprisonment. These experiences of imprisonment, while important in determining the diminishment of the quality of life associated with punishment, are to some extent subjective, very difficult to measure, and almost impossible to quantify in any meaningful way. Smaller qualitative studies can illuminate some of these distinctions.

The consequences of imprisonment also vary across states. The extent to which imprisonment is stigmatizing certainly might vary across places. In places where large numbers of residents experience imprisonment, the stigma of having served time in prison is likely reduced (see Fagan, 2004). The collateral consequences of imprisonment, or 'invisible punishments,' as Jeremy Travis (2002) has called them, are also not experienced uniformly across places. Some states, for example, restrict an ex-offender's access to the franchise, welfare, food stamps, housing, and the like, while others do not (see Mauer, 2002; Rubenstein & Mukamal, 2002). Each of these distinctions might be captured in a more comprehensive measure of the intensity of imprisonment.

While an analysis across *offense types* was included in Chapter 9, there were no controls for *offense seriousness* in the calculations of imprisonment risk or average time served. Offense types were isolated based on the "offense with the longest sentence length" and then grouped in a way that most closely matched the traditional violent, property, drug, and other offense categories. While the offense with the longest sentence is likely the most serious offense committed, this offense type classification ignores differences in the range of offenses within each broad offense type. Clearly, murder is a more serious offense than robbery (each of which were classified as violent offenses), and even among murders, offense seriousness can vary quite dramatically (involuntary manslaughter is very different from premeditated murder). The offense classification used in this analysis also did not control for the number of offenses, the number of conviction charges, or the number of counts (though the NCRP data do allow for such refined analyses). Finally, the analysis across offense types also did not control for offender seriousness in terms of prior convictions, prior prison sentences, or prior time served (though again, the NCRP data do permit such analyses). These extra controls were not pursued in this study because the purpose of the analysis across offense types was a limited one – to simply explore whether variations in imprisonment risk and average time served overall across the states could be explained by the 'mix' of offenders admitted to or released from prison. In other words, the analysis across offense types was included to determine whether, for example, Maine's average time served in 2000 was so lengthy because most of those released were violent offenders. The analysis across offense types demonstrated that, for the most part, states that were punitive in either imprisonment risk or average time served overall were punitive regardless of the offense type at admission or release.

Some of the more interesting contrasts that emerged from the data analysis were the largely unexplored vast differences that exist within regions and between contiguous states. There have been numerous attempts account for regional differences in punishment. The South has traditionally been depicted as more punitive than other geographic regions, at least with regard to imprisonment rates. This southern state punitiveness is typically explained as a function of either the uniqueness of southern culture, the higher degree of religious fundamentalism, or lingering racism (Greenberg & West, 2001; Beckett, 1997).[11] In this analysis, all of the states with over-punitive imprisonment rates are Southern states, and all of those that are under-punitive are non-southern, typically northern, states. Yet across each of the regions, there is great variation across the states that comprise the region. Some of those states are contiguous, demographically comparable, and might be expected to look more similar in terms of punitiveness than they actually do. These regional differences in imprisonment rates, propensities, and intensity also merit further exploration.

Throughout this discussion, I have noted some of the potential directions for future research. The magnitude of differences in the propensity to imprison and the intensity in the duration of imprisonment, both between states and within states across offense types, calls for further study. Research analyzing these dual determinants in either single states, or in sets of theoretically interesting states (e.g. those that represent the upper and lower ends of the punitive continuum), might further clarify our understanding of the punitive turn. More comprehensive analyses of changes over time will likely also prove valuable in that regard.

CONCLUSION

Too Punitive?

Regardless of how much a place punishes, it could punish more. As Nils Christie (2000) points out, the very reason why the crime control industry is so successful is that there is an endless supply of crime for the industry to process. Given that reality, is there a point at which a place can be fairly deemed 'too punitive'? Some are quite unambiguous in their condemnation of current penal practices. Michael Tonry argued a few years ago that "much that we do in the name of public safety is cruel and excessive, ruining lives for no good reason, and will in time be deeply regretted" (2001c:178), and more recently that "the United States has a punishment system that no one would knowingly have built from the ground up", adding that, "it is often unjust, it is unduly severe, it is wasteful, and it does enormous damage to the lives of black Americans" (2004a:vii). Moreover, an emerging body of literature suggests that mass imprisonment of the scale currently exhibited across many of the states in the U.S. may have unintended and deleterious effects (see Lynch & Sabol, 2004; Meares, 2004; Piehl, 2004; Fagan, 2004).

Still, not all are convinced that the scale of imprisonment suggests that the United States is over-punitive. James Jacobs, for one, is "not persuaded that there is a methodology that allows us to determine objectively whether the level of U.S. incarceration is 'excessive,' that is to say, greater than is necessary to achieve its intended effect" (2001:185). While I agree that 'excessive' might be a value judgment, I think it can be argued, and indeed others have argued, that some states imprison at a level that could be considered in Jacob's words, "greater than is necessary to achieve its intended effect" (2001:185).[12] As numerous scholars have pointed out (see Spelman, 2000b; Wilson, 1994) escalating levels of imprisonment in states that already imprison a substantial proportion of criminal offenders results in marginal returns, at least in terms of crime reduction. It is perhaps unfortunate that those states that have been the most careful in their use of imprisonment might be the states that could see the most notable crime-reduction returns by exponentially increasing their levels of imprisonment (see Spelman, 2000b).[13] Nor is Jacobs persuaded that "criminologists have the data to back up the constantly repeated assertion that American offenders serve hugely greater sentences than similarly situated offenders in other countries" (2001:186). While he may be correct in terms of cross-national variation, in this study I have provided evidence that offenders in some American states "serve hugely greater sentences" than offenders in other, often quite comparable, states.

What Goes Up, Must Come Down?

After almost thirty years of continuous growth, the average imprisonment rate in the United States fell slightly for the first time in 2001 (Harrison & Karberg, 2004). While the U.S. imprisonment rate has since resumed its upward trend, growth has slowed quite substantially in the past few years and some states appear to be making attempts to reduce their prison populations (see, Butterfield, 2003; Schiraldi, 2003; von Zielbauer, 2003). There is also some evidence that states are beginning to roll back some of the more punitive sentencing initiatives. In a recent report commissioned by Families Against Mandatory Minimums, Judith Greene (2003) documents some of the "smart on crime" reforms made at the state level in the past few years. Michigan, for example, has repealed most of its mandatory minimum penalties for drug offenses and eighteen other states have repealed some of their mandatory minimum provisions. California, Arizona, and Hawaii each passed legislation that mandates treatment (rather than prison) for first time offenders charged with drug possession or use. Greene reports that in 1998, as the Ohio legislature initiated sentencing reforms, correctional administrators in the state instituted new parole guidelines, and since that time, Ohio has reduced its prison population by 4,000 and moved to close two prisons. In still more states, prison construction has been curbed or completely halted.[14]

While state budget crises seem to be one of the driving forces behind the effort to restrict the growth of – and in some states reduce – prison populations, Greene notes that there are other reasons for the rollback. According to Greene, "there is a growing awareness that the huge investment in incarceration has yielded only very modest gains in crime control" (2003:17) and the public has become less willing to embrace punitive responses, particularly with regard to certain types of offenders.[15] If the punitive turn continues to slow, or indeed reverses itself, a whole new set of theorists and researchers will likely set about attempting to explain punitive rollback.

Concluding Remarks

I, like many others, believe the punitive turn that has been documented over and over again by scholars of punishment and social control is troubling, and, although I never explicitly argue for any particular conception of "the right amount of punishment," I am of the belief that the overall levels of imprisonment, the growing propensity to imprison, and the increasing intensity in the duration of imprisonment across the states has, in most instances, eclipsed what seems reasonable in a democratic society allegedly so attached to (and certainly quick to espouse the supremacy of) the principles of "liberty and justice for all".

NOTES

[1] When the period is partitioned, the rise in crime in the earlier period (1980 to 1992) can explain approximately 22 percent of the growth in imprisonment (see Blumstein and Beck, 2005).

[2] In four of the states, the percent change in propensity could be measured only either between 1990 and 1995 or between 1995 and 2000.

[3] Clearly this division is imperfect in that deterrence would suggest some combination of certainty and severity. Some have argued, however, that

deterrence depends more on the certainty of imprisonment than it does on the severity. Spelman asserts that across deterrence studies "the marginal effects of the probability of arrest and incarceration were almost always greater than the marginal effects of the length of the prison sentence" (2000b, 473-73). Tonry (2004b) argues that "there is no credible evidence at all that longer prison sentences are better deterrents than shorter ones" (p.5) (see also Lynch, 1999). Others contend that increasing imprisonment risk might actually decrease the deterrent value of imprisonment, particularly in communities where imprisonment is highly concentrated (see Fagan 2004, at p. 45). Still more (Blumstein, 2004) argue that deterrence might be more effective among the middle classes "who have so much to lose from the condemnation and relative deprivation associated with a prison sentence" (p.67).

[4] As noted by Spelman (2000b:466), "some states give long sentences to a few (focusing presumably on desert and incapacitation at the expense of deterrence), while others give shorter sentences to many offenders (maximizing deterrence at the expense of incapacitation)."

[5] See Zimring & Hawkins (1994) for a study focused on just California's imprisonment growth between 1980 and 1991.

[6] In a technical report, Langan and Levin (1999) assess the accuracy of Bureau of Justice Statistic's prison statistics through comparing National Corrections Reporting Program (NCRP) and National Judicial Reporting Program (NJRP) data. NCRP data is derived from prison admission and release records and NJRP data from state court records. Despite differences in geographical coverage, Langan and Levin report "close correspondence" in prisoner characteristics between the two datasets and note that "[NCRP] statistics serve as one of the nation's most valuable sources of information on its prison population" (1999:1).

[7] In an early version of this analysis, I included only those sentenced to prison following a new court commitment to prison of more than one year and excluded probationers and those entering prison following the imposition of a suspended sentence. I justified the exclusion because (in my mind) imposing a suspended sentence or probation in the first instance is clearly less punitive than sending someone directly to prison. Upon going back and examining the individual state data, I noticed that while some states were very specific as to the type of commitment (with admission types in literally every category), other states had separated their admissions among just two types – court

commitments and parole violation admissions. Clearly these states had admissions following probation revocations, suspended sentences, and the like, they simply appear to have collapsed them all of these various admission types into the category of court commitments. The data were then re-subjected to the data reduction strategy described in Chapter 7, with court commitments, probations commitments, and suspended sentences all being included as "court commitments" and the data were reanalyzed.

[8] Measuring each variable in each year would permit the use of moving averages or smoothed averages.

[9] Moreover, given that the average time served is approximately 28 months, the time served measure is actually a measure of punitiveness several years before the year in which it is analyzed.

[10] See Pease (1994) for a discussion of variations in these other realms of experience.

[11] See Ayers (1984) for a history of the uniqueness of Southern culture.

[12] See Christie (2004) for an interesting discussion of the basis on which such value judgments might be justifiably made.

[13] Although the question of whether "prison works" was intentionally side-lined in this analysis and discussion, the question of punitiveness ultimately at some point raises the question of effectiveness.

[14] See Greene (2003) for a comprehensive review of such initiatives by state.

[15] Both California's Proposition 36 and Arizona's Proposition 100 (the initiatives that diverted first time drug offenders in those states) were passed by voter referenda.

APPENDIX A:

STATE SPECIFIC DATA ANOMALIES

GENERAL DATA CAVEATS

Although the National Corrections Reporting Program (NCRP) datasets are quite comprehensive in their coverage and extraordinary in their level of detail (containing an individual case file for every single inmate admitted to or released from prison in participating states), there are numerous data caveats worth noting. Before describing some of the state specific caveats, I briefly summarize some of the more general cautions when using NCRP data.

The NCRP data can be fairly easily filtered on a variety of dimensions. As described in Chapter 7, in this study they were filtered on jurisdiction, type of commitment, sentence length, type of release, and eventually offense type. Some of these filters require numerous recodes, and, in examining the data by state, some disparities of general interest emerge. In some states, as reported in the NCRP, very few admissions follow a new court commitment, while in others the majority of admissions do. It appears, for example, that most of those admitted to and released from prison in Louisiana in 2000 were admitted following a probation or parole revocation of one type or another (only 25% of Louisiana's admissions and only 4% of its releases in 2000 followed a new court commitment). Moreover, it seems the degree of specificity on type of admission varies quite significantly by state. Among its 2000 prison releases, Louisiana has releases following admissions in every one of the parole and probation revocation categories, while other states simply report all parole or probation revocations in one category each. For those using NCRP data, this suggests that the type of commitment should be grouped more generally into either court commitments (including court, probation, and suspended sentence commitments) or parole recommitments.

In a few states, all (or virtually all) admissions or releases were coded as following a court commitment.[1] Because the data for these states almost certainly include an unknown number of parole recommitments, the propensity to imprison, as operationalized in this study, is likely overestimated where admissions are over-reported as court commitments. Conversely, intensity in the duration of imprisonment is likely underestimated where releases are over-reported as court commitments. In these instances, the average time served includes the average time served of parole violators (who likely serve less time on average than new court commitments – particularly where there is no new offense).[2] This anomaly tended to occur more among the release files, and so tended to affect the time served estimates more than the imprisonment risk estimates.

STATE SPECIFIC DATA ANOMALIES

Eleven states did not participate in the NCRP in any of the years included in this study and are therefore excluded from all imprisonment risk and time served analyses.[3] Twenty-three states participated in the UCR and NCRP in 1990, 1995, and 2000 with no notable anomalies in the data and were therefore, included in all of the analyses.[4] The remaining sixteen states had missing or anomalous data on either one or more of the measures or in one or more of the years – these states were included in the analyses as detailed below.

Alaska

Alaska participated in the NCRP in 2000 only and was therefore completely excluded from the analysis over time. While included in the analysis of imprisonment risk overall, Alaska was excluded from the analysis of imprisonment risk across offense types. 66% of Alaska's prison admissions in 2000 were coded as admissions for other offenses (e.g. not violent, property, or drug) – most of those were admissions for probation violations (code 500), minor traffic offenses (code 550), or driving while intoxicated (code 560). The filtering of Alaska's data left very few cases for the analysis across offense types, so it was excluded from these analyses.

Alaska is also excluded from the time served analysis due to a lack of cases. For 93% of Alaska's 1,494 releases in 2000, the type of commitment to prison was coded as a "transfer". Because Alaska has a mixed jail/prison system, these were likely transfers from jail to prison to begin serving a prison sentence of more than one year. While Alaska's data could have been recoded to include 'transfer' as a 'court commitment,' it seemed more prudent to simply exclude Alaska from the time served analyses. As noted above, Alaska only participated in the NCRP in 2000 and is therefore excluded from the analysis over time anyway.

Florida

Florida participated in the NCRP in 1990, 1995, and 2000; however, there are several data exceptions to note. In the 1990 NCRP, Florida reported only admissions and is therefore excluded from the analysis of average time served in that year. Moreover, there are no UCR data for Florida in 1989, and it is therefore excluded from all imprisonment risk analyses in 1990. Data on arrests in Florida in 1999 were drawn from the annual report "Crime in the United States." (U.S. Department of Justice, Federal Bureau of Investigation, 2000).

Hawaii

Hawaii participated in the UCR and the NCRP in 1990, 1995, and 2000. All of Hawaii's 1990 and 1995 admissions and releases were coded as 'court commitments'. Hawaii was included in all analyses (though as explained above, in 1990 and 1995, Hawaii's imprisonment risk is likely an overestimate and its time served likely an underestimate).

Illinois

Illinois participated in the NCRP in 1990, 1995, and 2000; however, the 1999 UCR arrest data for Illinois were unreliable (with only one jurisdiction reporting and no estimates for the other jurisdictions), it is therefore excluded from all imprisonment risk analyses in 2000.

Louisiana

Louisiana participated in the NCRP in 1995 and 2000 only. Louisiana is therefore included in all imprisonment risk and time served analyses in those years, but excluded from 1990 analyses.

Maine

Maine participated in the NCRP in 1995 and 2000 only. Maine is therefore included in all imprisonment risk and time served analyses in those years, but excluded from 1990 analyses.

Maryland

Maryland participated in the UCR and the NCRP in 1990, 1995, and 2000. In each of those years, all of Maryland's admissions and releases were coded as 'court commitments'. The NCRP codebook reports that Maryland is unable to provide data broken down by type of admission. As explained above, Maryland's imprisonment risk is likely an overestimate and its time served likely an underestimate.

Massachusetts

Massachusetts participated in the NCRP in 1990 and 1995, but not in 2000. Additionally, in 1995 Massachusetts submitted NCRP admission data but no release data. Massachusetts is included in imprisonment risk analyses for 1990 and 1995, and the time served analyses for 1990 only. In 1995, all of Massachusetts' admissions were coded as court commitment – imprisonment risk is therefore likely an over-estimate in that year. Finally, although it did not directly impact this study, in 1990, the offense type for virtually all (97.8%) of Massachusetts' admissions were coded as "unknown".

North Carolina

In 1995 and 2000, the vast majority of North Carolina's releases were coded as following 'court commitments'. As explained above, North Carolina's average time served is likely an underestimate in those years.

Ohio

When presenting an early version of this initial analysis based on 1998 data at the American Society of Criminology's annual conference (Frost, 2003), an employee of the Ohio Department of Corrections pointed out that Ohio had released an unusually large number of long-term inmates in that year.[5] It appears Ohio was still releasing long-term inmates in 2000. The exceptionally long time served in Ohio is not only an outlier relative to other states, but also an outlier compared to Ohio's own data for earlier periods.

Oklahoma

In 1995, the type of commitment for all of Oklahoma's releases was coded as "not known." As per BJS filtering instructions, unknown commitment types were re-coded to 'court commitments'. As explained above, Oklahoma's average time served is likely an underestimate in 1995.

Oregon

Although it did not directly impact the analyses in this study, it is worth noting that only six of Oregon's 2,937 admissions in 1990 were coded as admissions for drug offenses. 36% of Oregon's admissions were coded as either an "illegal entry" or "unknown" offense type - it is likely that some of these were admissions for drug offenses. In 1990 and 2000, the vast majority of Oregon's releases were coded as following 'court commitments' (as were the majority of its 2000 admissions). As explained above, Oregon's imprisonment risk is likely an overestimate in 2000 and its time served likely an underestimate in 1990 and 2000.

South Dakota

South Dakota participated in the NCRP in 1995 and 2000 only. South Dakota is therefore included in all imprisonment risk and time served analyses in those years, but excluded from 1990 analyses.

Tennessee

Tennessee participated in the UCR and the NCRP in 1990, 1995, and 2000; however, Tennessee's average time served data appeared to be highly irregular. In 1990, Tennessee reported only "time served on current admission" and its average time served both overall and across offense types were relatively high. In 1995 and 2000, however, Tennessee reported both time served on current admission (for virtually all releases) and total time served (for only some). The difference between the time served on current admission and total time served was substantial in 1995 (for drug offenses the time served on current admission averaged 8.96 months while total time served averaged 41.50 months, for property offenses 9.29 versus 37.63 months, and for violent offenses 13.91 versus 49.15 months). This suggested that many of Tennessee's offenders were serving a substantial portion of their sentence prior to the current admission; however, Tennessee reported total time served for less than half of their releases in 1995 and less than a quarter in 2000. In 2000, this resulted in the bizarre finding that the total time served was actually shorter than the time served on current admission. Because Tennessee's time served data were fraught with complications, it seemed prudent to exclude Tennessee from all time served analyses.

Texas

Texas participated in the UCR and the NCRP in 1990, 1995, and 2000. While in 1990 and 1995, Texas reported only time served on current admission, in 2000 it reported only total time served. It is unclear whether this was a coding error, or whether the 2000 time served averages actually do reflect the total time served. In 1995, all of Texas' releases were coded as following the imposition of a suspended sentence (and therefore all counted as 'court commitments'). The average time served for Texas in both 1995 and 2000 is likely an overestimate.

Wisconsin

Wisconsin participated in the NCRP in 1990, 1995, and 2000; however, UCR arrest data for Wisconsin were unavailable in 1999, and it is therefore excluded from all imprisonment risk analyses in 2000.

NOTES

[1]Hawaii for admissions and releases in 1990 and 1995; Maryland for admissions and releases in all years; Florida for admissions and releases in 2000; Massachusetts for only admissions in 1995; North Carolina for only releases in 1995 and 2000; Oklahoma for only releases in 1995 (coded "not known"); Oregon for only releases in 1990 and for admissions and releases in 2000; Tennessee for only releases in 1990 (all coded 'illegal entry'); and Texas for only releases in 1990 and 1995 (all coded 'illegal entry' in 1990 and 'suspended sentence imposed in 1995).

[2] As an aside, it is worth noting that 54% of Hawaii's 1995 admissions were coded as 'other offenses.' A closer inspection of Hawaii's data revealed that 40% of those 'other offenses' were admissions for parole violations (NCRP code 490). This closer inspection suggests that utilizing the offense type

breakdowns in the NCRP datasets can allow for greater specificity in regard to inclusion and exclusion of specific cases.

[3] The excluded states include: Arizona, Connecticut, Delaware, Idaho, Indiana, Kansas, Montana, New Mexico, Rhode Island, Vermont, and Wyoming.

[4] States included in all analyses with no data anomalies to report were: Alabama, Arkansas, California, Colorado, Georgia, Iowa, Kentucky, Michigan, Minnesota, Mississippi, Missouri, Nebraska, Nevada, New Hampshire, New Jersey, New York, North Dakota, Pennsylvania, South Carolina, Utah, Virginia, Washington, and West Virginia.

[5] As Judith Greene (2003) noted, the Ohio legislature restructured sentencing, and correctional officials modified parole guidelines in 1998.

APPENDIX B

SUPPLEMENTAL TABLES

The tables in this Appendix, which supplement the data and methodology chapter, are referred to at various points in the text of Chapter 8. Tables B1 through B3 document the beginning and ending sample sizes for prison admissions and releases by state for each of the years included in the analysis. Table B4 identifies the states excluded from the analyses in each of the years (noting their imprisonment rates in that year). Table B5 lists the number of inmates serving life sentences using data reported in the 2001 Corrections Yearbook (Camp & Camp, 2002). Tables B6, B7, and B8 supplement the time served methodology section and document the differences in time served based on actual release cohort averages and stock/flow estimates (Table B6), time served on current admission and total time served (Table B7) and mean versus median time served (Table B8).

Table B1: NCRP Data Reduction by State (2000)

	Admissions NCRP 2000	*After Data Reduction*	*Releases NCRP 2000*	*After Data Reduction*
Alabama	7,661	5,402	8,847	6,035
Alaska	5,060	1,217	1,494	49
Arkansas	7,953	4,534	7,793	4,404
California	127,843	40,875	131,832	43,046
Colorado	7,086	4,387	5,899	3,616
Florida	25,886	22,830	26,018	22,027
Georgia	20,923	10,948	11,077	5,498
Hawaii	1,728	1,215	1,058	507
Illinois	29,315	16,550	28,716	16,897
Iowa	4,072	3,379	5,162	3,477
Kentucky	8,295	5,238	7,917	4,929
Louisiana	15,616	7,089	15,493	3,908
Maine	807	614	782	573
Maryland	12,205	6,988	14,774	9,332
Michigan	12,841	7,651	11,694	5,886
Minnesota	4,249	3,021	3,903	2,525
Mississippi	8,501	6,054	6,753	3,803
Missouri	16,577	9,937	14,822	7,783
Nebraska	1,878	1,444	1,677	1,115
Nevada	4,605	3,589	4,336	3,462
NH	1,130	653	1,017	627
New Jersey	14,071	9,529	15,592	9,935
New York	27,920	15,525	29,220	14,975
N. Carolina	22,028	9,661	22,395	9,638
North Dakota	742	520	623	391
Ohio	20,902	8,637	8,455	4,982
Oklahoma	7,217	6,521	6,442	5,958
Oregon	4,139	3,932	3,417	2,975
Pennsylvania	11,865	7,208	10,596	5,812
S. Carolina	11,239	7,079	11,501	7,075
South Dakota	1,640	742	1,537	747
Tennessee	12,416	9,075	14,042	8,463
Texas	38,304	26,989	38,474	27,187
Utah	3,287	1,515	2,893	1,141
Virginia	12,516	7,940	9,886	7,077
Washington	7,102	5,720	6,795	5,202
West Virginia	1,203	1,015	1,065	898
Wisconsin	8,438	5,913	8,276	5,280
Total	**529,416**	**291,136**	**502,494**	**267,235**

Table B2: NCRP Data Reduction by State (1995)

	Admissions NCRP 1995	*After Data Reduction*	*Releases NCRP 1995*	*After Data Reduction*
Alabama	7,945	5,383	7,285	4,491
Arkansas	5,454	3,836	5,291	3,696
California	117,760	45,635	107,509	39,320
Colorado	5,000	3,735	4,633	3,116
Florida	21,031	17,984	19,904	18,141
Georgia	16,021	11,764	15,174	9,630
Hawaii	937	909	1,074	729
Illinois	23,345	16,657	22,083	16,262
Iowa	3,802	2,872	5,083	3,535
Kentucky	7,330	4,486	6,168	3,524
Louisiana	12,849	7,429	11,760	6,704
Maine	750	662	759	601
Maryland	12,973	8,664	13,933	9,532
Massachusetts	3,252	2,851	n/d	n/d
Michigan	11,715	7,656	11,211	5,189
Minnesota	3,068	2,240	2,878	1,902
Mississippi	5,893	4,749	4,182	3,139
Missouri	11,316	6,652	6,279	1,728
Nebraska	1,788	1,288	1,322	871
Nevada	3,960	2,827	3,657	2,619
New Hampshire	974	646	954	642
New Jersey	16,229	10,906	13,660	8,744
New York	34,678	19,030	32,956	15,696
North Carolina	24,213	13,473	18,873	14,095
North Dakota	496	321	437	244
Ohio	21,877	13,769	19,611	11,258
Oklahoma	5,272	4,385	2,747	2,013
Oregon	7,198	2,129	6,323	1,747
Pennsylvania	10,877	6,065	6,099	3,151
South Carolina	10,355	6,487	9,157	5,297
South Dakota	1,004	618	870	496
Tennessee	13,092	6,927	12,092	4,954
Texas	53,653	37,753	22,561	22,548
Utah	2,585	1,238	2,057	818
Virginia	12,431	9,346	10,074	6,982
Washington	6,062	4,765	5,248	3,903
West Virginia	1,266	1,097	721	653
Wisconsin	5,345	4,134	4,989	3,438
Total	**504,815**	**301,368**	**420,949**	**241,408**

Table B3: NCRP Data Reduction by State (1990)

	Admissions NCRP 1990	*After Data Reduction*	*Releases NCRP 1990*	*After Data Reduction*
Alabama	6,619	4,093	5,693	3,223
Arkansas	2,676	2,314	2,255	1,668
California	95,893	39,229	85,816	32,374
Colorado	3,331	2,514	2,981	2,258
Florida	41,513	38,005	n/d	n/d
Georgia	20,618	13,034	19,329	11,608
Hawaii	460	460	451	434
Illinois	17,967	12,739	15,088	9,503
Iowa	2,896	2,053	3,575	1,993
Kentucky	4,857	2,884	4,022	2,361
Maryland	9,181	6,902	8,741	6,499
Massachusetts	3,989	1,795	5,222	2,110
Michigan	13,208	9,214	10,699	5,931
Minnesota	2,419	1,763	2,289	1,621
Mississippi	2,600	1,675	3,474	2,490
Missouri	8,170	5,665	6,660	5,603
Nebraska	1,488	1,031	1,385	897
Nevada	3,277	2,215	3,278	2,795
NewHampshire	677	446	471	293
New Jersey	11,001	8,382	9,314	6,559
New York	30,176	22,645	26,488	24,123
North Carolina	23,088	15,761	22,120	15,201
North Dakota	478	272	443	216
Ohio	18,229	11,297	15,133	9,177
Oklahoma	5,572	3,736	7,090	5,481
Oregon	5,798	2,937	5,421	5,370
Pennsylvania	9,090	6,338	7,007	3,516
South Carolina	11,584	5,953	10,413	4,692
Tennessee	12,805	8,814	7,650	7,137
Texas	45,668	29,586	37,023	36,758
Utah	1,530	698	1,398	629
Virginia	10,672	8,105	9,455	6,808
Washington	4,490	3,532	3,403	2,557
West Virginia	614	599	605	588
Wisconsin	3,540	2,792	2,890	2,100
Total	**470,353**	**279,478**	**382,276**	**224,573**

Table B4: Imprisonment Rates of States Excluded from the 1990, 1995, and 2000 Analyses of Imprisonment Propensity and Intensity

	Imp. Rate 1990	Rank	**Imp. Rate 1995**	Rank	**Imp. Rate 2000**	Rank
Arizona	375	5	473	6	515	9
Connecticut	238	24	318	23	398	22
Delaware	323	12	413	13	513	10
Idaho	190	33	283	29	430	16
Indiana	223	29	275	30	335	33
Kansas	227	27	274	31	312	35
Montana	176	36	228	35	348	30
New Mexico	196	32	231	34	279	38
Rhode Island	157	38	186	41	197	45
Vermont	117	47	179	43	218	43
Wyoming	237	25	289	27	349	29
Excluded in Only One Period						
Louisiana	427	3				
Maine	118	45				
South Dakota	187	34				
Massachusetts					152	48
Illinois					371*	26
Wisconsin					376*	24

* Illinois and Wisconsin did participate in the 2000 NCRP data collection effort and are included in the intensity (time served) analysis, but they are excluded from the imprisonment propensity analysis because of insufficient UCR arrest data.

Table B5: Inmates Serving 20+ Years or Life without Parole and Death Sentences by State (2000)*

	Total Inmates	*20 + Years*	*% of all Inmates*	*LWOP or Death*	*% of all Inmates*
Alabama	24,123	10,165	42.14%	1,435	5.95%
Alaska	2,128	465	21.85%	27	1.27%
Arizona	25,412	2,851	11.22%	224	0.88%
Arkansas	11,851	5,314	44.84%	448	3.78%
California	160,412	29,618	18.46%	3,202	2.00%
Colorado	16,833	2,946	17.50%	264	1.57%
Connecticut	13,155	1,422	10.81%	184	1.40%
Delaware	3,937	484	12.29%	195	4.95%
Florida	71,318	13,511	18.94%	3,420	4.80%
Georgia	44,141	6,265	14.19%	6,082	13.78%
Hawaii	3,553	451	12.69%	24	0.68%
Idaho	5,526	650	11.76%	91	1.65%
Illinois	45,281	9,633	21.27%	1,252	2.76%
Indiana	20,081	6,506	32.40%	96	0.48%
Iowa	7,955	1,452	18.25%	512	6.44%
Kansas	8,344	3,105	37.21%	4	0.05%
Kentucky	14,919	2,715	18.20%	56	0.38%
Louisiana	35,047	4,597	13.12%	3,677	10.49%
Maine	1,635			38	2.32%
Maryland	22,490	6,804	30.25%	195	0.87%
Mass	9,479	1,126	11.88%	700	7.38%
Michigan	47,718	6,273	13.15%	2,600	5.45%
Minnesota	6,238	832	13.34%	21	0.34%
Mississippi	19,239	3,542	18.41%	758	3.94%
Missouri	27,299	4,403	16.13%	696	2.55%
Montana	3,105	827	26.63%	28	0.90%
Nebraska	3,816	662	17.35%	185	4.85%
Nevada	9,921	1,287	12.97%	410	4.13%
New Hamp.	2,257	361	15.99%	56	2.48%
New Jersey	29,784	4,452	14.95%	25	0.08%
New Mexico	4,887	665	13.61%	10	0.20%
New York	70,198	19,487	27.76%	80	0.11%
N. Carolina	27,043	3,229	11.94%	402	1.49%
North Dakota	994	99	9.96%	6	0.60%
Ohio	45,833	16,091	35.11%	280	0.61%
Oklahoma	23,181	6,422	27.70%	478	2.06%

	Total Inmates	*20 + Years*	*% of all Inmates*	*LWOP or Death*	*% of all Inmates*
Oregon	10,603	1,653	15.59%	107	1.01%
Pennsylvania	36,844	1,324	3.59%	3,868	10.50%
Rhode Island	1,966	419	21.31%	17	0.86%
S. Carolina	21,017	5,695	27.10%	408	1.94%
South Dakota	2,613	260	9.95%	145	5.55%
Tennessee	22,166	6,103	27.53%	264	1.19%
Texas	150,107	52,761	35.15%	437	0.29%
Utah	5,526	1,271	23.00%	18	0.33%
Vermont	1,313	69	5.26%	6	0.46%
Virginia	29,643	9,756	32.91%	426	1.44%
Washington	14,666	1,955	13.33%	412	2.81%
West Virginia	3,795	308	8.12%	209	5.51%
Wisconsin	20,013	4,498	22.48%	64	0.32%
Wyoming	1,680	162	9.64%	150	8.93%
Totals /Averages	**1,191,085**	**264,946**	**19.37%**	**34,692**	**2.90%**

* Source: Camp & Camp (2002).

Table B6: Mean Time Served of the 2000 NCRP Release Cohort and Estimated Time Served Based on the 2000 Stock/Flow Ratio

	Mean Time Served	*Rank*	*Stock/Flow Ratio*	*Rank*	*Dif.*
Ohio	72.97	1	63.68	3	-9.29
Maine	49.60	2	31.95	30	-17.64
Texas	45.09	3	66.74	2	21.66
Pennsylvania	41.46	4	61.34	4	19.88
Maryland	40.42	5	38.62	18	-1.80
Oklahoma	39.49	6	42.66	14	3.16
Florida	36.90	7	37.49	21	0.59
Michigan	36.66	8	74.84	1	38.18
North Carolina	34.12	9	33.59	25	-0.53
New York	31.33	10	54.26	6	22.93
Mississippi	30.43	11	38.13	19	7.70
Hawaii	29.93	12	35.09	23	5.16
South Carolina	29.61	13	35.63	22	6.01
New Hampshire	29.57	14	41.48	16	11.91
Nevada	28.48	15	33.17	26	4.69
Georgia	28.20	16	48.38	8	20.18
Virginia	27.76	17	44.80	12	17.04
Colorado	27.53	18	46.04	10	18.52
Iowa	27.44	19	28.25	35	0.81
Utah	26.85	20	43.77	13	16.92
Louisiana	26.58	21	59.33	5	32.74
Alabama	26.35	22	53.59	7	27.24
Oregon	26.29	23	32.36	29	6.07
Washington	25.74	24	30.77	33	5.03
New Jersey	25.64	25	37.51	20	11.87
Nebraska	25.24	26	31.71	31	6.47
Wisconsin	24.64	27	40.61	17	15.97
California	24.19	28	47.09	9	22.90
Kentucky	22.47	29	33.60	24	11.13
Arkansas	21.12	30	31.37	32	10.25
South Dakota	20.35	31	42.26	15	21.91
Illinois	19.91	32	32.83	28	12.92
Minnesota	18.23	33	24.78	36	6.55
North Dakota	17.97	34	22.94	37	4.97
West Virginia	17.75	35	44.87	11	27.11
Missouri	16.70	36	32.97	27	16.26

$r^s = .43$, $p = .01$

Table B7: Time Served on Current Admission and Total Time Served (2000)

	Time Served on Current Admission	*Total Time Served*	*Difference*
Ohio	72.97	72.94	-0.03
Maine	49.60	55.55	5.95
Texas	45.09		
Pennsylvania	41.46		
Maryland	40.42	43.75	3.33
Oklahoma	39.49	44.92	5.43
Florida	36.90	42.41	5.51
Michigan	36.66	43.99	7.33
North Carolina	34.12	37.12	3.00
New York	31.33	37.93	6.60
Mississippi	30.43	32.66	2.23
Hawaii	29.93	29.97	0.04
South Carolina	29.61	31.94	2.33
New Hampshire	29.57	33.11	3.54
Nevada	28.48	34.55	6.07
Georgia	28.20	41.13	12.93
Virginia	27.76	34.89	7.13
Colorado	27.53	30.46	2.93
Iowa	27.44	31.49	4.05
Utah	26.85		
Louisiana	26.58	37.10	10.52
Alabama	26.35	31.40	5.05
Oregon	26.29	34.86	8.57
Washington	25.74	28.82	3.08
New Jersey	25.64	30.59	4.95
Nebraska	25.24	28.74	3.50
Wisconsin	24.64	32.49	7.85
California	24.19	32.32	8.13
Kentucky	22.47	30.52	8.05
Arkansas	21.12		
South Dakota	20.35	22.36	2.01
Illinois	19.91	22.34	2.43
Minnesota	18.23	22.39	4.16
North Dakota	17.97	22.62	4.65
West Virginia	17.75	24.46	6.71
Missouri	16.70	19.65	2.95

$r^s = .86$, $p = .00$

Table B8: Mean and Median Average Time Served (2000)

	Mean	*Rank*	*Median*	*Rank*
Ohio	72.97	1	63.50	1
Maine	49.60	2	33.55	2
Texas	45.09	3	29.90	3
Pennsylvania	41.46	4	28.60	4
Maryland	40.42	5	24.80	6
Oklahoma	39.49	6	22.80	8
Florida	36.90	7	22.70	9
Michigan	36.66	8	25.10	5
North Carolina	34.12	9	18.00	18
New York	31.33	10	22.10	10
Mississippi	30.43	11	19.00	16
Hawaii	29.93	12	24.70	7
South Carolina	29.61	13	17.00	24
New Hampshire	29.57	14	21.30	11
Nevada	28.48	15	19.60	14
Georgia	28.20	16	18.20	17
Virginia	27.76	17	17.10	23
Colorado	27.53	18	20.00	13
Iowa	27.44	19	20.60	12
Utah	26.85	20	16.90	25
Louisiana	26.58	21	17.40	22
Alabama	26.35	22	17.60	21
Oregon	26.29	23	15.60	27
Washington	25.74	24	16.40	26
New Jersey	25.64	25	19.50	15
Nebraska	25.24	26	17.70	20
Wisconsin	24.64	27	17.70	20
California	24.19	28	12.90	30
Kentucky	22.47	29	15.10	28
Arkansas	21.12	30	11.40	32
South Dakota	20.35	31	10.90	33
Illinois	19.91	32	11.70	31
Minnesota	18.23	33	10.10	35
North Dakota	17.97	34	14.60	29
West Virginia	17.75	35	10.25	34
Missouri	16.70	36	5.50	36

$r^s = .91$, $p = .00$

REFERENCES

Anderson, E. (1999). *Code of the Street: Decency, Violence, and the Moral Life of the Inner City.* New York: Norton.

Altschuler, A.W. (1991). The failure of sentencing guidelines: A plea for less aggregation. *University of Chicago Law Review,* 58:901-951.

Arvanites, T.M. (1993). Increasing imprisonment: A function of crime or socioeconomic factors? *American Journal of Criminal Justice,* 17:19-38.

Arvanites, T.M. and Asher, M.A. (1995). The direct and indirect effects of socioeconomic variables on state imprisonment rates. *Criminal Justice Policy Review,* 7:27-53.

Arvanites, T.M. and Asher, M.A. (1998). State and county incarceration rates: The direct and indirect effects of race and inequality. *The American Journal of Economics and Sociology,* 57:207-222.

Associated Press (2003). Justice Kennedy says federal prison terms should be shorter, some mandatory minimum terms scrapped. *The Associated Press* (August 9).

Austin, J. and Brown, M. (1989). *Ranking the Nation's Most Punitive and Costly States.* San Francisco, CA: National Council on Crime and Delinquency.

Austin, J., Clark, J., Hardyman, P., and Henry, D.A. (2000). *Three Strikes and You're Out: The Implementation and Impact of Strikes Laws.* Final Report to the National Institute of Justice (NCJ 181297). Washington, D.C.: National Institute of Justice, U.S. Department of Justice.

Austin, J. and Irwin, J. (2001). *It's About Time: America's Imprisonment Binge.* 3rd Edition. Belmont, CA: Wadsworth.

Austin, J. and Tillman, R. (1988). *Ranking the Nation's Most Punitive States.* San Francisco, CA: National Council on Crime and Delinquency.

Austin, J., Marino A.B., Carroll L., McCall, P.L. and Richards, S.C. (2001). The use of incarceration in the United States. *Critical Criminology,* 10:17-41.

Austin, J., Clarke, J., Hardyman, P. and Henry, D.A. (1999). The impact of 'three-strikes and you're out'. *Punishment & Society,* 1:131-162.

Ayers, E.L. (1984). *Vengeance & Justice: Crime and Punishment in the 19th-Century American South.* New York: Oxford University Press.

Ayers, C., Craig, J., Cribbs, S., Miller, D. and Yancey, C. (2001). *Sentencing Policy and Pragmatism: A Survey of Systems across the United States.* MD: Maryland State Commission on Criminal Sentencing Policy.

Baadsager, P., Sims, B., Baer, J., and Chambliss, W.J. (2000). The overrepresentation of minorities in America's imprisonment binge: How did we get here? *Corrections Management Quarterly,* 4:1-7.

Baeur, L. and Owens, S.D. (2004). *Justice Expenditures and Employment in the United States, 2001.* Bureau of Justice Statistics Bulletin (NCJ 202792). Washington, D.C.: Bureau of Justice Statistics, U.S. Department of Justice.

Beck, A.J. and Harrison, P.M. (2001). *Prisoners in 2000.* Washington, D.C.: U.S. Department of Justice.

Beckett, K. (1994). Setting the public agenda: 'Street crime' and drug use in American politics. *Social Problems*, 41:425-447.

Beckett, K. (1996). Culture and the politics of signification: The case of child sexual abuse. *Social Problems*, 43:57-76.

Beckett, K. (1997) *Making Crime Pay: Law and Order in Contemporary American Politics*. New York: Oxford University Press.

Beckett, K. and Sasson, T. (2000). *The Politics of Injustice: Crime and Punishment in America*. Thousand Oaks, CA: Sage, Pine Forge Press.

Beckett, K. and Western, B. (2001). Governing social marginality: Welfare, incarceration, and the transformation of state policy. *Punishment & Society,* 3:43-59.

Beha, J.A. (1977). 'And nobody can get you out': The impact of a mandatory prison sentence for the illegal carrying of a firearm on the use of firearms and on the administration of criminal justice in Boston. *Boston University Law Review,* 57:96-146;289-333.
Bennett, W.L. (1980). *Public Opinion in American Politics.* New York: Harcourt Brace Jovanovich.
Berry, W.D., Ringquist, E.J., Fording, R.C., and Hanson, R.L. (1998). Measuring citizen and government ideology in the American states, 1960-1993. *American Journal of Political Science,* 42:327-348.
Blumstein, A. (1982). On the racial disproportionality of United States' prison populations. *Journal of Criminal Law and Criminology,* 73:1259-1281.
Blumstein, A. (1988). Prison populations: A system out of control? In M. Tonry and N. Morris (Eds.), *Crime and Justice: An Annual Review of the Research, 10.* Chicago, IL: University of Chicago Press.
Blumstein, A. (1993). Racial disproportionality of U.S. prison populations revisited. *University of Colorado Law Review,* 64:743-760.
Blumstein, A. (2002). Prisons: A policy challenge. In J.Q. Wilson & J. Petersilia (Eds.), *Crime* (pp. 451-482). San Francisco, CA: Institute for Contemporary Studies.
Blumstein, A. (2004). Restoring rationality in punishment policy. In M. Tonry (Ed.), *The Future of Imprisonment* (pp. 61-80). New York, NY: Oxford University Press.
Blumstein, A. and Beck, A.J. (1999). Population growth in U.S. Prisons, 1980-1996. In M. Tonry and J. Petersilia (eds.), *Prisons* (pp. 17-61). Chicago, IL: University of Chicago Press.
Blumstein, A. and Beck, A.J. (2005). Reentry as a transient state between liberty and recommitment. In J. Travis and C. Visher (eds.), *Prisoner Reentry and Crime in America* (pp. 50-79). New York, NY: Cambridge University Press.
Blumstein, A. and Cohen, J. (1973) A theory of the stability of punishment. *Journal of Criminal Law, Criminology, and Police Science,* 63:198-207.

Blumstein, A., Cohen, J. and Nagin, D. (1977). The dynamics of a homeostatic punishment process. *Journal of Criminal Law and Criminology,* 67:317-334.

Blumstein, A., Cohen, J. and Nagin, D. (1978). *Deterrence and Incapacitation: Estimating the Effects of Criminal Sanctions on Crime Rates.* Washington, D.C.: National Academy Press.

Blumstein, A. and Moitra, S. (1979). An analysis of the time-series of the imprisonment rate in the states of the United States: A further test of the stability of punishment hypothesis. *Journal of Criminal Law and Criminology,* 70:376-390.

Bonczar, T.P. (2003). *Prevalence of Imprisonment in the U.S. Population, 1974-2001.* Bureau of Justice Statistics Special Report (NCJ 197976). Washington, D.C.: Bureau of Justice Statistics, U.S. Department of Justice.

Bottoms, A. (1995). The philosophy and politics of punishment and sentencing. In C. Clarkson and R. Morgan (Eds.) *The Politics of Sentencing Reform.* New York: Oxford University Press.

Bourgois, P. (1995). *In Search of Respect.* Cambridge: Cambridge University Press.

Bowker, L.H. (1981). Crime and the use of prisons in the United States: A time series anaysis. *Crime & Delinquency,* 27:206-212.

Braithwaite, J. (1999). *Crime, Shame and Reintegration.* New York, NY: Cambridge University Press.

Bureau of Justice Assistance (1998). *1996 National Survey of State Sentencing Structures.* (NCJ 169270). Washington, DC: Government Printing Office.

Bushway, S.D., Piquero, A.R., Broidy, L.M., Cauffman, E., and Mazerolle, P. (2001). An empirical framework for studying desistance as a process. *Criminology,* 39:491-515.

Butterfield, F. (2003). With cash tight, states reassess long jail terms. *New York Times,* November 10:A1.

Bynum, T. (1982). Prosecutorial discretion and the implementation of a legislative mandate. In M. Morash (ed.) *Implementing Criminal Justice Policies.* Beverly Hills, CA: Sage Publications.

Brown, J. and Langan, P. (1999). *Felony Sentences in the United States, 1996.* Bureau of Justice Statistics Bulletin. Washington, D.C.: U.S. Department of Justice, Bureau of Justice Statistics.

Camp, C.G., and Camp, G.M. (2002). *The 2001 Corrections Yearbook.* Middletown, CT: Criminal Justice Institute, Inc.

Caplow, T. and Simon, J. (1999). Understanding prison policy and population trends. In M. Tonry & J. Petersilia (eds.), *Prisons* (pp. 63-120). Chicago, IL: University of Chicago Press.

Carroll, L. and Cornell, C.P. (1985). Racial composition, sentencing reforms, and rates of incarceration, 1970-1980. *Justice Quarterly*, 2:475-490.

Carroll, L. and Doubet, M.B. (1983). U.S. social structure and imprisonment. *Criminology*, 21:449-456.

Chambliss, William J. (2001). *Power, Politics, & Crime*. Boulder, CO: Westview Press.

Chiricos, T.G. and Delone, M. (1992). Labor surplus and punishment: A review and assessment of theory and evidence. *Social Problems,* 39:421-446.

Christie, N. (2000). *Crime Control as Industry: Toward Gulags, Western Style*. 3rd Ed. New York, NY: Routledge.

Christie, N. (2004). *A Suitable Amount of Crime.* New York, NY: Routledge.

Clarke, J., Austin, J. and Henry, D.A. (1997). 'Three-strikes and you're out': A review of state legislation. *National Institute of Justice, Research in Brief.* (NCJ 165369). Washington, DC: National Institute of Justice.

Clear, T.R. (1994). *Harm in American Penology.* New York: State University of New York Press.

Clear, T.R. (1996). Backfire: When incarceration increases crime. In Vera Institute (ed.). *The Unintended Consequences of Incarceration.* New York: Vera Institute of Justice.

Clear, T.R. (2002). The problem with "addition by subtraction": The prison-crime relationship in low-income communities. In M. Mauer & M. Chesney-Lind (eds.), *Invisible Punishment: The Collateral Consequences of Mass Imprisonment.* (pp. 181-193). New York: The New Press.

Clear, T.R. and Cole, G.F. (2003). *American Corrections*. 6th Ed. Belmont, CA: Wadsworth.

Clear, T.R., Rose, D., Waring, E., and Scully, K. (2003). Coercive mobility and crime: A preliminary examination of concentrated incarceration and social disorganization. *Justice Quarterly,* 20:33-64.

Cohen, J. and Canela-Cacho, J.A. (1994). Incarceration and violent crime – 1965-1988. In A.J. Reiss & J.A. Roth (Eds.), *Understanding and Preventing Violence, Vol. 4* (pp.296-388). Washington, D.C.: National Academy of Sciences.

Cohen, S. (1985). *Visions of Social Control.* New York, NY: Polity Press.

Cullen, F.T. (1995). Assessing the penal harm movement. *Journal of Research in Crime and Delinquency,* 32:338-358.

Cullen, F.T. (1999). Rehabilitation and treatment programs. In J.Q. Wilson and J. Petersilia (Eds.), *Crime: Public Policies for Crime Control* (pp.253-289). San Francisco, CA: Institute for Contemporary Studies.

Cullen, F.T., Fisher, B.S. and Applegate, B.K. (2000). Public opinion about punishment and corrections. In M. Tonry (Ed.), *Crime and Justice: A Review of Research, 27* (pp. 1-79). Chicago: University of Chicago Press.

Cullen, F.T., Van Voorhis, P., and Sundt, J.L. (1996). Prisons in crisis: The American experience. In R. Matthews and P. Francis (Eds.) *Prisons 2000: An International Perspective on the Current State and Future of Imprisonment.* New York: St. Martin's Press, Inc.

Currie, E. (1998). *Crime and Punishment in America*. New York: Henry Holt and Company, Inc.

DeFina, R.H. and Arvanites, T.M. (2002). The weak effect of imprisonment on crime: 1971-1998. *Social Science Quarterly,* 83:635-653.

DiIulio, J.J., Jr. (1994a). The question of black crime. *Public Interest,* 117 (Fall):3-32.

DiIulio, J.J., Jr. (1994b). Let em' rot. *Wall Street Journal,* January 26:A14.

DiIulio, J.J., Jr. (1996). Prisons are a bargain, by any measure. *New York Times,* January 16:A17.
DiIulio, J.J, Jr. (1999a) Against mandatory minimums: Drug sentencing run amok. *National Review,* 51(9):46-51.
DiIulio, J.J., Jr. (1999b). Two million prisoners are enough. *Wall Street Journal*, March 12:A14.
DiIulio (2000). An easy ride for felons on probation. *New York Times*, August 29:A23.
DiIulio, J. and Piehl, A.M. (1991). Does prison pay? *Brookings Review,* 9(4):28-36.
DiIulio, J. and Piehl, A.M. (1995) Does prison pay? Revisited. *Brookings Review,* 13(1):20-26.
Ditton, P.M. and Wilson, D.J. (1999). *Truth in Sentencing in State Prisons.* Bureau of Justice Statistics Special Report (NCJ 170032). Washington, D.C.: Bureau of Justice Statistics, U.S. Department of Justice.
Donziger, S.R. (Ed.) (1996). *The Real War on Crime: The Report of the National Criminal Justice Commission.* New York: Harper Perennial.
Fagan, J. (2004). Crime, law and the community: Dynamics of incarceration in New York City. In Michael Tonry (Ed.), *The Future of Imprisonment* (pp. 27-59). New York, NY: Oxford University Press.
Farrington, D. (1986). Age and crime. In M. Tonry and N. Morris (Eds.), *Crime and Justice: An Annual Review of Research, 7.* Chicago, IL: University of Chicago Press.
Feeley, M. (2003). Review essay: Crime, social order and the rise of neo-conservative politics. *Theoretical Criminology,* 7:111-130.
Frase, R.S. (1995). State sentencing guidelines: Still going strong. *Judicature,* 78:173-179.
Frase, R.S. (2000). Is guided discretion sufficient?: Overview of state sentencing guidelines. *St. Louis University Law Journal,* 44:425-446.
Frost, N.A. (2003). Modeling punitiveness: Assessing state-level variations in punishment. Paper presented at the 55th Annual Meeting of the American Society of Criminology, Denver, CO.

Frost, N.A. (2006). Editorial introduction: Mandatory minimum sentencing. *Criminology & Public Policy,* 5:1-4.
Garafalo, J. (1980). Social structure and rates of imprisonment: A research note. *Justice System Journal,* 5:299-305.
Garland, D. (1985). *Punishment and Welfare: A History of Penal Strategies.* Aldershot: Gower.
Garland, D. (2000). The culture of high crime societies: Some preconditions of recent 'law and order' policies. *British Journal of Criminology*, 40:347-375.
Garland, D. (2001). *The Culture of Control: Crime and Social Order in Contemporary Society.* New York, NY: Oxford University Press.
Greenberg, D.F. (2001). *Novus ordo saeclorum*: A commentary on Downes and on Beckett and Western. *Punishment & Society*, 3:81-93.
Greenberg, D.F. and West, V. (2001). State prison populations and their growth, 1971-1991. *Criminology*, 39:615-653.
Greene, J.A. (2003). *Positive Trends in State-Level Sentencing and Corrections Policy.* Washington, DC: Families Against Mandatory Minimums.
Greenwood, P. and Abrahamse, A. (1982). *Selective Incapacitation.* Santa Monica, CA: Rand Corporation.
Gordon, D. (1990). *The Justice Juggernaut: Fighting Street Crime, Controlling Citizens.* New Brunswick, NJ: Rutgers University Press.
Hallsworth, S. (2000). Rethinking the punitive turn: Economies of excess and the criminology of the other. *Punishment & Society,* 2:145-160.
Harrison, P.M. (2000). *Incarceration rates for prisoners under State or Federal jurisdiction, per 100,000 residents* [Computer file: corpop25.wk1]. Washington, DC: U.S. Department of Justice, Bureau of Justice Statistics.
Harrison, P.M. and Beck, A.J. (2005a). *Prison and Jail Inmates at Midyear 2004.* Bureau of Justice Statistics Bulletin (NCJ 208801). Washington, D.C.: U.S. Department of Justice, Bureau of Justice Statistics.

Harrison, P.M. and Beck, A.J. (2005b). *Prisoners in 2004.* Bureau of Justice Statistics Bulletin (NCJ 210677). Washington, D.C.: U.S. Department of Justice, Bureau of Justice Statistics.

Harrison, P.M. and Karberg, J.C. (2003). *Prison and Jail Inmates at Midyear 2002.* Bureau of Justice Statistics Bulletin (NCJ 198877). Washington, DC: U.S. Department of Justice, Bureau of Justice Statistics.

Harrison, P.M. and Karberg, J.C. (2004) *Prison and Jail Inmates at Midyear 2003.* Bureau of Justice Statistics Bulletin (NCJ 203947). Washington, D.C.: U.S. Department of Justice, Bureau of Justice Statistics.

Holleran, D. and Spohn, C. (2004). On the use of the total incarceration variable in sentencing research. *Criminology,* 42:211-240.

Jacobs, D. and Carmichael, J.T. (2001) The politics of punishment across time and space: A pooled time-series analysis of imprisonment rates. *Social Forces*, 80:61-91.

Jacobs, D. and Helms, R.E. (1996) Toward a political model of incarceration: A time-series examination of multiple explanations for prison admission rates. *American Journal of Sociology,* 102:323-357.

Jacobs, D. and Helms, R.E. (1997). Testing coercive explanations for order. *Social Forces,* 75:1361-1392.

Jacobs, D. and Helms, R.E. (2001). Toward a political sociology of punishment: Politics and changes in the incarcerated population. *Social Science Research,* 30:171-194.

Jacobs, J.B. (2001). Facts, values and prison policies: A commentary on Zimring and Tonry. *Punishment & Society,* 3:183-188.

Johnstone, G. (2000). Penal policy making: Elitist, populist or participatory. *Punishment & Society,* 2:161-180.

Joint Committee on New York Drug Law Evaluation (1978). *The Nation's Toughest Drug Law: Evaluating the New York Experience.* Washington, D.C.: Government Printing Office.

Joubert, P.E., Picou, J.S., and McIntosh, W.A. (1981). U.S. social structure, crime and imprisonment. *Criminology,* 19:344-359.

Kahan, D.M. (1996). What do alternative sanctions mean? *University of Chicago Law Review,* 63:591-653.

Kahan, D.M. (1999). Unthinkable misrepresentations: A response to Tonry. *UCLA Law Review,* 46:1933-1940.
Katz, M.B. (1989). *The Undeserving Poor: From the War on Poverty to the War on Welfare.* New York: Pantheon Books.
Kinder, D.R. (1998). Opinion and action in the realm of politics. In D.T. Gilbert, S.T. Fiske, and G. Lindzey (Eds.), *The Handbook of Social Psychology,* 4th Ed. Boston, MA: McGraw Hill.
Langan, P.A. (1985). Racism on trial: New evidence to explain the racial composition of prisons in the United States. *Journal of Criminal Law and Criminology,* 76:666-683.
Langan, P.A. (1991). America's soaring prison population. *Science,* 251:1568-1573.
Langan, P.A. & Levin, D. (1999). Assessing the accuracy of state prisoner statistics. Bureau of Justice Statistics Technical Report (NCJ 173413). Washington, D.C.: U.S. Department of Justice, Bureau of Justice Statistics.
Levitt, S. (1996). The effect of prison population size on crime rates: Evidence from prison over-crowding litigation. *Quarterly Journal of Economics,* 111:319-351.
Lynch, J.P. (1988). A comparison of prison use in England, Canada, West Germany, and the United States: A limited test of the punitiveness hypothesis. *The Journal of Criminal Law and Criminology,* 79:180-217.
Lynch, J.P. (1993). A cross-national comparison of the length of custodial sentences for serious crimes. *Justice Quarterly,* 10:639-660.
Lynch, J.P. (1995). Crime in international perspective. In J.Q. Wilson and J. Petersilia (Eds.), *Crime* (pp. 5-41). San Francisco, CA: Institute for Contemporary Studies.
Lynch, J.P. (2002). Crime in international perspective. In J.Q. Wilson and J. Petersilia (Eds.), *Crime: Public Policies for Crime Control* (pp. 5-41). San Francisco, CA: Institute for Contemporary Studies.
Lynch, J.P. & Sabol, W.J. (2004). Assessing the effects of mass incarceration on informal social control in communities. *Criminology & Public Policy,* 3:267-294.

Lynch, M.J. (1999). Beating a dead horse: Is there any basic empirical evidence for the deterrent effect of imprisonment? *Crime, Law and Social Change,* 31:347-362.
Lyons, W. (2000). Review Essay: Violence and the politics of law and order. *Law & Society Review,* 34.
Macleod, J. (1995). *Ain't No Makin It.* Boulder, CO: Westview Press.
Maguire, A.L. and Pastore, K. (Eds.) (2003). *Sourcebook of Criminal Justice Statistics, 1994-2001 Annual Editions.* [CD ROM: NCJ 197533]. Washington, D.C.: U.S. Department of Justice, Bureau of Justice Statistics.
Martinson, R. (1974). What works? Questions and answers about prison reform. *Public Interest,* 35:22-54.
Marvell, T.B. (1995). Sentencing guidelines and prison population growth. *Journal of Criminal Law and Criminology,* 85:101-115.
Marvell, T.B. and Moody, C.E. (1994). Prison population growth and crime reduction. *Journal of Quantitative Criminology,* 10:109-140.
Marvell, T.B. and Moody, C.E. (1996). Determinate sentencing and abolishing parole: The long-term impacts on prisons and crime. *Criminology,* 34:107-128.
Matthews, R. (2005). The myth of punitiveness. *Theoretical Criminology,* 9:175-201.
Mauer, M. (1999). Race to Incarcerate. New York, NY: The New Press.
Mauer, M. (2001). The causes and consequences of prison growth in theUSA. *Punishment & Society,* 3:9-20.
Mauer, M. (2002). Mass imprisonment and the disappearing voters. In M. Mauer and M. Chesney-Lind (Eds.), *Invisible Punishment* (pp.50-58). New York: The New Press.
McGarrell, E.F. (1993). Institutional theory and the stability of a conflict model of the incarceration rate. *Justice Quarterly,* 10:7-28.
McGuire, W.J. and Sheehan, R.G. (1983). Relationship between crime rates and incarceration rates – Further analysis. *Journal of Research in Crime and Delinquency,* 20:73-85.
Meares, T. (2004). Mass incarceration: Who pays the price for criminal offending? *Criminology & Public Policy,* 3:295-302.

Melossi, D. (1993). Gazette of morality and social whip: Punishment, hegemony, and the case of the USA, 1970-1992. *Social and Legal Studies,* 2:259-279.

Merritt, N., Fain, T. and Turner, S. (2006). Oregon's get tough sentencing reform: A lesson in justice system adaptation. *Criminology & Public Policy,* 5:

Michalowski, R.J. and Pearson, M.A. (1990). Punishment and social structure at the state level: A cross-sectional comparison of 1970 and 1980. *Journal of Research in Crime and Delinquency,* 27:52-78.

Millie, A., Jacobson, J., and Hough, M. (2003). Understanding the growth in the prison population in England and Wales. *Criminal Justice,* 3:369-387.

Murray, C. (1997). *Does Prison Work?* London, England: Institute of Economic Affairs.

Newman, G. (1995). *Just and Painful: A Case for the Corporal Punishment of Criminals.* 2nd Edition. Albany, NY: Harrow and Heston.

Nicholson-Crotty, S. (2004). The impact of sentencing guidelines on state-level sanctions: An analysis over time. *Crime & Delinquency,* 50:395-411.

Nicholson-Crotty, S. and Meier, K.J. (2002). Size doesn't matter: In defense of single state studies. *State Politics and Policy Quarterly,* 2:411-422.

Oleson, J.C. (2002). The punitive coma. *California Law Review*, 90: 829-901.

Ouimet, M. and Tremblay, P. (1996). A normative theory of the relationship between crime rates and imprisonment rates: An analysis of penal behavior of U.S. states from 1972-1992. *Journal of Research in Crime and Delinquency,* 33:109-125.

Parenti, C. (2000). *Lockdown America: Police and Prisons in the Age of Crisis.* New York: Verso.

Pease, K. (1994). Cross-national imprisonment rates: Limitations of method and possible conclusions. *British Journal of Criminology,* 34:116-130.

Piehl, A.M. (2004). The challenge of mass incarceration. *Criminology & Public Policy,* 3:303-308.

Reiss, A.J., and Roth, J. (1993). *Understanding and Controlling Violence.* Washington, D.C.: National Academy Press.

Reitz, K.R. (2001). The disassembly and reassembly of U.S. sentencing practices. In M. Tonry and R.S. Frase (eds.), *Sentencing and Sanctions in Western Countries* (pp.222-258). New York: Oxford University Press.

Reitz, K.R. (2004). Questioning the conventional wisdom of parole release authority. In M. Tonry (ed.), *The Future of Imprisonment* (pp.199-235). New York: Oxford University Press.

Roberts, J.V. (1992). Public opinion, crime and criminal justice. *Crime and Justice: A Review of Research, 16* (pp. 99-180). Chicago: University of Chicago Press.

Roberts, J.V., Stalans, L.J., Indermaur, D., and Hough, M. (2003). *Penal Populism and Public Opinion: Lessons from Five Countries.* New York, NY: Oxford University Press.

Roberts, J.V. and Stalans, L.J. (1997). *Public Opinion, Crime and Criminal Justice.* Boulder, CO: Westview Press.

Rose, D. and Clear, T. (1998). Incarceration, social control and crime: Implications for social disorganization theory. *Criminology,* 36:441-480.

Rossman, D., Froyd, P., Pierce, G.L., McDevitt, J., and Bowers, W.J. (1979). *The Impact of the Mandatory Gun Law in Massachusetts.* Law Enforcement Assistance Administration, U.S. Department of Justice. Washington, D.C.: U.S. Government Printing Office.

Rubenstein, G. and Mukamal, D. (2002). Welfare and housing – Denial of benefits to drug offenders. In M. Mauer and M. Chesney-Lind (Eds.), *Invisible Punishment* (pp.37-49). New York: The New Press.

Rutherford, A. (1997). Beyond crime control. In C. Murray, *Does Prison Work?* (pp.46-48). London, England: Institute of Economic Affairs.

Rusche, G. and Kircheimer, O. (1939). *Punishment and Social Structure.* New York: Columbia University Press.

Sabol, W.J., Rosich, K., Kane, K.M., Kirk, D.P. and Dubin, G. (2002). *The Influences of Truth-in-Sentencing Reforms on Changes in State's Sentencing Practices and Prison Populations.* Washington, DC: Urban Institute, Justice Policy Center.

Sampson, R.J., and Laub, J.H. (2003). Life-course desisters: Trajectories of crime among delinquent boys followed to age 70. *Criminology,* 41:555-592.

Saunders, P. and Billante, N. (2002-03). Does prison work? *Policy,* 18:3-8.

Savelsberg, J. (1992). Law that does not fit society: Sentencing guidelines as neoclassical reaction to the dilemmas of substantivized law. *American Journal of Sociology,* 97:1346-1381.

Selke, W.L. and Andersson, S.A. (1992). A model for ranking the punitiveness of the states. *Journal of Quantitative Criminology,* 8:217-232.

Selke, W.L. and Andersson, S.A. (2003). A test of social stress theory as applied to the study of imprisonment rates. *The Prison Journal,* 83:426-441.

Simon, J. (2001). 'Entitlement to cruelty': Neo-liberalism and the punitive mentality in the United States. In K. Stenson and R.R. Sullivan (Eds.), *Crime, Risk and Justice: The Politics of Crime Control in Liberal Democracies* (pp. 125-143). Devon, England: Willan.

Simon, J. (2002). Book review: 'Making crime pay: law and order in contemporary American politics'. *Theoretical Criminology,* 4:504-507.

Sorenson, J. and Stemen, D. (2002). The effect of state sentencing policies on incarceration rates. *Crime & Delinquency,* 48:456-475.

Sparks, R. (2000). The media and penal politics. *Punishment & Society,* 2:98-105.

Spelman, W. (2000a). The limited importance of prison expansion. In A. Blumstein & J. Wallman (eds.), *The Crime Drop in America.* New York: Cambridge.

Spelman, W. (2000b). What recent studies do (and don't) tell us about imprisonment and crime. In M. Tonry (Ed.), *Crime and Justice: A Review of Research, 27.* Chicago, IL: University of Chicago Press.

Stemen, D., Wilson, J. & Rengifo, A. (2003). *Of fragmentation and ferment: State sentencing and corrections reforms, 1975-2002.* Paper presented at the 55th Annual Meeting of the American Society of Criminology. Denver, CO.

Stephan, J.J. (2001). *Census of Jails, 1999.* Bureau of Justice Statistics. NCJ 186633. Washington, D.C.: U.S. Department of Justice, Bureau of Justice Statistics.

Stephan, J.J. (2004). *State Prison Expenditures, 2001.* Bureau of Justice Statistics Special Report (NCJ 202949). Washington, D.C.: U.S. Department of Justice, Bureau of Justice Statistics.

Taggart, W.A. & Winn, R.G. (1993). Imprisonment in the American states. *Social Science Quarterly,* 74:736-749.

Tonry, M. (1993). The success of Judge Frankel's sentencing commission. *University of Colorado Law Review,* 64:713-722.

Tonry, M. (1995). *Malign Neglect: Race, Crime and Punishment in America.* New York, NY: Oxford University Press.

Tonry, M. (1996). *Sentencing Matters*. New York, NY: Oxford University Press.

Tonry, M. (1999a). Why are U.S. incarceration rates so high? *Crime & Delinquency,* 45:419-437.

Tonry, M. (1999b). Rethinking unthinkable punishment policies in America. *UCLA Law Review,* 46:1751-1791.

Tonry, M. (2001a). Punishment policies and patterns in western countries. In M. Tonry and R.S. Frase (eds.) *Sentencing and Sanctions in Western Countries* (pp. 3-28). New York: Oxford University Press.

Tonry, M. (2001b). Symbol, substance, and severity in western penal policies. *Punishment & Society*, 3:517-536.

Tonry, M. (2001c). Unthought thoughts: The influence of changing sensibilities on penal policies. *Punishment & Society*, 3:167-181.

Tonry, M. (2004a) *Thinking About Crime: Sense and Sensibility in American Penal Culture.* New York, NY: Oxford University Press.

Tonry, M. (2004b). Has the prison a future? In M. Tonry (Ed.), *The Future of Imprisonment* (pp. 3-24). New York, NY: Oxford University Press.

Tonry, M. (2006). Mandatory minimums, criminology, and public policy. *Criminology & Public Policy,* 5:

Travis, J. (2002). Invisible punishment: An instrument of social exclusion. In M. Mauer and M. Chesney-Lind (Eds.), *Invisible Punishment* (pp.15-36). New York: The New Press.

Tyler, T.R. and Boeckmann, R.J. (1997). Three-strikes and you're out, but why?: The psychology of public support for punishing rule breakers. *Law & Society Review*, 31:237-265.

U.S. Census Bureau. (2002). *Time Series of Intercensal State Population Estimates: April 1, 1990 to April 1, 2000.* [Table CO-EST2001-12-00, Release Date: April 11, 2002]. Washington, D.C.: U.S. Census Bureau, Population Division.

U.S. Department of Justice, Bureau of Justice Statistics. (1997). *National Corrections Reporting Program, 1990: [United States] [Computer file].* Conducted by U.S. Department of Commerce, Bureau of the Census. ICPSR ed. Ann Arbor, MI: Inter-university Consortium for Political and Social Research [producer and distributor].

U.S. Department of Justice, Bureau of Justice Statistics. (1998). *National Corrections Reporting Program, 1995: [United States] [Computer file].* Conducted by U.S. Department of Commerce, Bureau of the Census. ICPSR ed. Ann Arbor, MI: Inter-university Consortium for Political and Social Research [producer and distributor].

U.S. Department of Justice, Bureau of Justice Statistics. (2001). *National Corrections Reporting Program, 1998: [United States] [Computer file].* Conducted by U.S. Department of Commerce, Bureau of the Census. ICPSR ed. Ann Arbor, MI: Inter-university Consortium for Political and Social Research [producer and distributor].

U.S. Department of Justice, Bureau of Justice Statistics. (2003). *National Corrections Reporting Program, 2000: [United States] [Computer file].* Conducted by U.S. Department of Commerce, Bureau of the Census. ICPSR ed. Ann Arbor, MI: Inter-university Consortium for Political and Social Research [producer and distributor].

U.S. Department of Justice, Federal Bureau of Investigation. (1997). *Uniform Crime Reporting Program Data [United States]: County-Level Detailed Arrest and Offense Data, 1989 [Computer file].* ICPSR version. Washington, DC: U.S. Department of Justice, Federal Bureau of Investigation [producer], 1989. Ann Arbor, MI: Interuniversity Consortium for Political and Social Research [distributor], 1997.

U.S. Department of Justice, Federal Bureau of Investigation. (2000) *Crime in the United States, 1999.* Washington, D.C.: U.S. Department of Justice.

U.S. Department of Justice, Federal Bureau of Investigation. (2001) *Uniform Crime Reporting Program Data [United States]: County-Level Detailed Arrest and Offense Data, 1994 [Computer file].* 3rd ICPSR ed. Ann Arbor, MI: Inter-university Consortium for Political and Social Research [producer and distributor].

U.S. Department of Justice, Federal Bureau of Investigation. (2002). *Uniform Crime Reporting Program Data [United States]: County-Level Detailed Arrest and Offense Data, 1999 [Computer file].* 3rd ICPSR ed. Ann Arbor, MI: Inter-university Consortium for Political and Social Research [producer and distributor].

U.S. Sentencing Commission. (1991). *Special Report to Congress: Mandatory Minimum Penalties in the Federal Criminal Justice System.* Washington, D.C.: U.S. Sentencing Commission.

Useem, B., Liedka, R.V. and Piehl, A.M. (2003). Popular support for the prison build-up. *Punishment & Society,* 5:1-32.

Von Zielbauer, P. (2003). Rethinking the key thrown away: As Ashcroft cracks down, states cut prison terms. *New York Times*, September 28:N41.

Walmsley, R. (2003). *World Prison Population List, 4th Edition.* Home Office Findings 188. London, England: Home Office.

Western, B. and Beckett, K. (1999). How unregulated is the U.S. labor market?: The penal system as a labor market institution. *American Journal of Sociology*, 104:1030-1060.

Western, B. and Guetzkow, J. (2002). Punitive policy and neoliberalism in the U.S. labor market. Paper presented at the Annual Meeting of the American Sociological Society, Chicago.

Western, B., Kleykamp, M., and Rosenfeld, J. (2003). Crime, punishment, and American inequality. *Unpublished Manuscript.*

Whitman, J.Q. (2003). *Harsh Justice: Criminal Punishment and the Widening Divide Between America and Europe.* New York, NY: Oxford University Press.

Wilson, J.Q. (1975). *Thinking About Crime.* New York: Basic Books.

Wilson, J.Q. (1994). Prisons in a free society. *Public Interest,* 117:37-41.

Wilson, J.Q. (1995). Crime and public policy. In J.Q. Wilson and J. Petersilia (Eds.), *Crime* (pp. 489-507). San Francisco, CA: Institute for Contemporary Studies.

Wilson, J.Q. (2002) Crime and public policy. In J.Q. Wilson and J. Petersilia (Eds.), *Crime: Public Policies for Crime Control* (pp.537-557). San Francisco, CA: Institute for Contemporary Studies.

Yates, J. (1997). Racial incarceration disparity among states. *Social Science Quarterly,* 78:1001-1010.

Young, J. (1997). Charles Murray and the American prison experiment: The dilemmas of a libertarian. In C. Murray, *Does Prison Work?* (pp. 31-39). London, England: Institute of Economic Affairs.

Young, J. (1999a). *The Exclusive Society.* Thousand Oaks, CA: Sage Publications.

Young, J. (1999b). Cannibalism and bulimia: Patterns of social control in late modernity. *Theoretical Criminology,* 3:387-407.

Young, J. (2002) Searching for a new criminology of everyday life: A review of 'The Culture of Control'. *British Journal of Criminology,* 42:228-243.

Young, J. (2003a). In praise of dangerous thoughts. *Punishment & Society,* 5:97-107.

Young, J. (2003b). Merton with energy, Katz with structure: The sociology of vindictiveness and the criminology of transgression. *Theoretical Criminology,* 7:389-414.

Zedlewski, E.W. (1987). Making confinement decisions. *National Institute of Justice Research in Brief.* Washington, D.C.: U.S. Department of Justice, National Institute of Justice.

Zimring, F.E. (2001). Imprisonment rates and the new politics of criminal punishment. *Punishment & Society,* 3:161-166.
Zimring, F.E. and Hawkins, G. (1991). The new mathematics of imprisonment. *Crime & Delinquency,* 34:425-436.
Zimring, F.E. and Hawkins, G. (1991). *The Scale of Imprisonment.* Chicago, IL: University of Chicago Press.
Zimring, F.E. and Hawkins, G. (1994). The growth of imprisonment in California. *British Journal of Criminology,* 34:83-96.
Zimring, F.E. and Hawkins, G. (1995) *Incapacitation: Penal Confinement and the Restraint of Crime.* New York: Oxford University Press, Inc.
Zimring, F.E., Hawkins, G., and Kamin, S. (2001) *Punishment and Democracy: Three-strikes and You're Out in California.* New York: Oxford University Press.
Zimring, F.E. and Hawkins, G. (2004) Democracy and the limits of punishment: A preface to prisoners' rights. In Michael Tonry (ed.), *The Future of Imprisonment* (pp. 157-178). New York: Oxford University Press.

INDEX

Lightning Source UK Ltd.
Milton Keynes UK
UKOW050007220113

205181UK00003B/3/P

9 781593 321765